DIRECTORY
OF LITERARY
MAGAZINES
1991–92

DIRECTORY
OF LITERARY
MAGAZINES
1991–92

Prepared in Cooperation with the
Council of Literary Magazines and Presses

Moyer Bell Limited : Mount Kisco, New York & London

LIBRARY OF CONGRESS
CATALOGING-IN-PUBLICATION DATA

Directory of literary magazines / prepared with the Council of Literary
Magazines and Presses*—1984—New York: The Council c1984-

v.;22cm

Annual.
Continues:CLMP literary magazine directory
ISSN 0884-6006 = Directory of literary magazines

1. Literature—Periodicals—Bibliography. 2. American periodicals—
Directories. 3. Little magazines—United States—Directories. I. Council
of Literary Magazines and Presses (U.S.)

Z6513.C37   85-648720
PN2   AACR 2 MARC-S

ISBN 1-55921-050-8 Pb

Printed in the United States of America

---

* Council of Literary Magazines and Presses (CLMP) was
known as the Coordinating Council of Literary Magazines
(CCLM)

> The little magazine is something I have always fostered, for without it, I myself would have been early silenced. To me it is one magazine, not several. . . . When it is in any way successful it is because it fills a need in someone's mind to keep going. When it dies, someone else takes it up in some other part of the country—quite by accident—out of a desire to get the writing down on paper.
>
> —William Carlos Williams*

The *Directory of Literary Magazines* has been compiled as a guide to the changing world of literary magazines of which Williams speaks. The literary magazine is a particularly American tradition that has provided early publishing opportunities for most of our important writers—including T.S. Eliot, E.L. Doctorow, Elizabeth Bishop, Ernest Hemingway, Ralph Ellison, Robert Lowell, Katherine Anne Porter, Raymond Carver, Richard Wright, Ezra Pound, Maxine Hong Kingston and Amiri Baraka. Through the medium of literary magazines, writers see their art in print, are given a place in our culture and find a readership.

This year's *Directory* includes almost 500 magazines from 49 states, the Virgin Islands and the District of Columbia. Entries are designed to include information asked for by **readers, writers, librarians, publishers,** and others.

Entries include:

• descriptions of each magazine in the editor's own words in order to clarify for prospective **writers** the magazine's editorial directions and interests. Writers are strongly urged to research magazines before submitting work, by using these entries, and most importantly, by purchasing and supporting the magazines that interest them.

---

* *The Autobiography of William Carlos Williams*, © 1951 William Carlos Williams. Reprinted by permission of New Directions Publishing Corporation.

- listings of types of material published by each magazine, subscription rates, ISSN numbers for use by **librarians** in selecting additions to their collections, and distributors for use by **bookstores** interested in increasing their magazine sections.

- advertising information for **publishers'** use, including ad rates and sizes as a complement to the activities of CLMP's Ad Program, which offers advertising space in specially designed packages of literary magazines to interested publishers. For more information on ad rates and CLMP's advertising services to publishers, please contact CLMP.

For the past 23 years, the Coordinating Council of Literary Magazines (CCLM) has been the primary organization serving America's literary magazines. Over the years, its programs have grown and changed as the field of literary magazines changed. This year, 1991, will see many major changes at the organization. The board, staff, mission, goals, programs and fundraising of CLMP will all grow and change this year and continue to move in new directions in the following 2 or 3 years, as it responds to new needs and trends in noncommercial literary publishing in America.

CLMP's newly refined mission is to preserve, promote, and support literary magazines and presses. Historically, literary magazines and presses have been an important open door to freedom of expression in America. In addition to economic, technological and demographic trends, the great vitality of today's writers contributes to the great changes occurring in the publishing of serious literature in America. Experimental literature, work by emerging writers and writing by minority groups, are primarily presented by the independent literary magazines and presses of our country. Publishers of periodicals and books that are primarily literary exist in all regions, all populations, cultures and nationalities of our country. The number, size, goals, and needs of literary publishers are changing, CLMP is changing to become the primary service organization and advocate for this dynamic field. If you would like further information about CLMP, please write to us at CLMP, 666 Broadway, New York, NY 10012-2317.

This **Directory** will continue to change and improve in the coming years in several ways. We hope you are well-served by this edition and will be even more pleased in the future. CLMP would like to thank the staff of Moyer Bell Limited for the commitment, patience, good-cheer and dedication to this project. CLMP would also like to thank the National Endowment for the Arts, the New York State Arts Council and *Harper's Magazine* for their general support.

KEY

NAME OF MAGAZINE
Editor(s)
Address
Telephone number

Material published
Magazine description
Recent contributors
Payment to contributors
Reporting time
Copyright
First year of publication; frequency; circulation
Subscription rate; single copy price; discount for resale
Number of pages; size of magazine
Advertising rates and sizes
International Standard Serial Number
Distributors

Abbreviations

ea—each
ind—individual
inst—institutional
irreg—irregular
pp—pages
var—varies
v—volume
yr—year

All entries contain the fullest information available at date of *Directory* publication.

Index by State (see p. 209)

A

ABACUS

Peter Ganick

181 Edgemont Avenue

Elmwood, CT 06110

(203) 233-2023

Poetry

A 12 to 18 page, newsletter format, single-author-per-issue periodical devoted to experimental and language poetry.

Clark Coolidge, Jackson MacLow, Carla Harryman, Laura Moriarty, Joan Retallack, Leslie Scalapino.

Payment: 12 copies.

Reporting time: variable.

Copyright: author.

No ads

ISSN: 0886-4047

Small Press Distribution, Small Press Traffic, Segue Foundation

ABRAXAS

Ingrid Swanberg, Warren Woessner, David Hilton

2518 Gregory Street

Madison, WI 53711

(608) 238-0175

Poetry, criticism, essays, reviews, translations, photographs, graphics/artwork, "found" cultural artifacts.

Contemporary poetry: (non-academic). Some emphasis on lyric forms. Unusual graphics and "found" poems. Interested in poetry in translation, especially from Latin America and Eastern Europe. Criticism and essays on the contemporary scene.

Ivan Arguelles, Gerald Locklin, Próspero Saíz, Andrei Codrescu, Denise Levertov.

Payment: in copies.

Reporting time: 3 weeks–5 months.

Copyright held by Abraxas Press, Inc; reverts to author upon publication.

1968; 4/year; 500

$12/4 issues; $3/ea; 40%

80 pp; 6 x 9

Ad rates: $60/page/5 x 8; $35/½ page/5 x 3½

ISSN: 0361-1663

Bookslinger

ACM (Another Chicago Magazine)

Barry Silesky

3709 N. Kenmore

Chicago, IL 60613

(312) 248-7665

Poetry, fiction, reviews, essays, interviews.

Literary, contemporary, non-regional, socio-political outlook.

S.L. Wisenberg, Tom McGrath, Pablo Antonio Cuadra, Ariel Dorfman, Maxine Chernoff, Lore Segal, Sterling Plumpp.
Payment: $5–$25.
Reporting time: 8 weeks.
Copyright held by **ACM**; reverts to author upon publication.
1977; 2/yr; 750
$15/ind; $15/inst; $8/ea; 40%
220 pp; 5½ x 8½
Ad rates: $150/page/5 x 8; $75/½ page/5 x 3⅞
ISSN: 0272-4359
Ingram, Total, ILPA

ACTS: A Journal of New Writing
David Levi Strauss, Benjamin Hollander
514 Guerrero St.
San Francisco, CA 94110
(415) 431-8297
Poetry, criticism, essays, reviews, translation, interviews, graphics/ artwork, photographs, word/ image work.
Contemporary radical poetry, "analytic lyric," word/image work and photography.
Also book issues on selected writers (Jack Spicer, Paul Celan, Robert Duncan) and subjects.
Nate Mackey, Susan Howe, Aaron Shurin, Norma Cole, Michael Palmer.

Payment: in copies.
Reporting time: 2–4 months.
Copyright held by Acts; reverts to author upon publication.
1982; 2/yr; 600–1,500
$12/yr ind; $16/yr inst; $10/ea; 40%
120 pp; 8½ x 11
Ad rates: $100/page/7½ x 10¼; $60/½ page/3 x 9
ISSN: 0749-3908
Small Press Distribution, Segue, Inland Book Co., Sun & Moon, Ubiquity

AEGEAN REVIEW
Dino Siotis
220 West 19th Street/2A
New York, NY 10011
Modern Greek literature in translation. Works inspired by Greece by American authors.
Fiction, essays, interviews, poetry, art and photography.
Jorge Luis Borges, Lawrence Durrell, Truman Capote, Yannis Ritsos, Alice Bloom.
Payment: $25–$50.
Reporting time: 6 weeks.
1985; 2/yr.; 4,000
$10/yr ind; $18/yr inst; $5/ea; 40%
80 pp; 7½ x 10
Ad rates: $265 per page
ISSN: 0891-7213
DeBoer

AERIAL

Rod Smith
P.O. Box 25642
Washington, D.C. 20007
(202) 333-1544, 965-5200

Poetry, fiction, criticism, essays, reviews, translations, photos, graphics.

AERIAL is interested in what writing is, might be. Many of our contributors are familiar with the works of writers such as Pound, Stein, Bunting, Oppen, Zukofsky, the Black Mountain Community, "structuralist linguistics from Saussure to Derrida," the Beats, $L = A = N = G = U = A = G = E$, Ashbery, O'Hara, Poetics Journal, Temblor, etc.

John Cage, Janet Gray, Rachel Blau DuPlessis, Charles Bernstein, Harrison Fisher.

Payment: copies.

Copyright held by AERIAL; reverts to author upon publication.

1985; 1–2/yr; 500

$15/yr ind; $17.50/3 issues inst; $7.50/ea; 40%

100–160 pp; 6 x 9

Ad rates available. Contact CLMP for information.

Sun & Moon (issue #4 only), Paul Green (U.K.), Ubiquity, and S.P.D.

THE AFRO-HISPANIC REVIEW

Marvin Lewis & Edward Mullen
Department of Romance Languages
U Missouri: 143 Arts & Science Building
Columbia, MO 65211
(314) 882-2030

Scholarly articles, translations of Afro-Hispanic texts.

A bilingual journal of Afro-Hispanic literature and culture, publishing literary criticism, book reviews, translations, creative writing, and relevant developments in the field. Jointly published by the Department of Romance Languages and the Black Studies Program of the University of Missouri-Columbia.

William W. Megenney, E. Valerie Smith, Jerry Williams, Guillermo Bowie, Miriam DeCosta-Willis.

Payment: none.

Reporting time: 3 months.

Copyright held by University of Missouri.

1982; 3/yr; 500

$15/yr inst; $5/ea; $1 off inst. rate

8½ x 11

No ads

ISSN: 0278-8969

Faxon, Ebsco

AGADA

Reuven Goldfarb
2020 Essex Street
Berkeley, CA 94703
(415) 848-0965
Poetry, fiction, midrash, memoir, essay, translation, graphics, artwork.

AGADA has a specifically Jewish orientation and emphasis in a universalist perspective, and publishes work touching on traditional Jewish themes and contemporary concerns. Seeks to share insights, memories, and vision of creative Jewish people with people everywhere.
Lou Barrett, Barry Brown, Shlomo Carlebach, Charles Fishman, Lyn Lifshin.
Payment: in copies.
Reporting time: 2–3 months.
Copyright reverts to author.
1981; 1yr; 1,000
$14/2 issues/$7.50/ea; 40%
64 pp; 7 x 10
ISSN: 0740-2392

AGNI

Boston University Creative Writing Program
Askold Melnyczuk, Editor
236 Bay State Road
Boston, MA 02215
Poetry, fiction, artwork, essays.
AGNI publishes poetry and fiction, and the occasional commissioned essay. Our special interests are new and underappreciated writers. Every issue features the work of a poet who has not yet published a full-length collection.
Thom Gunn, Marilynne Robinson, Rita Dove, John Updike, Frank Bidart, Ha Jin, Martin Espada, Sharon Olds, Robert Pinsky, Seamus Heaney, Tom Sleigh, Derek Walcott.
Payment: varies.
Reporting time: 2–10 weeks.
Copyright held by The Agni Review, Inc.; reverts to author upon publication.
1972; 2/yr; 1,400
$12/yr; $6/ea; 40%
250–300 pp; 5½ x 8½
Ad rates: $200/page/4½ x 7; $125/½ page/4½ x 3½
ISSN: 0191-3352
DeBoer, Inc.

ALASKA QUARTERLY REVIEW

Ronald Spatz, James Liszka, Thomas Sexton
University of Alaska Anchorage
College of Arts & Sciences
3221 Providence Drive
Anchorage, AK 99508
(907) 786-4775

Poetry, fiction, criticism, philosophy.

A journal devoted to contemporary literature and philosophy of literature.

Stuart Dybek, Jerome Charyn, Maura Stanton, Sam Hamill, Bill Van Wert, Grace Paley, Amy Hempel, Tobias Wolff.

Payment: in copies; other payment depends on grants.

Reporting time: 3–12 weeks.

Copyright held by University of Alaska Anchorage.

1981; 2/yr; 1,000

$8/yr ind; $10/yr inst; $4/ea; 50%

140 pp; 6 x 9

ISSN: 0737-268X

B. DeBoer

ALBATROSS

Richard Smyth, Richard Brobst

13498 Darnell Avenue

Port Charlotte, FL 33981

Poetry, interviews, graphics/artwork.

Since we see the albatross as a metaphor for an environment that must survive, we are primarily interested in ecological/environmental/nature themes, written in a narrative style; however, this is not to say that we do not consider other themes and forms.

Walter Griffin, Daniel Comiskey,

Stephen Meats, Duane Locke, Peter Meinke.

Payment: in contributor's copies.

1986; 2/yr; 500

$5/yr ind/inst; $3/ea; 40%

32–44 pp; 5½ x 8

ISSN: 0887-4239

AMBERGRIS

Mark Kissling

P.O. Box 29919

Cincinnati, OH 45229

Poetry, fiction, essays, photographs, graphics/artwork.

AMBERGRIS gives special, but not exclusive consideration to works by Ohio writers and artists, and to works with Midwestern themes in general.

Payment: two copies.

Reporting time: 6–8 weeks, 1st Round; up to 1 year, and readings.

Copyright held by magazine; reverts to author upon publication.

1987; 2/yr; 500

$6/yr; $3/ea; 40%

84 pp; 5½ x 8½

ISSN: 1044-2006

AMELIA

Frederick A. Raborg, Jr.

329 "E" Street

Bakersfield, CA 93304

(805) 323-4064

Fiction, poetry, plays, graphics/ artwork, criticism, reviews, essays, photographs, translation. **AMELIA** is a reader's magazine, intended to be enjoyed over a period of time, offering a unique blend of the traditional with the contemporary in virtually every printed artform by both "name" and unknown writers and artists of superior talents. Contributors from its pages have been included in Pushcart Prizes, The Artist Market and other prestigious reprint anthologies.

Pattiann Rogers, David Ray, Lawrence P. Spingarn, Larry Rubin, Stuart Friebert, Merrill Joan Gerber, Maxine Kumin.

Payment: poetry/$2–$25; fiction/$10–$35; non-fiction/$10/1,000 words; artwork/$5–$50.

Reporting time: 2 weeks–3 months.

Copyright held by magazine; reverts to author upon publication.

1984; 4/yr; 1,250

$25/yr ind; $25/yr inst; $7.95/ea; 40%

124 pp; 5½ x 8½

Ad rates: $250/page/4½ x 7½; $140/½ page/4½ x 3¾; $80/¼ page/4½ x 1¾

ISSN: 0743-2755

AMERICAN BOOK REVIEW

Ronald Sukenick, Rochelle Ratner, John Tytell, Don Laing (Managing Editor)

English Department Publications Center

Campus Box 494

University of Colorado

Boulder, CO 80309-0494

(303) 492-8947

Criticism, essays, reviews. **AMERICAN BOOK REVIEW** is offered as a guide to current books of literary interest published by the small, large, university, regional, third world, women's and other presses. It is edited and produced by writers for writers and the general public.

Hayden Carruth, Robert Creeley, Diane Wakoski, Marge Piercy, Daniel Berrigan.

Payment: $50 per review.

Reporting time: 2 weeks to 2 months.

Copyright held by ABR; reverts to author upon publication.

1977; 6/yr; 12,000

$18/yr ind; $23/yr inst; $3/ea; 40%

32 pp; 10 x 14

Ad rates: $425/page/10 x 14; $260/½ page/5 x 14; $150/¼ page/5 x 7; $100/½ col/ 2¼ x 6¾; $60/¼ col/2¼ x 3¾; discounts available.

Trade distribution by Ingram Periodicals, Interstate Distributors, Fine Print, Armadillo, and LS Distributors

AMERICAN DANE
Jennifer C. Denning
3717 Harney St.
Omaha, NE 68131
(402) 341-5049
Fiction, historical, essays.
The **AMERICAN DANE** Magazine is the official publication of the Danish Brotherhood in America—whose purpose is "to promote and perpetuate Danish culture and traditions and to provide fraternal benefits and family protection."
Payment: appx. $50.
Reporting time: 2 weeks.
Copyright returns to contributor after publication.
1916; 12/yr; 8,000
$12 domestic, $15 foreign; $1/ea; No resale disc.
8¼ x 11
Query for ad rates
ISSN: 0739-9170
Danish Brotherhood in America

THE AMERICAN POETRY REVIEW
Stephen Berg, David Bonanno, Arthur Vogelsang

1721 Walnut Street
Philadelphia, PA 19103
(215) 496-0439
Poetry, translation, criticism, reviews, interviews, essays.
Lucille Clifton, Sam Hamill, W.S. Merwin, Jane Miller, Howard Nemerov.
Payment: $1.00/line for poetry; $50/page for prose.
Reporting time: 10 weeks.
Copyright held by World Poetry, Inc.; reverts to author upon publication.
1972; 6/yr; 20,000
$12/yr ind; $12/yr inst; $2.50/ea; 50%
48 pp; 9¾ x 13¾
Ad rates: $600/page/9¾ x 13¾; $360/½ page/9¾ x 6¾; $200/¼ page/4¾ x 6¾
ISSN: 0360-3709
Eastern News Distributors

THE AMERICAN VOICE
Frederick Smock, Sallie Bingham
332 W. Broadway, Suite 1215
Louisville, KY 40202
(502) 562-0045
Fiction, poetry, essays, criticism, photographs.
THE AMERICAN VOICE publishes daring new writers and the more radical work of established writers. Feminist, Pan-American.

Susan Griffin, Kay Boyle, Marjorie Agosin, Brian Swann, Eduardo Galeano, Michelle Cliff, Linda Hogan, Doris Grumbach, Brenda Marie Osbey.
Payment: $400/prose; $150/poem; $75–150/translator fee.
Copyright: first rights held by magazine; reverts to author upon publication.
1985; 4/yr; 2,000
$12/yr ind; $20/2 yr; $5/ea; 40%
100 pp
ISSN: 0884-4536
Bernhard DeBoer, Ingram Periodicals

THE AMERICAS REVIEW
(formerly **REVISTA CHICANO-RIQUENA**)
Julian Olivares, Evangelina Vigil-Pinon
Arte Publico Press
University of Houston
Houston, TX 77204-3784
(713) 749-4833
Poetry, fiction, criticism, review, interviews, photographs, graphics/artwork.
THE AMERICAS REVIEW, A Review of Hispanic Literature and Art of the USA, is the oldest (16 years) and most prestigious U.S. Hispanic literary magazine. It publishes works by outstanding Hispanic writers and artists of the USA, as well as works by new and emerging writers and artists. Analysis, interviews, commentary and reviews of U.S. Hispanic works and writers.
Sandra Cisneros, Denise Chavez, Tato Laviera, Ed Vega, Gary Soto.
Payment: varies.
Reporting time: 3–4 months.
Copyright held by Arte Publico Press.
1972; triquarter (2 + double issue); 3,000
$15/yr ind; $20/yr inst; $5/$10 (double issue) ea; 40%
128 pp; 224 pp double issue; 5½ x 8½
Ad rates: $200/page/5 x 8; $125/½ page/4 x 5; $75/¼ page/2½ x 4
ISSN: 0360-7860
EBSCO, Ubiquity Distributors, Homing Pigeon, Armadillo & Co.

ANEMONE
Nanette Morin, Editor; Bill Griffin, Art Editor
Box 369
Chester, VT 05143
Poetry, reviews, interviews, translations, photographs, graphics/artwork, paintings.
ANEMONE is a quarterly literary

arts journal publishing the expressive voice of the people. Our purpose is to help bring the spirit of man closer to his true self through art. We look for work that is different, always looking for the new voice. **ANEMONE** encourages "political" and "social" poetry.

Robert Chute, Arthur Winfield Knight, Teresa Volta, Sesshu Foster, John Oliver Simon.

Payment: one year's plus subscription and five gifts.

Reporting time: 8 weeks.

Copyright held by Anemone Press; permission given to publish with mention.

1984; 4/yr; 3,000

$10/yr ind; $10/yr inst; $2.50/ea; 40%

24 pp; 10 x 15

Ad rates: $200/page/10 x 15; $100/½ page/10 x 7 or 5 x 15; $50/¼ page/5 x 7

ISSN: 8756-7709

ANERCA/COMPOST

Adeena Karasick, Kedrick James, Wreford Miller

3989 Arbutus St.

Vancouver, BC V6J 4T2

604-253-5755

Poetry, criticism, graphics, word/text/image games/speculation.

A low-budget erratic mocking magazine devoted to experimental writing (although we also publish more traditional work if it shows great vision and might not get attention elsewhere). Mainly 'young' authors, testing the constraints of language.

Bill Bissett, Bruce Andrews, B.P. Nichol, Christopher Dewdney, Jerome Rothenberg, Roy Kiyooka.

Payment: 2 copies.

Reporting time: 1 to 4 months.

Copyright held by author.

1986; irregular; 400

$12/4 copies; $3 each; 60

40 pp; 8½ x 11

No ads

Direct Mail Dist., Faxon

ANTAEUS

Daniel Halpern

26 West 17th Street

New York, NY 10011

(212) 645-2214

Poetry, fiction, essays, criticism, translation, interviews.

ANTAEUS features a broad spectrum of current, previously unpublished fiction and poetry by both new and established authors, as well as essays and documents. Frequently publishes special issues offering essays on particular subjects (nature, autobiography, art, etc.).

Czeslaw Milosz, Robert Hass, Jorie Graham, Gail Godwin, Paul Bowles.

Payment: $10/page.

Reporting time: 10 weeks.

Copyright held by Antaeus; reverts to the author upon publication.

1970; 2/yr; 7,500

$30/2 yr ind; $30/2 yr inst; $10/ ea; 20%

280 pp; 6 ½ x 9

Ad rates: $500/page/5½ x 8; $300/½ page/2¾ x 8; $200/¼ page/2¾ x 4

ISSN: 0003-5319

W.W. Norton & Co., Ingram Periodicals, B. DeBoer & Co.

ANTIETAM REVIEW

Ann B. Knox, Crystal Brown
82 West Washington Street
Hagerstown, MD 21740
(301) 791-3132

Poetry, fiction, photographs.

The **ANTIETAM REVIEW** is a regional literary magazine for fiction writers, poets and photographers from Delaware, Maryland, Pennsylvania, Virginia, West Virginia, and the District of Columbia; however, we look for strong literary and artistic quality rather than local interest.

Wayne Karlin, David McKain, Geraldine Connolly, Linda Pasten, Ann Darr, Myra Sklarew.

Payment: $100 for fiction; $20 for poems.

Reporting time: 6 weeks to 4 months depending on pub. date.

Copyright held by Washington County Arts Council; reverts to author upon publication.

1984; 1 or 2/yr; 1,000

$5/yr; $5/ea; 20%

44 pp; 8½ x 11

No ads

ANTIOCH REVIEW

Robert S. Fogarty
P.O. Box 148
Yellow Springs, OH 45387

Poetry, fiction, criticism, essays, reviews.

ANTIOCH REVIEW is an independent quarterly of critical and creative thought which prints articles of interest to both the liberal scholar and the educated layman. Authors of articles on the arts, politics, social and cultural problems as well as short fiction and poetry find a friendly reception regardless of formal reputation.

Emile Capouya, Raymond Carver, Perri Klass, Gordon Lish, Joyce Carol Oates.

Payment: $15 per published page.

Reporting time: 3–6 weeks. *
Copyright held by **ANTIOCH REVIEW**.
1941; 4/yr; 4,500
$20/yr ind; $30/yr inst; $5.00/ea
128 pp; 6 x 9
Ad rates: $250/page/4½ x 7⅞;
$150/½ page; $100/¼ page
ISSN: 0003-5769
Eastern News Distributors, Inc.

ANTIPHONY
Patrick Pritchett
4422 Whitsett Ave., #8
Studio City, CA 91604
Poetry, essays, criticism, reviews,
fiction, translation.
ANTIPHONY is a twice yearly
publication devoted primarily to
poetry and essays about poetry.
Fiction, book and film reviews,
and socio-political articles are
also welcome. Humor, whimsi-
cal or trenchant, is not to be
despised. Essays on feminism
and the emergent Gaian poli-
tique are encouraged. The only
axe we have to grind is the
grassblade of eleutheria.
Herman J. Fong, Morin Sorescu,
Arwo F. Kuus, Denise Dumars,
Steven Tracey, Fuschia.
Payment: in copies.
Reporting time: 3–8 weeks.
Copyright held by Crow's Mouth
Press; reverts to author.

1989; 2/yr; 1,000
$9/yr ind; $12/yr inst.; $5.00/ea;
40%
60–75 pp.; 5½ x 8½.
Ad rates: $100/page; $50/½ page
Pending ISSN

ANTIPODES
Marian Arkin, Robert Ross
190 Sixth Avenue
Brooklyn, NY 11217
(718) 482-5680 or (718) 789-5826
Fiction, Reviews, Criticism, Essays, Poetry, Interviews, Photographs, Graphics/Artwork
Focus is on Australian literature.
Thomas Keneally, A.D. Hope,
Judith Wright, Thea Astley,
Olga Masters
Payment: in copies.
1987; 2/yr; 600
$20/yr ind; $24/yr inst; (Domestic); $25/ overseas; $2.00 Canadian postage; single copies: $12
Ind.; $14 Inst. (+ $3.50 overseas, $1.00 Canadian postage)
60–75 pp; 8½ x 11
Ad rates: $300/page/7½ x 10;
$175/½ page/7½ x 5 or 3½ x
10; $90/¼ page/7½ x 2½ or
3½ x 5

APALACHEE QUARTERLY
Barbara Hamby, Pam Ball, Clau-
dia Johnson, Bruce Boehrer,
Paul McCall

P.O. Box 20106
Tallahassee, FL 32316
Poetry, fiction, reviews, translation, photographs, graphics/artwork.
We are interested in well-crafted, modern fiction and poetry. Stylistic innovation is encouraged except when it interferes with narrative intent.
Peter Meinke, G.S. Sharat Chandra, Janet Burroway, Michael Shaara, David Kirby.
Payment: in copies and money when grants permit.
Reporting time: 12 weeks.
Copyright reverts to author upon publication.
1971; 3/yr; 500
$15/yr; $5/ea
100–200 pp; 6 x 9
Ad rates: $50/page

APPEARANCES

Robert Witz, Joe Lewis, Bill Mutter
165 West 26th Street
New York, NY 10001
(212) 675-3026
Poetry, fiction, interviews, photographs, graphics/artwork.
APPEARANCES. Literature, art, civilization. New talent. The works. Why wait.
Hal Sirowitz, j-poet, Nathaniel

Burkins, Michael LaBombarda, Jack Wark, Rodolpho Torres.
Payment: is occasional.
Copyright held by magazine; reverts to author upon publication.
1976; 2/yr; 900
$15/3 issues; $5/ea; 40%
76 pp; 8½ x 11
Ad rates: $180/page/7½ x 10; $110/½ page/7 x 5½; $80/¼ page/3½ x 5

ARACHNE

Susan L. Leach
162 Sturges Street
Jamestown, NY 14701
(716) 488-2601
Poetry, fiction.
ARACHNE is a small press dedicated to publishing well written poetry with a largely, but not exclusively, rural theme. We are interested in new poets and in poets who have been writing but have not been largely published. We publish four contributors' issues yearly.
Gary Fincke, Penny Kemp, Norbert Krapf, Walt Franklin, Wallace Whatley.
Payment: in copies.
Reporting time: 1 week to 2 months.
1980; 4/yr; 250

$18/yr ind; $20/yr inst; $5/ea;
40%
28 pp; 5¼ x 8¼

ARARAT QUARTERLY

585 Saddle River Road
Saddle Brook, NJ 07662
(201) 797-7600
Poetry, fiction, criticism, essays,
reviews, translation, interviews,
photographs.
Although all writing of merit is
considered for publication, the
magazine strongly prefers mate-
rial pertaining to subjects of
Armenian interest.
Joel Oppenheimer, Peter Balakian,
David Kherdian, Elizabeth
Young-Bruehl, Laura Kalpa-
kian, Odysseas Elytis, Kenneth
Rexroth.
Payment: arranged with editor.
Reporting time: 6–8 weeks.
Copyright held by author.
1958; 4/yr; 1,800
$24/yr ind; $7/ea
72 pp; 8 x 11
Ads accepted by inquiry

ARTFUL DODGE

Daniel Bourne and Karen Kovacik
Department of English
The College of Wooster
Wooster, OH 44691
(216) 262-8353

Poetry, fiction, translation, graphics, reviews.
ARTFUL DODGE is open not
just to American work combin-
ing the human and the aesthetic,
but also to translation, especially from Eastern Europe and
the Third World. We also have
an ongoing section on American
poets who translate, featuring
the poet's own work and his or
her adaptations of work going
on in landscapes other than English.
Stuart Dybek, Naomi Shihab Nye,
William S. Burroughs, Katharyn
Machan Aal, William Stafford,
Zbigniew Herbert
Payment: in copies, plus $5 hono-
rarium, as funding allows.
Reporting time: 1–4 months.
Copyright reverts to author.
1979; 2/yr; 1,000
$10/2 issues; $5/ea
150-200 pp; 6 x 9
ISSN: 0196-691X
DeBoer

ASCENT

Audrey Curley
P.O. Box 967
Urbana, IL 61801
Fiction, Poetry.
Eclectic.
Edith Pearlman, Lisa Steinman,

Elisavietta Ritchie, E.G. Burrows, K.C. Frederick.
Payment: three copies to author
Reporting time: 1 week to 2 months.
Copyright held by Ascent; reverts to author upon publication.
1975; 3/yr; 600
$3/yr; $1.50/ea; 40%
64 pp; 6 x 9
ISSN: 0098-9363

ASYLUM

Greg Boyd
P.O. Box 6203
Santa Maria, CA 93456
(805) 934-4570

Fiction, poetry, prose poems, essays, criticism, reviews, translation, photographs, graphics/artwork.
Contemporary literature: some emphasis on short prose forms, experimental writing, dream works and surrealism.
Kenneth Bernard, Stephen Dixon, Richard Kostelanetz, Stephen-Paul Martin, Edward Roditi, T. Wiloch.
Payment: in copies.
Reporting time: 2 weeks–3 months.
Copyright held by **ASYLUM**; reverts to author upon publication.
1985; 2/yr; 750

$10/yr; $3/ea; 40%
100 pp; 5½ x 8½
$40/page; $20/½ page
ISSN: 0896-1344

ATTICUS REVIEW

Harry Polkinhorn
720 Heber Avenue
Calexico, CA 92231
Verbal/visual, poetry, short fiction.
Payment: 1 copy.
Reporting time: 1 month.
Copyright reverts to author.
1983; 2/yr; 150
$6/yr; $3/ea + $1 transportation
40 pp; 8½ x 11

AURA LITERARY/ARTS REVIEW

Adam Pierce, Stefanie Truelove
P.O. Box 76
University Center UAB
Birmingham, AL 35294
(205) 934-3216

Poetry, fiction, interviews, essay
Contemporary poetry and prose. Experimental, traditional or genre. Looking for work that distinguishes itself from the crowd yet remains successful. Interested in documentary photography.
Payment: 2 copies.
Reporting time: 3 months.

Copyright reverts to author.
1974; 2/yr; 500
$6/yr; $2.50
20 pp; 6 x 9
ISSN: 0889-7433

A/B: AUTO/BIOGRAPHY STUDIES

Rebecca Hogan
English Department
University of Wisconsin
Whitewater, WI 53190
Timothy Dow Adams
English Department
University of West Virginia
Morgantown, WV 26506

Criticism, Reviews, Bibliographical and Newsletter information.

Purpose of magazine is to publish essays—literary and critical— about autobiography and biography. Emphasis of recent issues has been on special topics: women's autobiography, Mexican, therapeutic (forthcoming), European, etc. The journal serves also as a clearinghouse for information about convention panels, members' interests, etc.

Lynn Bloom, Janet Verner Gunn, Richard D. Woods, G. Thomas Couser, Silonie Smith.

Payment: none.
Copyright held by author.
1985; 4/yr; 200
$15/yr ind; $45/yr inst
70 pp; 7 x 8½

Ad rates: $150/page/7 x 8½;
$75/½ page/7 x 4¼; $40/¼
page/3½ x 4¼

AVEC

Cydney Chadwick
P.O. Box 1059
Penngrove, CA 94951
(707) 762-2370
Fax (707) 769-0880

Contemporary poetry, prose, translations, line art, photographs. Innovative, challenging work from established and emerging writers. **AVEC** is particularly interested in translation from the French.

Norma Cole, Michael Davidson, Lydia Davis, Dominique Fourcade, Jackson Mac Low, Michael Palmer, Claude Royet-Journoud, Leslie Scalapino.

Reporting time: Eight Weeks
Copyright reverts to author upon publication
1988; 2 issues yearly
2 issues/$12; $7.50/ea; 40%
(bookstores)
168 pages
Ad rates: Full page/7½ x 10/$130;
Half page/7½ x 4¾/$65 (horizontal); ¼ page/3¼ x 4¾/$40
ISSN: 0899-3750
Inland, Book People, Small Press Dist, Segue, Spectacular Diseases (U.K.)

B

B-CITY

Connie Deanovich
619 West Surf Street #2
Chicago, IL 60657
(312) 871-6175

Poetry, fiction, interviews.
Paul Hoover, Anne Waldman, Clark Coolidge, Jim McManus, Bernadette Mayer, Maxine Chernoff, Jerome Sala.
Small honorarium when available.
$5/yr ind; $6/yr inst; $5/ea; 40%
Illinois Literary Publishers Association

BAMBOO RIDGE: The Hawaii Writers' Quarterly

Eric Chock and Darrell Lum
P.O. Box 61781
Honolulu, HI 96839-1781

Poetry, fiction.
BAMBOO RIDGE has special interest in literature reflecting the multi-ethnic cultures and peoples of the Hawaiian Islands.
Juliet Kono, Wing Tek Lum, Garrett Hongo, Sylvia Watanabe, Rodney Morales, Cathy Song.
Payment: $10/poem; $20/short story.
Reporting time: 3–6 months.
Copyright held by Bamboo Ridge Press; reverts to author upon publication.
1978; 4/yr; 1,000
$12/yr; varies; 40%
120 pp, 6 x 9
Ad rates: $100/page/5¼ x 8¼
ISSN: 0733-0308
Small Press Distribution

BASTARD REVIEW

Thomas Aveva. Jennifer Wollin, Ellen Romano
P.O. Box 11837
San Francisco, CA 94101-7837

Poetry, fiction, translations, photographs.
Arkadii Dragomoshchenko, Adrienne Rich, William Gibson, Essex Hemphill, Amy Gerstler, August Kleinzahler, Carolyn Lau, William Dickey, Stephen Mitchell.
Payment: none
Copyright reverts to author on publication. For reproduction, please acknowledge BASTARD REVIEW.
$7/copy
80; 8½ x 11

BEAT SCENE

Kevin Ring
27 Court Leet

Binley Woods
Coventry, England CV32JQ
(020) 354-3604
Beat influenced/interviews/reviews.
SOS America onwards. Heavy emphasis on beat generation writers such as Jack Kerouac, William Burroughs, Charles Bukowski. Interviews, features, and information magazine. Full colour covers/glossy pages.
Charles Bukowski, Carolyn Cassady, Anne Waldman, Jack Micheline.
Copyright with contributors
1988; Quarterly; 6,000
$30.00; &7.00; 30%
60 p.
Ad rates: Full page $285; ½ page $150; ¼ page $75
Caroline International and Beat Scene

BELLES LETTRES: A Review of Books by Women
Janet Mullaney
11151 Captain's Walk Ct.
Gaithersburg, MD 20878
(301) 294-0278
Reviews, criticism, essays, interviews, photographs, graphics/artwork.
BELLES LETTRES reviews literature by women in all genres. Our purpose is to promote and celebrate writing by women and to inform and entertain. Interviews, rediscoveries, retrospectives, theme reviews, and publishing news are regularly featured. Queries from writers are welcome.
Jewelle Gomez, Cheryl Clarke, Margaret Randall, Evelyn Beck, Merrill Joan Gerber, Faye Moskowitz.
Payment: in subscriptions, copies & $25 per column, depending on grant funding.
Copyright held by magazine; reverts to author upon publication.
1985; 4/yr; 5,000
$20/yr ind; $40/yr inst; $5/ea; 40%
48 pp; 8½ x 11
Ad rates: Full page/7½ x 10/$400; Back page/7¼ x 8½ or 8½ 7¼/ $350; ⅔ page/4¾ x 10 or 7½ x 6½/$300; ½ page/3½ x 10 or 7½ x 5/$250; ¼ page/3½ x 5 or 7½ x 2½/$125
ISSN: 0084-2957
Ubiquity, Small Changes, Inland

THE BELLINGHAM REVIEW
Susan Hilton, Editor; Knute Skinner, Advisory Editor
The Signpost Press, Inc.
1007 Queen St.
Bellingham, WA 98226

(206) 734-9781

Poetry, fiction, reviews, plays, photographs, graphics/artwork. The focus is primarily on poetry, fiction and drama.

Richard Martin, Joseph Green, Nancy King, Maria Winston, Grace Grafton.

Payment: 1 year's subscription.

Reporting time: 2–3 months.

Copyright reverts to author upon publication.

1977; 2/yr; 800

$5/yr; $5.50 if agencied; $2.50/ea; 40% on 5 or more

60 pp; 5½ x 8½

Exchange ads only

ISSN: 0734-2934

BELLOWING ARK

Robert R. Ward

P.O. Box 45637

Seattle, WA 98145

(206) 545-8302

Poetry, fiction, essays, graphics/ artwork, novel serializations, short autobiography.

We feature work in the American Romantic tradition, i.e. editorial content is concerned with universal truths and the idea of transcending individual limitation. Content of a work is the primary consideration; form is a distant second, leading to a wryly eclectic mix (we are just concluding the serialization of a 14,000 line epic, for instance).

Nelson Bentley, Susan McCaslin, John Elrod, Harold Witt, Natalie Reciputi, Jon Jech, Bethany Reid.

Payment: 2 copies, upon publication.

Copyright held by **BELLOWING ARK**; reverts to author upon request.

1984; 6/yr; 800

$12/yr ind; $12/yr inst; $2/ea; 40%; comp to libraries on request

24 pp; 11 x 16

Ad rates: only in special circumstances

ISSN: 0887-4115

Ubiquity, Faxon, Popular Subscription Service

THE BELOIT POETRY JOURNAL

Marion K. Stocking

Box 154, R.F.D. 2

Ellsworth, ME 04605

(207) 667-5598

Poetry, reviews.

We publish the best poems we receive without bias as to length, form, subject, or tradition. We especially hope to discover new voices. Occasional chapbooks; recently Afro-

American, American Indian, and new Chinese poetry. Susan Tichy, Bruce Cutler, Hillel Schwartz, Brooks Haxton, Lola Haskins. Payment: 3 copies. Reporting time: immediately to four months. Copyright held by magazine; reverts to author upon publication.

1950; 4/yr; 1,200

$8/yr ind; $12/yr inst; $2/ea; 20%

40 pp; 5½ x 8½

No ads

ISSN: 0005-8661

B. DeBoer, Inc.; Maine Writer's and Publisher's Alliance

THE BERKELEY POETRY REVIEW

Natalia Apostolos & Jonathan Brennan

700 Eshleman Hall

University of California at Berkeley

Berkeley, CA 94720

Poetry, fiction, translation, interviews, photographs, graphics/ artwork

THE BERKELEY POETRY REVIEW is a small but longstanding literary journal that publishes primarily poetry. We accept submission year-round (4 poems maximum). We are always on the lookout for emerging writers.

Victor Hernandez Cruz, Thom Gunn, Heather McHugh, Opal Palmer-Adisa, Ishmael Reed. Payment: in 1 copy, upon publication.

Copyright held by author.

1973; 1–2/yr; 500–1,000

$10/yr ind; $12/yr inst; $10/ea; 40%

100 pp; 5 x 8

Ad rates: $55/page/4 x 7; $30/½ page/2½ x 3½

BETWEEN C & D

Joel Rose and Catherine Texier

255 East 7th Street

New York, NY 10009

Note Well: **BETWEEN C & D** will neither be reading manuscripts, nor offering subscriptions during the 1991-92 period. Fiction.

Sex, drugs, violence, danger, computers. Writers on the edge. David Foster Wallace, Reinaldo Povod, Patrick McGrath, Dennis Cooper, Kathy Acker. Payment: in copies. Reporting time: 3 months. Copyright reverts to author.

1984; 3/yr; 600

$15/yr issues post. included; $4/ea

50 pp; 9½ x 11

New York Newpapers

BIG CIGARS

José Padua, Michael Randall,
Stephen Ciacciarelli
1625 Hobart St., NW
Washington, DC 20009
Poetry, fiction, graphics/artwork.
BIG CIGARS is hand-assembled,
limited editions, the purpose of
which is to publish new writing
from mostly non-established
writers, reaching as wide an
audience as possible. We are
interested in short, lucid poetry
and fiction, the more daring the
better. While we do not print
great quantities, we reach both
coasts and several countries.
Ron Kolm, Hal Sirowitz, Lyn Lifshin, Todd Moore, Rollo White-
head.
Payment: in copies.
Reporting time: 2 to 3 months.
Copyright held by The P.O.N.
Press; reverts to author upon
publication.
1986; 2/yr; 350
$3.00/ea
40 pp; 8½ x 11
No ads
St. Marks Books, Sohazat, Spring
St. Books, City Lights

THE BILINGUAL REVIEW/LA REVISTA BILINGÜE

Gary D. Keller
Hispanic Research Center
Arizona State University
Tempe, AZ 85287-2702
(602) 965-3867
Poetry, fiction, criticism, reviews,
scholarly articles.
Devoted to the linguistics and lit-
erature of bilingualism, prima-
rily Spanish/English, in the
United States. We publish cre-
ative literature by and/or about
United States Hispanics, literary
criticism and reviews of United
States Hispanic literature. We
do not publish translations.
Martín Espada, Carolina Hospital,
Rosaura Sánchez, Alberto Ríos.
Payment: in copies.
Reporting time: 30 days.
Copyright held by magazine.
1974; 3/yr; 1,000
$16/yr ind; $26/yr inst; sample
copies: $6 ind/$9 inst
96 pp; 7 x 10
Ad rates: $150/page/5½ x 8½;
$90/½ page/5½ x 4
ISSN: 0094-5366

BITTERROOT

Menke Katz
P.O. Box 489
Spring Glen, NY 12483
Poetry, translation, reviews.
To inspire and encourage talented
poets who have difficulty get-
ting published, as well as estab-
lished poets who seek their own

identity through original poetry, realistic or fantastic. No rejection slips, always a personal reply. The William Kushner Awards and Heershe Dovid Badonneh Awards sponsored annually.

Payment: in copies
Reporting time: One month-6 weeks
Copyright: Held by the author.
1962; 1,000
$12/yr; $4/ea
70; 5½ x 8½
$200/page/4 x 6½; $100/½ page/4 x 3¼

BLACK AMERICAN LITERATURE FORUM

Joe Weixlmann
Department of English
Indiana State University
Terre Haute, IN 47809
(812) 237-2968

Poetry, criticism, reviews, interviews, photographs, graphics/ artwork, bibliographies.
Critical and pedagogical essays on black American literature, interviews, bibliographies, book reviews, poems, and graphics on black themes.
Amiri Baraka, Gwendolyn Brooks, Ishmael Reed, Houston A. Baker, Jr., Rita Dove, Henry Louis Gates, Jr.

Payment: depends on grants.
Reporting time: 3 months.
Copyright held by author.
1967; 4/yr; 1,200
$19/yr ind; $30/yr inst; $7.50/ea; 40%
192 pp; 6 x 9
$150/page/4⅜ x 7½; $90/½ page/4⅜ x 3¾.
ISSN: 0148-6179

BLACK BEAR REVIEW

Ave Jeanne & Ron Zettlemoyer
1916 Lincoln St.
Croydon, PA 19021

Poetry, reviews, graphics, market listings, current poetry news.
BLACK BEAR REVIEW is an international literary/fine arts magazine published twice a year. We welcome poetry that shows knowledge of / the craft, the world around us / human nature. We attempt to get into print as much poetry as possible and chapbooks. Social, environmental, and political topics welcomed.
Arthur Winfield Knight, A. D. Winans, James Humphrey, Tony Moffeit, Alan Catlin, Harry Calhoun, Gina Bergamino.
Payment: in copy.
Copyright: held by magazine; reverts to author upon publication.

1984; 2/yr; 500
$8/yr ind; $10/yr inst; $4/ea; 40%
64 pp; 5½ x 8
ISSN: 8756-0666

BLACK ICE

Editor: Ron Sukenick; Associate
   Editor: Dallas Wiebe; Assistant
   Editor: Mark Amerika
English Dept. Publications Center
Campus Box 494
Boulder, CO 80309-0494
(303) 492-8947
Fiction.
BLACK ICE publishes only fic-
   tion, with emphasis on non-
   traditional fiction. We intend to
   take risks with the fiction we
   publish and encourage writers to
   do the same.
Steve Katz, Erik Belgum, Thomas
   Glynn, Harold Jaffe, Cris
   Mazza.
Payment: in 2 contributors copies.
Copyright held by **BLACK ICE**;
   reverts to author upon publica-
   tion.
1984; 3/yr; 500
$7/ea; 40%
100 pp; 5½ x 8½
Ad rates: $150/page/5 x 8
ISSN: 1047-515X

BLACK JACK/VALLEY
GRAPEVINE

Art Cuelho
P.O. Box 249
Big Timber, MT 59011

Poetry, fiction, photographs,
   graphics/artwork.
BLACK JACK's focus is on rural
   America; regional writing; and
   interests are on the the Dust-
   bowl; Okie migration; southern
   Appalachia; Hoboes; American
   Indians; the West. **VALLEY
   GRAPEVINE** focuses on any-
   thing in the San Joaquin Valey
   in Central California.
Bill Rintoul, Gerry Haslam,
   Wilma McDaniel, Dorothy
   Rose, Frank Cross.
Payment: in copies.
Reporting time: 1 week.
Copyright held by Seven Buffa-
   loes Press; reverts to author
   upon publication.
1973; 1/yr; 750
$10/yr; $6/ea; 20%–40%
85 pp; 5¼ x 8¼

BLACK RIVER REVIEW

Kaye Collier
855 Mildred Ave
Lorain, OH 44052
(216) 244-9654
Poetry, fiction, critical essay, book
   review.
BRR presents contemporary writing of diverse styles and genres
   aimed toward a broad audience.
   We print work that exhibits
   originality, craftsmanship, vivid
   style, by writers both well-

known and as-yet-to-be-discovered. More detailed guidelines are available for SASE.

John M. Bennett, Diane Glancy, Prescott Foster, Bayla Winters, Robert Cooperman, Li Mia Hua.

Payment: in copies.

Reporting time: 2 weeks–6 months. Submissions are accepted between Jan. 1 and May 1 of each year. Those received at any other time are returned unread. No response without an SASE.

Copyright reverts to author upon publication.

1985; 1/yr; 400

$3.50 per issue

60 pp; 8½ x 11

Query for ad rates

THE BLACK SCHOLAR

Robert Chrisman, Editor: JoNina Abron, Managing Editor

P.O. Box 2869

Oakland, CA 94606

(415) 547-6633

Poetry, fiction, sociology, politics, economy, education, book reviews.

A journal of black studies and research, addressing such issues as black culture, black politics, black education, economics, Southern Africa, etc. . . . A journal on the cutting edge of contemporary black thought.

Jesse Jackson, Jayne Cortez, Johnnotta B. Cole, Gwendolyn Brooks, Haki R. Madhubuti, P.P. Sarduy

Payment: subscription plus 10 copies.

Reporting time: 2 months.

Copyright held by Black World Foundation.

1969; 6/yr; 10,000

$30/ind; $50/inst; $5/ea; 20%–40%

64 pp; 7 x 10

$1,000/page; $600/½ page; query

ISSN: 0006-4246

L-S Dist., B. DeBoer

BLACK WARRIOR REVIEW

Mark Dawson

P.O. Box 2936

Tuscaloosa, AL 35486-2936

(205) 348-4518

Poetry, fiction, essays, reviews, translations, interviews, photographs, graphics/artwork.

The **BLACK WARRIOR REVIEW** publishes the best of contemporary writing by the best of contemporary writers.

Andre Dubus, Michael S. Harper, Howard Nemerov, John Irving, Jorie Graham, Jane Miller, David St. John.

Payment: $5–10/page.

Reporting time: 1–3 months.

Copyright held by magazine; reverts to author upon publication.

1974; 2/yr; 1,800

$7.50/yr ind; $11.00/yr inst; $4/ea

144 pp; 6 x 9

Ad rates: $150/page/5 x 8; $75/½ page/5 x 3½; $37.50/¼ page/ 5 x 1¾

ISSN: 0193-6301

BLATANT ARTIFICE

Edmund Cardoni

Hallwalls Contemporary Arts Center

700 Main Street

Buffalo, NY 14202

(716) 854-5828

Fiction, graphics/artwork.

An annual anthology of short fiction and performance texts by visitors to Hallwalls, dedicated to innovative prose writing.

Robie McCauley, Karen Finley, Holly Hughes, Oscar Hijuelos, Victor Montejo.

Payment: $35.

Copyright reverts to author upon publication.

1986; annual; 1,000

$10; 40%

168 pp; 7 x 9

Printed Matter (New York), Contemporary Arts Press (San Fran-

cisco), Marginal Distribution (Toronto), Central Books Warehouse (London)

BLIND ALLEYS

Michael S. Weaver

29 S. Munn Ave, #3H

East Orange, NJ 07018

(201) 677-1114

Poetry, fiction, criticism, essays, reviews, graphics/artwork.

BLIND ALLEYS is a semiannual magazine which has a primary focus on the third world, but it does not limit itself to a specific literary approach or political beat.

Lucille Clifton, Andrei Codrescu, Jerry Ward, Ethelbert Miller, Eric Abrahamson.

Payment: in copies.

Reporting time: 3 to 4 months.

Copyright reverts to author.

1982; 2/yr; 300

$11/yr ind; $13/yr inst; $5/ea

45 pp; 5¼ x 8⅜

Ad rates: $100/page; $50/½ page; $25/¼ page

THE BLOOMSBURY REVIEW

Tom Auer, Publisher; Marilyn Auer, Assoc. Publisher

1028 Bannock Street

Denver, CO 80204

(303) 892-0620
FAX (303) 892-5620
Reviews, graphics/artwork, poetry, interviews, photographs, essays.

THE BLOOMSBURY REVIEW is a "Book Magazine" that includes reviews, interviews, essays, poetry, profiles, and previews of new titles, with an emphasis on new titles from small, medium-sized, and university presses.

Harlan Ellison, Gregory Mc-Namee, John Nichols, Linda Hogan, Peter Wild.
Payment: $15/review; $10/poetry; $20/interviews.
Reporting time: 6–8 weeks.
Copyright reverts to author.
1980; 8/yr; 50,000
$18/yr; $3.00/ea; 40%; less discount through distributors.
32 pp; 10 x 12
Ad rates: $2,790/9⅞ x 15¼; $1490/4⅞ x 15¼; $775/ 4⅞ x 7½
ISSN: 0276-1564

BLUE BUILDINGS

Tom Urban, Ruth Doty, Guillaume Williams
Drake University
Department of English
Des Moines, IA 50311
(515) 277-2060

Poetry, translations, and art.
Michael Benedikt, Marge Piercy, William Stafford, Richard Shelton, George Garrett, Alberto Rios, Gary Fincke.
Payment: none.
Reporting time: 6–8 weeks, sometimes longer.
Copyright reverts to author.
1979; 2/yr; 750
$8/ea
50 pp; 8½ x 11

BLUE LIGHT RED LIGHT

Alma Rodriguez, Joy Parker
496A Hudson Street, Suite F-42
New York, NY 10014
(212) 432-3245

Fusion of contemporary writing, magic surrealism, and mainstream writing together with speculative fiction.

BLUE LIGHT RED LIGHT, a periodical of speculative fiction and the arts, welcomes all international writers, poets and storytellers inspired by the literature of personal myth, dream images and folklore.

Gloria Naylor, Harlan Ellison, Peter Wortsman, E. S. Creamer.
Payment: small honorarium, plus issues.
Reporting time: 6 weeks.
Copyright held by BLRL; reverts to author.
1988; 1–3/yr

$15/yr; $5.50/ea; 40%
176 pp; 9 x 6
$250/page; $150/½ page
ISSN: 10456-0012

BLUE UNICORN

Ruth G. Iodice, Harold Witt,
Daniel J. Langton; Art Editor:
Robert L. Bradley; Contest
Chairperson: Ila F. Berry
22 Avon Road
Kensington, CA 94707
(415) 526-8439

Poetry, translation, artwork.

We are looking for excellence of
the individual poetic voice,
whether that voice comes
through in form or freer verse,
rhyme or not. We want originality of image, thought and music, poems which are
memorable and communicative.
We publish both well-known
poets and unknowns who de-
serve to be known better.

John Ciardi, Charles Edward
Eaton, Emilie Glen, Diana
O'Hehir, William Stafford.
Payment: in copies.
Reporting time: 3–4 months.
Copyright held by magazine; re-
verts to author upon publica-
tion.
1977; 3/yr; 500
$12/yr; $4/ea; $18 foreign.

56 pp; 5½ x 8½
ISSN: 0197-7016

BLUELINE

Anthony Tyler
English Dept.
SUNY
Potsdam, NY 13676
Poetry, fiction, essays, reviews,
graphics/artwork, oral history,
journals.
BLUELINE is dedicated to prose
and poetry about the Adiron-
dacks and other regions similar
in geography and spirit. We are
interested in historic and contemporary writing, from new
and established writers, that
interprets the region as well as
describes it.
Joseph Bruchac, Paul Corrigan,
Roger Mitchell, Noelle Oxen-
handler, Lloyd Van Brunt.
Payment: in copies.
Reporting time: 2–10 weeks.
Copyright held by magazine; reverts to author upon publication.
1989; 1/yr double issue; 600
$6/yr; $6/ea; $4 per copy to dis-
tributors
112 pp; 6 x 9
ISSN: 0198-9901

BOGG

John Elsberg, George Cairncross
422 North Cleveland

Arlington, VA 22201

Poetry, prose poems, criticism, essays, reviews, interviews, graphics/artwork.

Editing is a subjective affair, and we print what takes our fancy. **BOGG** is an Anglo-American literary journal, with contributions from the U.S., Canada, England, and Australia/New Zealand.

Ann Menebroker, Ron Androla, Harold Witt, Robert Peters, John Millett, Tina Fulker, Richard Peabody, Jon Silkin.

Payment: in copies.

Reporting time: immediately.

Copyright held by author.

1968; 2–3/yr; 750

$10/3 issues; $4/ea; $3/sample; 40%

64 pp; 6 x 9

ISSN: 0882-648X

BOMB MAGAZINE

Betsy Sussler

P.O. Box 2003

Canal Station

New York, NY 10013

(212) 431-3943

Interviews, poetry, fiction, photographs, art.

BOMB MAGAZINE is a spokespiece for new art, fiction, theatre and film in New York. Named after Wyndham Lewis's "Blast," it promotes and encourages conversations throughout the arts.

Kathy Acker, Gary Indiana, Patrick McGram, Lynn Tillman.

Payment: $100.

Copyright reverts to author.

1981; 4/yr; 8,500

$18/yr; $5/ea; 40%

100 pp; 10 x 14½

Ad rates: on request

BONE & FLESH

Frederick Moe/Lester Hirsh

P.O. Box 349

Concord, NH 03302-0349

(603) 228-5723

Poetry, short fiction, essays, reviews, artwork.

BONE & FLESH is an eclectic blend of styles and voices. We are oriented towards spiritual and interpersonal growth. We look for work that has emotional impact.

Joel Oppenheimer, Jean Battlo, Jack Veasey, Carolyn Page, Chelsea Adams, Alan Catlin.

Payment: in copies.

Reporting time: usually within 8 weeks.

Copyright reverts to author.

1988; 2/yr; 250+

$8/yr; $5/ea

pp varies; 8½ x 11

ISSN: 9130-1040

BOSTON LITERARY REVIEW (BLUR)

Gloria Mindock
Box 357
W. Somerville, MA 02144
(617) 625-6087

Poetry, short fiction (under 3,000 words).

We seek work that pushes form or content, and that has a unique, even idiosyncratic voice. 5–10 poems are welcome, as we prefer to publish several poems by each author.

Eric Pankey, David Ray, Stuart Freibert, Richard Kostelanetz.

Payment: 2 copies.

Reporting time: 2–4 weeks.

Copyright reverts to author upon publication.

1984; 2/yr; 500
$6/yr; $4/ea
24 pp; 5½ x 13

BOSTON REVIEW

Margaret Ann Roth, Editor
33 Harrison Avenue
Boston, MA 02111
(617) 350-5353

THE BOSTON REVIEW is an award-winning national magazine with the distinctive voice of Boston—unconventional coverage of culture and all the arts. Meet the next generation of gifted young writers alongside with established authors saying what's really on their minds. People like Helen Vendler, David Leavitt, Rosellen Brown, Seamus Heaney.

Payment: $40–$250/depending on length and author.

Copyright held by Boston Critic, Inc.; reverts to author upon publication.

1975; 6/yr; 10,000
$15/yr ind; $18/yr inst
28–44 pp; 11⅜ x 14½

Ad rates: $800/page/10 x 14; $550/½ page/10 x 6¾; $250/¼ page/4¾ x 6¾

ISSN: 0734-2306

Interstate, Ingram, Total

BOTTOMFISH

Robert Scott
DeAnza College
21250 Stevens Creek Blvd.
Cupertino, CA 95014
(408) 864-8538 or 864-8547

Poetry, fiction.

BOTTOMFISH accepts lyric poems and short fiction of 5,000 words or less, including portions of novels. We publish some experimental fiction. We are interested only in carefully crafted work.

Naomi Clark, Janice Dabney, William Dickey, Edward Kleinschmidt, Martin Nakell.

Payment: in copies.
Copyright held by magazine; reverts to author upon publication.
1986; 1/yr; 500
$4.00/ea; 40%
70–80 pp; 17.5 x 21 cm.
No ads

Rights; reverts to author upon
publication.
1986; 3/yr; 2,500
$12/yr ind; $9/yr inst; $5/ea. 40%
200 pp
Ad rates available. Contact CLMP
for information.
ISSN: 0885-9337
Bernhard DeBoer Inc.

BOULEVARD
Richard Burgin, Editor
2400 Chestnut St., #2208
Philadelphia, PA 19103
(215) 561-1723

Poetry, fiction, criticism, essays,
translations, interviews, photos,
graphics.

BOULEVARD publishes excep-
tional fiction and poetry by im-
pressive new talent as well as
established literary voices. The
editors believe a critical dimension is essential to an outstanding literary publication; thus,
each issue publishes essays on
literature and the other arts.
BOULEVARD believes in the
school of talent.

John Ashbery, Isaac Bashevis
Singer, Joyce Carol Oates, Al-
ice Adams, Kenneth Koch.
Payment: $25–150/poetry; $50–
150/fiction & other prose.
Copyright held by Opojaz Inc. for
First North American Serial

BOUNDARY 2
William V. Spanos
SUNY/Binghamton
Binghamton, NY 13901
(607) 798-2743

Poetry, fiction, criticism, essays,
plays, translation, interviews,
photographs, graphics/artwork.

BOUNDARY 2 publishes poetry,
fiction and literary criticism that
try to break out of the impasse
that traditional, including modernist, literature and literary
criticism have become stalled
in. We are especially interested
in providing a forum for experi-
ments in open forms that ulti-
mately interrogate the literary
tradition and the dominant culture this tradition supports.

Armand Schwerner, Jerome Rothenberg, John Taggart, Charles
Bernstein and the
l=a=n=g=u=a=g=e
poets.
Payment: none.

37

Reporting time: 4–6 months.
1972; 3/yr; 1,000
$15/yr ind; $13/yr students; $25/yr
inst; $8/ea; 40%
300 pp; 9 x 5¾
Ad rates: $100/page; $50/½ page;
$25/¼ page

BRIEF

Jim Hydock
P.O. Box 33
Canyon, CA 94516
(415) 376-5509

Poetry, fiction, post-modern fiction/poetry.
Subscription only. Sold in select bookstores.
Larry Eigner, Fielding Dawson, August Kleinzahler, Anselm Hollo, Martha King.
Payment: none.
Reporting time: 2–4 weeks.
Copyright held by magazine; reverts to author upon publication.
1988; 3/yr; 250
$10/yr ind; $12/yr inst.; $2.50/ea; 40%
25 pp; 5½ x 8½
No ads

BROOKLYN REVIEW

English Dept., Brooklyn College
Brooklyn, NY 11210
(718) 780-5195

Poetry, fiction, playwriting.
A magazine of contemporary poetry, fiction and playwriting. No specifications as to style, length, form or content.
James Schuyler, Alice Notley, Joan Larkin, Eileen Myles, Elaine Equi, David Trinidad, Ronna Levy.
Payment: 2 copies.
Reporting time: 2 weeks–2 months.
Copyright reverts to author upon publication.
1984; 1/yr; 500
$5/yr; $5/ea
50–80 pp; 4¼ x 5½

BRUSSELS SPROUT

Francine Porad
P.O. Box 1551
Mercer Island, WA 98040
(206) 232-3239

Haiku Poetry, senryu, essays, book reviews dealing with haiku, graphics/artwork.
A journal of contemporary English language haiku and art, with international contributors and subscribers. Seeking haiku and senryu in a variety of styles and forms, from one to four lines. Subject matter is open. BRUSSELS SPROUT looks for haiku that capture "the haiku moment" in a fresh way.

Marlene Mountain, Anne McKay, George Swede, Paul O. Williams, Robert Spiess, Vincent Tripi.
Payment: none, 3–$10 editor's awards.
Reporting time: 3 weeks.
Copyright reverts to author upon publication.
1980; 3/yr; 300
$12 domestic/Canada, $18 elsewhere; $5.00/$6.00
48 pp; 8½ x 5½
ISSN: 0897-7356
U. Book Store, Elliot Bay Book Co., ISLAND BOOKS

C

CAFE SOLO

Glenna Luschei
Box 2814
Atascadero, CA 93422
(805) 466-0947

Poetry, fiction, criticism, essays, reviews, translation, photographs, graphics/artwork.
We seek excellence and the avant-garde: Subconscious navigation in strange waters and Columbus sighting land. We print new writers next to known ones. We emphasize poetry, but encour-age imaginative essays and new literary art forms.
Robert Bly, Denise Levertov, Gene Frumkin, Gary Snyder, Lawrence Ferlinghetti, Thomas McGrath, and prisoners from the California Men's Colony.
Payment: in copies.
Reporting time: 8 weeks.
Copyright held by Solo Press.
1969; 3/yr; 500
$20/yr; $5/ea; 40%
44 pp; 6 x 9
ISSN: 0773-1796

CALIBAN

Lawrence R. Smith
P.O. Box 4321
Ann Arbor, MI 48106
(517) 486-3548

Poetry, fiction, translation, interviews, graphics/artwork.
CALIBAN has redefined the literary and artistic avant-garde by cutting across partisan lines, making different writers and artists in serious pursuit of the new aware of each other. CALIBAN also insists that the avant-garde is not the exclusive domain of white, middle-class males, bohemian or otherwise.
Berssenbrugge, Bly, Creeley, Kingston, Wakoski.
Payment: $15–$20, plus 2 copies.

Reporting time: 2 weeks to 1 month.

Copyright held by **CALIBAN**; reverts to author upon publication.

1986; 2/yr; 1,700

$10/yr; $18/2 yr ind; $17/yr inst; $6/ea; 40%, 25% textbook orders

192 pp; 6 x 9

Ad rates: $100/page/5 x 8

ISSN: 0890-7269

DeBoer, Bookpeople, SPD, Fine Print

CQ (CALIFORNIA STATE POETRY QUARTERLY)

John M. Brander

1200 E. Ocean Blvd., #64

Long Beach, CA 90802

(213) 495-0925

Poetry, translation, graphics/artwork.

Poems may come from anywhere in the country. We like everything we've published in **CQ**, some of it a lot, but from now on we would like to receive not only poems like those we've printed but also those which are unlike anything we've ever printed.

Jennifer Olds, William James Kovanda, Sylvia Rosen, Joseph Kent, Aaron Kramer.

Payment: none.

Reporting time: 2–3 months.

Copyright held by California State Poetry Society and English Department, Chapman College, Orange, CA; reverts to author upon publicaton.

1972; 3 or 4/yr; 500

$5/ea; 20%

84 pp

No ads

Small Press Traffic (San Francisco), Midnight Special (Santa Monica), Dutton's (Brentwood, Los Angeles), CSULB Bookstore, Long Beach

CALLALOO

Charles H. Rowell

Department of English

Wilson Hall

University of Virginia

Charlottesville, VA 22903

(804) 924-6616

Bibliography, poetry, fiction, criticism, essays, reviews, plays, translation, photographs, graphics/artwork.

CALLALOO is a quarterly magazine which gives special attention to Black South arts and literature. **CALLALOO** also publishes black writers nationwide and black writers in the Caribbean and Africa.

Rita Dove, Chinua Achebe, John Edgar Wideman, Derek Walcott, Leopold S. Senghor, Alice Walker, Aimé Césaire.

Payment: (When grants are available from NEA.)

Copyright held by Johns Hopkins University Press; reversion to author depends upon situation.

1976; quarterly; 800

$20/yr ind; $41/yr inst (plus foreign postage); $6/ea ind; $9/ea inst; 40%

180 pp; 7 x 10

Ad rates: $150/page/5½ x 8; $90/½ page/5½ x 4; cover 2/$200; cover 3/$175

ISSN: 0161-2492

CALLIOPE

Martha Christina
Creative Writing Program
Roger Williams College
Bristol, RI 02809
(401) 253-1040, ext. 2217

Poetry, fiction.

Interested in both established and emerging writers, but need not have published elsewhere. Prefer concrete to abstract images, work that appeals to the emotions through the senses.

Thomas Lux, Mark Doty, Mark Cox, Lynne deCourcy, Lynda Sexson.

Payment: 2 copies and subscription.

Copyright held by magazine; re-verts to author upon publication.

1977; 2/yr; 300

$5.00/yr; $3/ea; 40%

5½ x 8½

CALYPSO: Journal of Narrative Poetry and Poetic Fiction

Susan Richardson, Frances Richardson
175 East Washington, #C
El Cajon, CA 92020

Poetry, fiction, interviews, essays, reviews.

We consider interviews, essays and reviews which concern narrative poetry and poetic fiction; we also publish additional types of poetry and fiction.

Paul Milenski, John Bradley, Geraldine C. Little, William Kloefkorn, Eve Shelnutt.

Payment: two copies

Reporting time: 1–2 months

Copyright reverts to author provided **CALYPSO** is acknowledged upon subsequent publication.

1989; Annual; 200

$6/yr; $6

60–100; 6 x 9

No ads

ISSN: 1051-1857

CALYX: A Journal of Art and Literature by Women

Margarita Donnelly, Catherine Holdorf, Bev McFarland, Linda Smith

P.O. Box B

Corvallis, OR 97339

(503) 753-9384

Poetry, fiction, essays, translations, reviews, photographs, visual art, interviews.

Considered one of the finest literary magazines in the U.S., CALYX publishes work by women artists and presents a wide spectrum of women's experience. CALYX is committed to publishing the finest work by women of color, working class women, lesbians, politically active women, and older women. Winner of 1988 OILA award for literary achievement in Oregon. Two-time winner of the CCLM Editor's Grant (1985 & 1990).

Robin Morgan, Gioconda Belli, Gloria Bird, Monica Sjöo, Terri Jewell, Ingrid Wendt, Carmen Naranjo.

Payment: in copies.

Reporting time: 3–6 months.

Copyright released to authors by magazine.

1976; 3/volume; 3,000

$18/yr ind; $22.50/yr inst; add for foreign postage $4/surface; $9/air; $8.00/ea + postage; 30%–40%

100–128 pp single; 200+ double.

Ad rates: $550/page/5¾ x 7; $285/½ page/5¾ x 3⅜

ISSN: 0147-1627

Small Changes, Inland, Bookpeople, Ingram, Small Press Dist., Ingram Periodicals, Airlift, Armadillo, Homing Pigeon

THE CAPE ROCK

Harvey Hecht

English Department

Southeast Missouri State University

Cape Girardeau, MO 63701

(314) 651-2636

Poetry, photographs.

We have no restrictions on subjects or forms. Our criterion for selection is the quality of the work rather than the bibliography of the authors. We prefer poems under 70 lines. We feature a single photographer each issue.

Laurel Speer, Laurie Taylor, Martin Robbins, Charles A. Waugaman.

Payment: each issue we award $200 for the best poem and $100 for the photography. All contributors are paid in copies.

Reporting time: 1–4 months. We

do not read poetry in May, June or July.

Copyright held by magazine; reprint rights granted upon request provided reprint credit is given The Cape Rock.

1964; 2/yr; 700
$2/ea; 40%
64pp; 5½ x 8½
ISSN: 0146-2199

THE CARIBBEAN WRITER

Erika J. Smilowitz
Caribbean Research Institute
University of the Virgin Islands
RR 02, Box 10,000 Kingshill
St. Croix, VI 00850
(809) 778-0246

Poetry, fiction, reviews, graphics/ artwork.

THE CARIBBEAN WRITER is an international magazine with a Caribbean focus. The Caribbean should be central to the work, or the work should reflect a Caribbean heritage, experience, or perspective.

Derek Walcott, Olive Senior, Julia Alvarez, O. R. Dathorne.

Payment: 1 copy.

Copyright held by Caribbean Research Institute; reverts to author upon publication.

1987; 1/yr; 1500
$7/ea; 12–24 = 30%, 25+ = 40%

100 pp; 6 x 9
Ad rates: $200/page/6 x 9; $150/½ page/3 x 10; $100/¼ page/3 x 4½
ISSN: 0893-1550

A CAROLINA LITERARY COMPANION

Nellvena Duncan Eutsler, Managing Editor; Michael Parker, Fiction; Patrick Bizzaro, Poetry
Community Council for the Arts
P.O. Box 3554
Kinston, NC 28502-3554
(919) 527-2517

Poetry, fiction.

A CAROLINA LITERARY COMPANION is published twice yearly, and is intended primarily as a vehicle for emerging Southern writers of poetry and short fiction. Primary consideration is given to writers who live in the South or are natives of that region. All selections are made on the basis of artistic merit.

Ron Rash, Becke Roughton, Marion Hodge, R. T. Smith, Ruth Moose.

Payment: in 2 copies of the volume in which contributors are published.

Reporting time: 2–3 weeks after each deadline (10/15 and 2/15 each year).

Copyright held by Community Council for the Arts; reverts to author upon publication.
1985; 2/yr; 400
$8.50/yr; $5/ea; 40% on 5 or more; 33% on 3 or 4 copies
67 pp; 5½ x 8½
No ads

CAROLINA QUARTERLY

David Kellogg
Greenlaw Hall CB #3520
University of North Carolina at Chapel Hill
Chapel Hill, NC 27599-3520
(919) 962-0244

Poetry, fiction, interviews, photographs.

A literary journal published three times yearly. Interested in fiction and poetry by both new and established writers— excellence is our only restriction.

R. T. Smith, Martha Collins, Ian MacMillan.

Payment: $15 per author, fiction and poetry.

Reporting time: 4–6 months.
Copyright held by magazine.
1944; 3/yr; 800
$10/yr ind; $12/yr inst; $5/ea
100 pp; 6 x 9
Ad rates; $95/page; $60/½ page; $40/¼ page
ISSN: 000-8-6797

CATALYST MAGAZINE

Pearl Cleage
34 Peachtree Street, Suite 2330
Atlanta, GA 30303
(404) 730-5785

Fiction, non-fiction, poetry, criticism, essays.

Focuses primarily on Southern writers, but welcomes all submissions in Fiction, poetry, drama and criticism. The magazine presents writers in a format designed to stimulate discussion and encourage the exchange of ideas.

Willie Woods, Zaron Burnett, Mari Evans.

Payment: $20–$200
Reporting time: 4 Months
Copyright authors
1986; biannual; 5,000
$10/2 yrs; $2.50
96; 7½ x 14
ISSN: 0896-7423
Sauacou; Marcus Books; The Shrine of The Black Madonna

THE CATHARTIC

Patrick M. Ellingham
P.O. Box 1391
Fort Lauderdale, FL 33302
(305) 967-9378

Poetry, reviews, photographs, artwork.

THE CATHARTIC is devoted to the unknown poet, with the understanding that most poets are unknown in America. All types of poetry except those that are racist or sexist. Avoid poems over 50 lines or rhyme for the sake of rhyme. Experiment with language and form. Poems that deal with or come from the dark side; intense poems that use words sparingly and forget the poet; poems that jar the reader's sensibilities, darkly erotic poems.

Eileen Eliot, Joy Walsh, Harry Knickerbocker.

Payment: 1 copy.

Copyright reverts to author upon publication.

1974; 2/yr; 200

$3.75/yr; $7/2 yrs; $2/ea

28 pp; 5½ x 8½

No ads

ISSN: 0145-8310

CEILIDH: AN INFORMAL GATHERING FOR STORY & SONG

P.O. Box 6367

San Mateo, CA 94403

(415) 378-2350 or (415) 591-9902

Fiction, poetry, plays, translation, photographs, graphics/artwork

Patrick Smith, John Moffitt, Traise Yamamoto, Richard Soos, Sarah Bliumis

$7.50/yr; $2.50/ea; 40%

CENTRAL PARK

Stephen-Paul Martin; Richard Royal: Prose and Visuals; Eve Ensler: Poetry

P.O. Box 1446

New York, NY 10023

(212) 691-0890 or (212) 242-0302

Experimental fiction, narrative fiction, theory, graphics/ artwork, poetry, photographs, translation, interviews, reviews.

CENTRAL PARK is moving in three main directions: poetry and fiction of an either experimental or aggressively political nature, essays in social or esthetic theory, and visual work that moves the eye to think about how it sees. Prospective contributors are advised to order a sample copy ($5.00) before submitting.

Marc Kaminsky, Rosmarie Waldrop, Rae Armantrout, Ron Silliman, Jackson MacLow.

Payment: one copy.

Reporting time: 8 weeks.

Copyright held by magazine.

1981; 2/yr; 1,000

$8/yr; $5/ea; 40%

100 pp; 7½ x 10

Ad rates: $100/page; $50/½ page; $25/¼ page

Ubiquity, Segue, Edge

CHAMINADE LITERARY REVIEW

Loretta Petrie
Chaminade University of Honolulu
3140 Waialae Avenue
Honolulu, HI 96816-1578
(808) 735-4723

Poetry, fiction, criticism, reviews. CHAMINADE LITERARY REVIEW intends to bring together work from both artists and writers, talented new ones along with those nationally or internationally recognized. We want writing from Hawaii side by side with writing from the mainland to demonstrate how well our local writers compare. We want a magazine at once regional and cosmopolitan. We hope to reflect the diversity of Hawaii's people, their writers, their interests.

Cathy Song, John Unterecker, Phyllis Thompson, William Stafford, Tony Quagliano.
Payment: one year's subscription, upon publication.
Copyright held by Chaminade Press; reverts to author upon publication.
1987; 2/yr; 350
$10/yr; $18/2 yrs ind & inst; $5/ea; 20%
175 pp; 6 x 9
Ad rates: $50/page/4 x 7¼; $25/½ page/4 x 3⅞
ISSN: 0894-6396

THE CHARIOTEER

Pella Publishing Company
337 West 36th Street
New York, NY 10018-6401
(212) 279-9586

Poetry, fiction, criticism, essays, reviews, plays, translation, graphics/artwork.
Purpose: to bring to English-speaking readers information on, appreciation of, and translations from modern Greek literature, with criticism and reproductions of modern Greek art and sculpture.
Payment: none.
Reporting time: 3 months.
Copyright held by Pella Publishing Company; reverts to author upon request.
1960; 1/yr; 1,500
$15/yr; $28/2 yrs; $40/3 yrs
200 pp; 5½ x 8½
Ad rates: $125/page/4⅛ x 7; $75/½ page/4⅛ x 3½
ISSN: 0577-5574

THE CHARITON REVIEW

Jim Barnes
Northeast Missouri State University
Kirksville, MO 63501
(816) 785-4499

Poetry, fiction, essays, reviews, translation.

Excellence in literature only. We like the old; we like the new. Jack Cady, Phyllis Barber, Barry Targan, David Ray, Robert Canzoneri, Patricia Goedicke, Gordon Weaver, Steve Heller, Elizabeth Moore.

Payment: $5/page.

Reporting time: 1 week to 1 month.

Copyright held by Northeast Missouri State University; reverts to author upon publication.

1975; 2/yr; 700

$5/yr; $2.50/ea; 0%

100 pp; 6 x 9

Ad rates: $100/page/4 x 7; $50/½ page/4 x 3½

ISSN: 0098-9452

Direct mail and bookstores only

THE CHATTAHOOCHEE REVIEW

Lamar York

DeKalb College

2101 Womack Road

Dunwoody, GA 30338-4497

(404) 551-3166

Poetry, fiction, criticism, essays, reviews, interviews.

THE CHATTAHOOCHEE REVIEW promotes fresh writing and encourages as yet unacknowledged writers by giving them space in print next to their acclaimed peers.

Leon Rooke, Fred Chappell, George Garrett, Jim Wayne Miller, Peter Meinke.

Payment: none.

Reporting time: 6 months.

Copyright held by DeKalb College; reverts to author upon publication.

1980; quarterly; 1,250

$15/yr; $3.50/ea; 30%

100 pp; 6 x 9

Ad rates: $125/page/4½ x 7; $75/½ page/4½ x 3½

ISSN: 0741-9155

CHELSEA

Sonia Raiziss, Alfredo de Palchi, Richard Foerster, Caila Rossi, Brian Swann

Box 5880

Grand Central Station

New York, NY 10163

Poetry, fiction, criticism, essays, translations, interviews, art.

Stress on style, variety, originality. No special biases or requirements. Flexible attitudes, eclectic material. Active interest, as always, in crosscultural exchanges, in superior translations. Leaning toward cosmopolitan avant-garde, interdisciplinary techniques, but no strictures against traditional modes. Annual competition (send for guidelines).

Meena Alexander, Bruce Bawer, Rita Dove, James Laughlin, Robert Phillips, Marjorie Stelmach, Elizabeth McBride, Michael Waters.
Payment: $5/page.
Reporting time: immediately to 4 months.
Copyright held by magazine; reverts to author upon publication.
1958; 2/yr; 1,300
$11/2 issues or 1 double issue; $6.00
132 pp; 6 x 9
$125/page/4½ x 7½; $75/½ page/4½ x 3½
ISSN: 0009-2185
Bernard DeBoer, Inc.; Faxon; EBSCO

CHICAGO REVIEW

Andy Winston
5801 S. Kenwood
Chicago, IL 60637
(312) 702-0887

Poetry, fiction, criticism, essays, reviews, translation, interviews, photographs, graphics/artwork.
CHICAGO REVIEW is dedicated to contemporary writing of excellence, regardless of stylistic biases or trends. A sure hand, demonstrating originality and precision of language and tone, is the sole requirement for inclusion, overriding formal affiliation, theme, regional basis, or previous history of publication.
Eavan Boland, Michael Donaghy, Turner Cassity, Mark Harris.
Payment: copies/subscription.
Reporting time: 2 months.
Copyright held by magazine; transfers to author upon request.
1946; 4/yr; 1,400
$20/yr ind; $25/yr inst; $5.00/ea; 40%
110 pp; 6 x 9
Ad rates: $150/page/4½ x 7½; $100/½ page/2½ x 7½
ISSN: 0009-3696

CIMARRON REVIEW

Gordon Weaver, Editor; Deborah Bransford, Managing Editor; Jack Myers, Randy Phillis, Sally Shigley, Poetry Editors; Gordon Weaver, Kathy Bedwell, Dennis Bormann, Steffie Corcoran, David Major, Fiction Editors; E.P. Walkiewicz, Nonfiction Editor; Thomas E. Kennedy, European Editor
205 Morrill Hall
Oklahoma State University
Stillwater, OK 74078-0135
(405) 744-9476

Poetry, fiction, essays, reviews.
Seeks well-written material, which emphasizes attempts to find

value and purpose in a dehumanized and dehumanizing world. Avoids "easy" answers of extremes and would not publish work which espouses any specific religious or political view or advocates simple escapism. It does not publish children's stories; but does publish stories about children aimed at adult understanding.
Payment: none.
Reporting time: 3–4 weeks.
Copyright held by magazine.
1967; 4/yr; 450
$12/yr; $3/ea
112 pp; 6 x 9
ISSN: 0009-6849

CINCINNATI POETRY REVIEW

Dallas Wiebe
English Department, 069
University of Cincinnati
Cincinnati, OH 45221
(513) 556-3922
Poetry.

CINCINNATI POETRY REVIEW sets local writers in a national context. One fourth to one third of each issue is local; the rest is national. "Local" means about 150 from the city. All types of poetry considered. Poetry contest each issue.

Alvin Greenberg, X.J. Kennedy, David Citino, Laurie Henry, Walter McDonald.
Payment: none.
Reporting time: 4–6 weeks.
Copyright held by magazine; reverts to author upon publication.
1985; 2/yr; 1,000
$9/yr; Samples; $2/ea; 40%; 50% for direct purchase by dealers
72 pp; 5½ x 8½

CLOCKWATCH REVIEW

James Plath, Editor; Lynn DeVore, Eric Gardner, James McGowan, Pamela Muirhead, Associate Editors
Dept. of English
Illinois Wesleyan University
Bloomington, IL 61702
(309) 828-4452, 556-3352
Fiction, poetry, interviews, essays, photographs, graphics/artwork.

CLOCKWATCH REVIEW seeks to present quality work in a format lively enough to attract a popular as well as literary/academic audience. Special feature: an ongoing interview series with contemporary artists and musicians.
Dawn Upshaw, Friz Freleng, Gary Gildner, Pat Hutchings, Peter Wild, Martha M. Vertreace.

Payment: in 3 copies, and a small cash award.
Reporting time: under 2 weeks; up to 2 months if under serious consideration.
Copyright held by author.
1983; 2/yr; 1,500
$8/yr; $4/ea
64–80 pp; 5½ x 8½
ISSN: 0740-9311
Ingram Periodicals

CLUES: A Journal of Detection
Pat Browne
Journals Department
Popular Press
Bowling Green State University
Bowling Green, OH 43403
(419) 372-2981
Fiction, articles.
A magazine focusing upon detective fiction.
1982; 2/yr; 700
$12.50/yr; $7.75/ea

COLLAGES & BRICOLAGES
Marie-José Fortis
P.O. Box 86
Clarion, PA 16214
or 212 Founders Hall
Clarion University of Pennsylvania
Clarion, PA 16214
(814) 226-2340 or 226-5799

Poetry, fiction, criticism, essays, reviews, plays, translation, interviews, photographs, graphics/artwork.
COLLAGES & BRICOLAGES wants mostly to involve experimental, post-modern writing, anything innovative, whether it is poetry, short fiction, or new criticism. We seek the unusual, the eccentric, the bold, the brave. This includes feminism, satire, parody, avant-garde, surrealism, dada, etc. We believe in the innovative writer who has read the classics. At this point in time (the after Eastern European Revolution Era), we would like to receive less egocentric, more politically engaged, pieces.
Marilou Awiahla, Marcia Yudkin, Daniel Quinn.
Payment: 1 or 2 copies/contributor. Extras: $5.00/copy.
1987; 1/yr; 400
$5/ea
120 pp; 11 x 18
Ad rates: $50/page/9 x 16; $30/½ page/5 x 8; $15/¼ page/2½ x 4

COLORADO REVIEW
Bill Tremblay, General Editor;
David Milofsky, Fiction Editor;
Mary Crow, Translations Editor
360 Eddy Building

English Department
Colorado State University
Fort Collins, CO 80523
Poetry, fiction, criticism, reviews, translation.
Although published in Colorado, **COLORADO REVIEW** is more than a regional literary magazine. We seek to print the best fiction, poetry, translations, interviews, reviews, and articles on contemporary literary subjects that we receive from a contributorship that is national and international. We continue to be interested in Magical Realist writing, but any writing that is vital, highly imaginative and highly realized in artistic terms and that avoids mere mannerism to embody important human concerns will find support here.
Reg Saner, Patricia Goedicke, Bin Ranke, Carole Oles, T. Alan Broughton, Rita Ciresi, David Huddle; interviews with Carolyn Forche; Gwendolyn Brooks, Gretel Ehrlich.
Payment: when funding permits.
1977; 2/yr 1,000
$5/yr ind/inst; $3/ea; 40%
112 pp; 6 x 9
Ad rates: $100/page/7½ x 5; $50/½ page

COLUMBIA: A Magazine of Poetry and Prose
Rotating Editors
404 Dodge Hall
Columbia University
New York, NY 10027
(212) 280-4391
Poetry, fiction essays.
Payment: in copies; Editors' awards, also.
Reporting time: 1–2 months.
Copyright reverts to author.
1977; 1–2/yr; 200
$15/3 issues; $11/2 issues; $6 ea
Approx. 220 pp; 5 x 8
Ad rates: on request

CONDITIONS
Cheryl Clarke, Dorothy Randall Gray, Sabrina Williams, Pam Parker, Melinda Goodman, Mariana Romo-Carmona
Box 150056
Van Brunt Station
Brooklyn, NY 11215-0001
(718) 788-8654
Poetry, fiction, criticism, essays, review, translation, interviews, photographs, graphics/artwork.
Writing by women with an emphasis on writing by lesbians, women of color, non-U.S. writers (in or with translation).
Audre Lorde, Mila Aquilar, Jacqueline Lapidus, Julia Alvarez, Cheryl Clarke.

Payment: in copies.

Reporting time: 3 months.

Copyright held by magazine; reverts to author upon publication.

1976; 1/yr; 2,500

$24/ind; $36/inst; $8.95/ea; 40%

225 pp; 5½ x 8½

Ad rates: $200-125/page/4½ x 7; $125-75/½ page/4½ x 3½; $75-50/¼ page/2 x 3½

ISSN: 0147-8311

CONFRONTATION

Martin Tucker

L.I.U. Dept. of English

C.W. Post

Greenvale, NY 11548

(516) 299-2391

Poetry, fiction, criticism, essays, plays, translation, interviews.

We are eclectic in our tastes, preferring a mix of traditional and experimental, of the known and relatively unknown writers. We have no prohibition except that of poor literary quality.

Cynthia Ozick, Wilfrid Sheed, Stephen Dixon, Joyce Carol Oates, Thomas Fleming, Joseph Brodsky.

Payment: $5 to $100.

Reporting time: 6 weeks.

Copyright held by Long Island University; reverts to author upon publication.

1968; 2/yr; 2,000

$10/yr ind; $10/yr inst; $6/ea

160–190 pp; 5½ x 8½

CONJUNCTIONS

Bradford Morrow

Bard College

P.O. Box 115

Annandale-on-Hudson, NY 12504

(914) 758-1539

Poetry, fiction, translation, interviews, photographs, graphics/artwork, reviews, essays.

CONJUNCTIONS publishes formally innovative writing, with equal emphasis on fiction and poetry; also essays on culture and the arts, book reviews, literary historical materials, special features. Editorial staff: Walter Abish, Mei-Mei Berssenbrugge, Guy Davenport, Kenneth Irby, William Gass, Ann Lauterbach, Nathaniel Tarn.

Payment: in copies, and $50–100.

Reporting time: 4–6 weeks.

Copyright reverts to author upon publication.

1981; 2/yr; 7,500

$18/yr paper; $45/yr cloth; $9.95/ea paper

320 pp; 6 x 9

Ad rates: $350/page/4⅜ x 7½; $250/½ page

ISSN: 0278-2324

New Writing Foundation

THE CONNECTICUT POETRY REVIEW

James Wm. Chichetto, J. Claire White
P.O. Box 3783
New Haven, CT 06525
Poetry, criticism, reviews, translations, interviews, excerpts from verse plays.
Marge Piercy, John Updike, Margaret Randall, Allen Ginsberg, Eugenio de Andrade.
Payment: $5/poem; $10/review; $20/interview; $20/verse play.
Reporting time: 3 months.
1981; 1/yr; 500
$3/ea
50 pp; 5¾ x 9¼
ISSN: 0277-7770

CONNECTICUT RIVER REVIEW

Robert Isaacs, Editor
P.O. Box 2171
Bridgeport, CT 06608
Poetry.
The **CRR** uses highest quality poetry, in which logic and emotion, picture and sound cohere, making for authentic music. All forms welcome, except haiku. Prefer poems of 40 lines or under; submit no more than 5 poems at a time.
Payment: 2 copies.
Reporting time: 2–8 weeks.

Copyright held by Connecticut Poetry Society; reverts to author upon publication.
1978; 2/yr; 600
$10; $5/ea; 40%
60 pp; 6 x 9

CONTACT II

Maurice Kenny, J.G. Gosciak
P.O. Box 451, Bowling Green
New York, NY 10004
(212) OR4-0911
Poetry, reviews, criticism, translation, interviews, photographs, graphics/artwork.
Contemporary American poetry.
Janice Mirikitani, Charlotte de Clue, Carolyn Stoloff, Shalin Hai-Jew, Karoniaktatie.
Payment: in copies; when payment is cash, $10/poem, $15/review.
Reporting time: 6 months.
Copyright held by Contact II Publications; reverts to author upon publication with credit.
1976; semi-annual; 2,500
$10/ind; $16/inst; $7/ea; 40%;
50% prepaid on 10 or more.
92 pp; 7¾ x 10½
Ad rates: $150/page; $80/½ page; $50/¼ page
ISSN: 0197-6796

CONTEXT SOUTH

David Breeden, Craig Taylor, J.F. Smith

Box 2244
State University, AR 72467
(501) 972-6095

Poetry, Fiction, Criticism, Graphics/Artwork.

A magazine based in the South, but not confined to it, **CONTEXT SOUTH** endeavors to be a collection of art by artists interested in pushing boundaries.

Wayne Dodd, Andrea Hollander Budy, Diane Glancy, William Greenway

Copyright author
2; 300
$12/yr; $5; 40%
65; 5½ x 8½
$100/page; $50/½ page; $25/¼ page
ISSN: 1045-2265

CORNFIELD REVIEW

Stuart Lishan, General Ed; Martha Bartter, Fiction; Terry Hermson, Poetry; Larry Sauselen, Art
OSU at Marion
1465 Mt. Vernon Ave
Marion, OH 43302
(614) 389-2361

Poetry, short stories, nonfiction essays; original art (black & white) and photography.

A "little" literary magazine showcasing the Midwest experience (but not limited to that topic). Submissions should be of high quality; fiction and non-fiction should not exceed 3500 words.

David Citano, Donald M. Hassler, Roas Maria DelVecchio, Will Wells.

Payment: 1 copy.
Reporting time: 2–4 months.
Copyright reverts to author.
1976; 1/yr; 1,500
$4.50/ea
64 pp
ISSN: 0363-4574

COTTON BOLL/ATLANTA REVIEW

Mary Hollingsworth
Sandy Springs P.O. Box 76757
Atlanta, GA 30358-0703

Poetry, fiction, essays, profiles, commentaries, interviews, book reviews.

Preference is for reflection of the contemporary South or for general applicability. No pornography, religion, lovelorn or racism, or genres such as sci-fi or romance.

Miller Williams, Gail Galloway Adams, Lawrence Naumoff, Madison Jones, Edward C. Lynskey.

Payment: for short stories is $10.00 per story on publication for stories *accepted after* January 1, 1990. Note: This payment CANNOT apply to stories

accepted and/or published *before* January 1, 1990.
Payment for poems is $5.00 per poem on publication for poems *accepted after* January 1, 1990. Note: This payment CANNOT apply to poems accepted and/or published *before* January 1, 1990.
Copyright held by magazine; reverts to author upon publication.
1985; 4/yr; 1,000
$20/yr ind/inst; $5.50/ea; 40%
125 pp; 8½ x 5½
No ads
ISSN: 0886-5051

COTTONWOOD

George Wedge, Editor; Phil Wedge, Poetry Editor; Jane Garrett, Fiction Editor
Box J, Kansas Union
Lawrence, KS 66045
(913) 864-4520
Poetry, fiction, reviews, interviews, photographs, graphics/artwork.
COTTONWOOD uses fiction and poetry with clear images and interesting narratives and reviews of books by writers or from publishers in our area. The magazine welcomes submissions from all parts of the country.
Robert Day, Rita Dove, Patricia Traxler, Gerald Early, William Stafford.
Payment: none.
Reporting time: 2–6 months.
Copyright held by magazine; reverts to author upon publication.
1965; 3/yr; 500
$12/yr; $5/ea; 30%
120 pp; 6 x 9
ISSN: 0147-149X

CRAB CREEK REVIEW

Linda Clifton, Carol Orlock (Fiction)
4462 Whitman Avenue, N.
Seattle, WA 98103
(206) 633-1090
Poetry, fiction, translation, essays, graphics/artwork.
. . . well-crafted and perceptive works . . . technically proficient and sensitive poems . . . powerfully expressed images . . . tightly controlled narrative . . . diverse enough to appeal to a variety of literary tastes . . ." Literary Magazine Review. Not accepting submissions until 1992.
William Stafford, Jana Harris, Maxine Kumin, David Lee.
Payment: 2 copies.
Reporting time: 4–8 weeks.
Copyright held by CCR; reverts to author upon publication.

1983; 3/yr; 350
$8/yr; $3/ea; 40%; 50% through
distributor Small Changes, 3443
12th W., Seattle, WA 98119
32 pp; 6 x 10
$120/page/6 x 10; $65/½ page/6 x
5; $35/¼ page/6 x 2½; $20/⅛
page/3 x 2½
ISSN: 07380-7008

CRAZYHORSE

Zabelle Stodola (Managing Edi-
tor); David Jauss (Fiction);
David Wojahn and Lynda Hull
(Poetry); Dennis Vanatta (Criti-
cism)
Poetry Submissions Only
David Wojahn and Lynda Hull
English Department
Ballantine Hall
Indiana University
Bloomington, IN 47405
Fiction, Criticism, and All Other
Correspondence
English Department
University of Arkansas at Little
Rock
2801 S. University
Little Rock, AR 72204
(501) 569-3160
Poetry, fiction criticism, reviews,
interviews.
A literary magazine which pub-
lishes quality work by estab-
lished and promising new
writers.

Andre Dubus, Bobbie Ann Ma-
son, Raymond Carver, Jorie
Graham, John Updike.
Payment: 2 copies and $10/page.
Annual fiction and poetry awards:
$500 each.
Reporting time: 2 weeks–1 month.
Copyright reverts to author upon
request.
1960; 2/yr; 1,000
$10/yr; $5/ea; 25%–40%
135 pp; 6 x 9
Ad rates: $85/page; $50/½ page
ISSN: 0011-0841

CRAZYQUILT

Marsh Cassady
P.O. Box 632729
San Diego, CA 92163-2729
(619) 688-1023
Poetry, fiction, criticism, essays,
plays, photographs, graphics/
artwork.
All kinds of poetry; short stories
with good character develop-
ment; nonfiction about writers;
literary criticism; one-act plays
and black and white photography and art work. Accept translations of poetry. Publish new
writers as well as established
authors. Annual contest: poetry,
short story.
Louis Phillips, Elizabeth Barret,
Brian Clark, Madeline Tiger,
Geraldine Little.

Payment: 2 copies.
Reporting time: 10–12 weeks.
Copyright held by Crazyquilt
Press; reverts to author upon
publication.
1986; quarterly; 180
$14.95/ind/inst; $25/2 yrs; $4.50
ea; 40%
80 pp
ISSN: 0887-5308

CREAM CITY REVIEW
Kit Pancoast, Editor-in-Chief
P.O. Box 413
University of Wisconsin-
Milwaukee
Milwaukee, WI 53201
(414) 229-4708
Poetry, fiction, reviews, essays,
interviews. Will consider: plays,
photographs, graphics/artwork.
The **CREAM CITY REVIEW** is
an eclectic literary magazine
affiliated with the University of
Wisconsin-Milwaukee; it strives
to publish the best of traditional
and non-traditional work by
new and established writers.
Eve Shelnutt, Stuart Dybek, Fred
Chappell, Denise Levertov,
David Ignatow, Marge Piercy,
Maxine Kumin, Amy Clampitt,
Derek Walcott, William Mat-
thews, Mary Oliver & William
Stafford.
Payment: varies with funding.

Reporting time: 2–8 weeks.
Copyright held by the Board of
Regents of the University of
Wisconsin; reverts to author
upon publication.
1975; 2/yr; 1,000
$10/yr; sample $4.50; 40%
185 pp; 5½ x 8½
Ad rates: $50/page

CREEPING BENT
Joseph P. Lucia
433 West Market Street
Bethlehem, PA 18018
(215) 866-5613
Poetry, reviews, fiction, essays,
translation.
Hewing to no orthodoxies but reflecting an awareness of the
broad spectrum of current writing and thought about writing,
CREEPING BENT is an independent, eclectic, and adventur-
ous magazine for serious (but
not solemn or humorless) readers and writers of contemporary
literature, with emphasis on
poetry.
Brigit Kelly, Charles Edward
Eaton, Turner Cassity, Robert
Gibb, Donald Revell.
Payment: none.
Copyright held by publishers; reverts to author upon publication.
1984; 2/yr; 250

$6/yr ind; $7/yr inst; $3/ea. 40%
No ads
ISSN: 8756-0291

THE CRESCENT REVIEW

Guy Nancekeville
P. O. Box 15065
Winston-Salem, NC 27113
(919) 924-1851

Short stories.
Payment: in copies.
Copyright reverts to author.
1983; 2/yr; 300
$10/yr; $6/backissue; $5/next issue
128 pp; 6 x 9
Ebsco, Faxon, Swets

CRITICAL TEXTS: A Review of Theory and Criticism

Joe Childers, Jon Anderson, Richard Moye, Martha Buskirk, James Buzard, Ina Lipkowitz, Susan Fraiman, Gary Hentzi, Eric Lott
602 Philosophy Hall
Columbia University
New York, NY 10027
(212) 854-3215

Articles, reviews, translations and interviews dealing with theory in the humanities.

We are an oppositional journal interested in printing articles and reviews on theoretical issues connected with the humanities and social sciences.

Payment: none.
Reporting time: 2 months.
Copyright held by **CRITICAL TEXTS.**
1982; 3/yr; 850
$9/yr ind; $3.75/ea; $5 back issues
120 pp; 6 x 9
$185/page; $100/½ page
ISSN: 0730-2304
Ubiquity

CROSSCURRENTS

Linda Brown Michelson
2200 Glastonbury Road
Westlake Village, CA 91361
(818) 991-1694

Fiction, graphics.

CROSSCURRENTS features previously unpublished, literary short fiction. Select pieces are highlighted by photos and line drawings. Reading period from June 1 through November 30. Two special issues each year.

Alice Adams, Saul Bellow, Josephine Jacobsen, Joyce Carol Oates, John Updike.
Payment: varies, $35 minimum per story.
Reporting time: 6 weeks.
Copyright reverts to author.
1980; 4/yr; 3,000
$18/yr; $6/ea; 40%
176 pp; 6 x 9
ISSN: 0739-2354
The Faxon Company; EBSCO

Subscription Service; Boley Internatinal Subscription Agency; L-S Distributors, Ingram

CUMBERLAND POETRY REVIEW

Editorial Board
P.O. Box 120128 Acklen Station
Nashville, TN 37212
(615) 371-9078

Poetry, criticism, interviews.
CUMBERLAND POETRY REVIEW is devoted to poetry and poetry criticism and presents poets of diverse origins to a widespread audience. We place no restrictions on form, subject, or style. Manuscripts will be selected for publication on the basis of the writer's perspicuous and compelling means of expression. We welcome translations of high quality poetry. Our aim is to support the poet's efforts to keep up the language.
Seamus Heaney, Lewis Horne, Emily Grosholz, Francis Blessington, Mairi McInnes.
Payment: in contributor's copies.
Reporting time: 6 months.
Copyright held by Poetics, Inc.; reverts to author upon publication.
1981; 2/yr; 500

$12/yr ind; $15/yr inst; $4/ea sample back issue; 40%
100 pp; 6 x 9
Ads: accepted only on exchange basis
ISSN: 0731-7980
Faxon, Swets, EBSCO, McGregor

CUZ

Richard Meyers
437 E. 12th Street
Apt. 25
New York, NY 10009

Poetry, primarily; also fiction, essays and interviews.
We lean towards what a decaying world-center like New York does best: Highly sophisticated aestheticism and violent/erotic self-display. We like to beautifully present (via advanced typography & design) a representative (largish) selection from each of the 10–15 writers, half of whom are regular contributors, that we publish per issue.
William Burroughs, Dennis Cooper, Eileen Myles, Richard Hell, John Ashbery, Susie Timmons.
Payment: 5 copies.
Reporting time: 3–6 months.
Copyright reverts to author.
1988; 2/yr; 1,000

$16/4 issues; $3.95/ea + .85 postage; 40%
100 pp; 4¼ x 7
$160/page

D

DENVER QUARTERLY
Donald Revell
University of Denver
Denver, CO 80210
(303) 871-2982
Poetry, fiction, reviews, criticism,
essays, interviews.
For twenty years the **DENVER
QUARTERLY** has been pub-
lishing work by distinguished as
well as promising new writers.
The magazine generally pub-
lishes material reflecting on
modern culture as it has devel-
oped over the past century. It is
recognized as the premiere liter-
ary publication of the Rocky
Mountain region.
James Tate, Carl Dennis, Charles
Baxter, Jorie Graham, Rachel
Hadas.
Payment: $5/page for fiction es-
says, reviews; $5/page for po-
etry.
Copyright held by magazine.
1966; 4/yr; 900

$15/yr ind; $18/yr inst; $5/ea;
30%
160 pp; 6 x 9
Ad rates: $150/page/6 x 9; $75/½
page/6 x 4½
ISSN: 0011-8869

DESCANT
Karen Mulhallen
245 Markham Street
Toronto, Ontario, M6G2J7
(416) 927-7059
Short fiction, poetry, essays,
plays, visual essays.
Literary magazine interested in all
the arts and their interrelation-
ship. Aims to publish works of
excellence from established and
emerging writers and artists.
Quality bound.
Leon Rooke, Isabel Allende, Joseph Skvorecky, Libby Scheier.
Payment: varies
Copyright 1st Canadian Rights
1970; Quarterly; 1,000
$21 Individual; $29 Institute; $10–
$13
130; 5¼ x 8¾
$225/B&W/5¾ x 8¾-one issue;
$400-two issues
ISSN: 0382-909-X
Canadian Magazine Publishers
Association

THE DIFFICULTIES
Tom Beckett
596 Marilyn Street

Kent, OH 44240

Criticism, poetry, reviews, interviews.

THE DIFFICULTIES is a journal devoted to new writing. Typically an issue will focus on an individual—presenting recent examples of his or her work, interviews, critical essays by others and bibliographic materials. The next issue will be a focus on the work of Susan Howe. Inquire before submitting.

Ron Silliman, Charles Bernstein, David Bromige, Michael Davidson, Rae Armantrout.

Payment: in copies.

Reporting time: usually a week. Generally no later than a month.

Copyright held by magazine; reverts to author upon publication.

1980; irreg.; 500

$7/ea; 40%

110 pp; 8½ x 11

No ads

Segue Foundation, Small Press Distribution

DIMENSION

A. Leslie Willson

P.O. Box 26673

Austin, TX 78755

(512) 345-0622

Poetry, fiction, essays, plays, translation, interviews, graphics/artwork, German literature in the original and translation: post 1945.

DIMENSION concentrates on established and non-established writers from all German-speaking countries, with original works with translations. Few essays.

Friedrich Dürrenmatt, Wolfgang Hildersheimer, Günter Grass, Günter Kunert, Peter Weiss.

Payment: modest, copies for translators.

Reporting time: varies.

Copyright held by magazine.

1968; 3/yr; 1,000

$20/yr ind; $24/yr inst; $10/ea; 20%

200 pp; 6 x 9

DOG RIVER REVIEW

Laurence F. Hawkins, Jr.

5976 Billings Road

Parkdale, OR 97041-0125

(503) 352-6494

Poetry, fiction, reviews, interviews, satire, criticism, B/W art/graphics.

Experimental and traditional. Descriptive and lyric stressed over the 'intellectual'. Prefer shorter, to 30 lines, poems and fiction to 2500 words. Longer material considered.

Gerald Locklin, Lyn Lifshin, Judson Crews, David Chorlton, Arthur Winfield Knight.

Payment: in copies.

Reporting time: 2–3 months.

Copyright reverts to author upon publication.

1982; 2/yr; 200

$6/yr; $3/ea; 40%

60 pp; 5½ x 8½

THE DRAMA REVIEW

Richard Schechner

MIT Press Journals

55 Hayward Street

Cambridge, MA 02142

(617) 253-2866

TDR is a quarterly journal of performance with a strong intercultural, intergeneric, and interdisciplinary focus. We consider everything from wrestling to ritual, from Peter Brook's Mahabharata to what is going on at "Downtown Beirut." **TDR** borrows from the fields of anthropology, performance theory, ethology, psychology, and politics. We combine scholarship and journalism in the form of essays, interviews, letters and editorials.

Payment: 2¢ per word.

Copyright held by MIT Press.

1955; 4/yr; 6,000

$25/yr ind; $55/yr inst; $7/ea

160 pp; 7 x 10

ISSN: 0012-5962

E

EARTH'S DAUGHTERS: A Feminist Arts Periodical

Editors: Kastle Brill, Elizabeth Conant, Camille Cox, Perrie Hill, Bonnie Johnson, Joy Walsh, Joyce Kessel, Robin Willoughby, Ryki Zuckerman

Box 622

Station C

Buffalo, NY 14209

(716) 886-2636

Poetry, fiction, plays, photographs, graphics/artwork.

EARTH'S DAUGHTERS is a feminist literary and art periodical published in Buffalo, New York. We believe ourselves to be the oldest feminist arts periodical extant, having published our first issue in February, 1971. Our focus is the experience and creative expression of women.

Jimmie Canfield, Lyn Lifshin, Marge Piercy, Kathryn Machan Aal, Susan Fantl Spivack.

Payment: 2 copies.

Reporting time: 3 months.

Copyright held by magazine; reverts to author upon publication.

1971; 3/yr; 1,000

$14/yr ind; $22/yr inst; $4/ea; 30%

60 pp; 6 x 9

No ads

ISSN: 0163-0989

EBSCO, Faxon, Burroughs Subscription Agencies

EARTHWISE REVIEW/ EARTHWISE PUBLICA- TIONS

Barbara Holley

P.O. Box 680536

Miami, FL 33168

(305) 653-2875

Poetry, fiction, criticism, essays, reviews, translations, interviews, photos, artwork, short stories.

EARTHWISE REVIEW is a bimonthly tabloid of poetry, fine arts, focuses on poetry and environment. Accepts interviews, critical essays, fiction, children's work and prison projects. Sponsors four annual competitions including the annual T. S. Eliot Memorial Chapbook Competition.

The annual **EARTHWISE LIT-**

ERARY CALENDAR appears for the tenth year and includes poetry of over 200 poets, quotes and excerpts from longer poems. We feature an annual Artist and this year we have featured Hand Adolf Seeberg of West Germany (Hamburg).

Calendar sells for $8.95. Free copy to members of the Earth Chapter, FSPA, Inc. ($15 annual dues)

Richard Wilbur, Lola Haskins, Galway Kinnell, Jorge Valls, William Stafford.

Payment: $5 and up.

Copyright reverts to author upon publication.

1978; 6/yr; 400

$25/yr ind

60–80 pp; 5½ x 8½

Ad rates: $100/page/4 x 6; $50/½ page/4 x 4; $30/¼ page/2 x 3½

ISSN: 0190-1761

ECHOES

Carol Lambert, Susan McIntosh

Box 365

Wappingers Falls, NY 12590

(914) 471-0226

Poetry, fiction, essays, plays, graphics/artwork.

ECHOES was created by Carol Lamber and Barbara Mindel who believe Hudson Valley Writers Association should and could publish a literary magazine which would showcase unknown area writers. It was designed, therefore, to introduce readers to writers from the Hudson Valley and beyond, to present a balance of notable prose and poetry from those writers, and to invite writers to submit their essays, illustrations, prose and poetry to our quarterly. Its emphasis has now grown to reflect writers from the country at large and the pool of shared writing has grown tremendously in the last four years.

Jodi Sterling, Barbara Mindel, Ken Wibecan, Claire Michaels, David Stalzer.

Payment: one copy, upon publication.

Copyright held by Hudson Valley Writers Association; reverts to author upon publication.

1985; 4/yr; 150

$15/yr ind & inst; $4.50/ea; 40%

44 pp; 8½ x 11

No ads

(415) 564-5291

Poetry, fiction, photographs, graphics/artwork.

An open-forum journal, **EIGHTY-NINE CENTS** seeks to publish a diverse collection of visions, both from established and emerging artists. We emphasize that we are a journal of writing and therefore don't actively seek visual art, although we would be interested in seeing any submissions. We try to balance the volume of poetry against that of fiction, and then to present varying approaches to literature.

William Dickey, Stephen Mitchell, Charlotte Painter, Carolyn Lau, Essex Hemphill.

Payment: none.

Copyright held by magazine; reverts to author conditionally.

1988; 3/yr; 500

$10/yr ind & inst; $3/ea ($.89 in S.F. Bay Area); 40%

28 pp; 8½ x 11

Ad rates: $400/page/8½ x 11; $200/½ page/ 8½ x 5½; $100/¼ page/4¼ x 5½

EIGHTY-NINE CENTS, A Journal of Writing

Thomas Avena, Gary Szabo, Ellen Romano, Jennifer Wollin
P.O. Box 11837
San Francisco, CA 94101-7837

EMBERS

Katrina Van Tassel, Mark Johnston, Charlotte Garrett
Box 404
Guilford, CT 06437
(203) 453-2328

Poetry.
A poetry journal. Editors are poets, interested in poets' voices. New writers encouraged. Submit 3–5 poems.
Margaret Gibson, Marilyn Waniek, Walter MacDonald, Brendan Galvin, Sue Ellen Thompson.
Payment: 2 copies.
Reporting time: Continuously.
Copyright held by poets; reverts to author upon publication.
1979; 2/yr; 500
$11/yr; $6/ea; $3/sample
48 pp; 6 x 9
ISSN: 0731-0382

THE EMRYS JOURNAL
Linda Julian
P.O. Box 8813
Greenville, SC 29604
(803) 294-3151
Poetry, fiction, essays.
Our journal is interested in publishing the work of new writers, especially that of women and other minorities. We are interested in maintaining a high literary standard.
Maxine Kumin, Carole Oles, Linda Paston, Amy Clampitt, Pattiann Rogers.
Payment: in copies.
Reporting time: 6 weeks.

Copyright held by The Emrys Foundation.
1984; 1/yr; 400
$8/ea; 40%
No ads

EPOCH
Michael Koch
251 Goldwin Smith Hall
Cornell University
Ithaca, NY 14853
(607) 255-3385
Poetry, fiction.
EPOCH is primarily a journal of fiction and poetry and we publish work by a wide range of writers, some established, some just beginning their careers.
Harriet Doerr, Rick DeMarinis, Stuart Dybek, Thylias Moss, Lee K. Abbott, Alice Dulton.
Payment: $10/magazine page (prose); $1/line (poetry).
Reporting time: 2 months.
Copyright held by Cornell University; reverts to author upon publication.
1947; 3/yr; 1,000
$11/yr; $4/ea
80 pp; 6 x 9
Ad rates: $180/page/5 x 8; $100/½ page/3 x 8
ISSN: 0145-1391
B. DeBoer

EVERYWHERE
Greg Booth, Mike Burbach
P.O. Box 5173
Grand Forks, ND 58206-5173
Poetry, fiction, criticism, photographs, graphics/artwork, essays.
Thomas McGrath, Jay Meek, Joel Sartore, Bill Alkofer, Louis Jenkins, Joan Hoffman.
$3 ea

EXQUISITE CORPSE
Andrei Codrescu
P.O. Box 25051
Baton Rouge, LA 70894
Poetry, criticism, essays, reviews, translation, photographs, graphics/artwork, polemics, letters, reports from many countries.
A review of books and ideas. We are a print cafe, hopeful that vigorous dialogue on general culture is still possible in Mandarin U.S.A. We encourage honesty, combativeness and openness. We have published wide-ranging polemics, as well as essays on various matters of literary interest. Our foreign bureaus report on goings-on in several European and Asian cities. We also publish translations, and reprint important but overlooked texts. Our contributors are both famous and unknown.
Lawrence Ferlinghetti, John Cage, James Laughlin, Janet Gray, Janet Hamill, Laura Rosenthal.
Payment: some payment to contributors.
Reporting time: 2 weeks.
Copyright held by authors.
1983; monthly; 3,500
$15/yr; $2.50/ea
20 pp; 6 x 15½
ISSN: 0740-7815
Inland Books

F

F MAGAZINE
John Schultz
1405 West Belle Plaine
Chicago, IL 60613
(312) 281-7642
Fiction, criticism, essays, reviews, translations, interviews, photos on query.
F MAGAZINE has the unique, contemporary purpose of being devoted to the publication of novels-in-progress that are part of a literary movement toward a synthesis of novelistic techniques, emphasizing story—content, imagery, character,

voice, style, a rich exploration of points of view, forms, dimensions of time, dramatic and self relationships. Award winning fiction.

Andrew Allegretti, Betty Shiflett, Beverlye Brown, Gary Johnson, Shawn Shiflett, John Schultz, Charles Johnson, Harry Mark Petrakis, Cyrus Colter, Paul Carter Harrison.

Payment: varies from $5.00 per page.

Reporting time: 4 months. No reading June 1 – Sept. 1.

Copyright held by magazine; reverts to author upon publication.

2/yr; 1,500

$6.95/ea; 40%

210 pp; 6 x 9

Ad rates available. Contact CLMP for information.

ISBN: 0-936959-00-2

Ingram, DeBoer

FAG RAG

John Wieners, Charles Shively, John Mitgel

Box 331

Kenmore Station

Boston, MA 02215

(617) 661-7534

Poetry, fiction, criticism, essays, reviews, plays, translation, interviews, photographs, graphics/artwork, gay autobiography.

Gay male journal in search of the unrestrained aesthetic with emphasis on the striking and astonishing. Prisoners, mental patients, children, pedophiles and other poets.

Payment: in copies.

Reporting time: 4–6 months.

Copyright held by magazine; reverts to author upon publication.

1971; 1–2/yr; 5,000

$10/yr ind; $20/yr inst; $5/ea; 40%

28–44 pp; quarterfold tabloid

ISSN: 0046-3167

FARMER'S MARKET

Jean C. Lee, John E. Hughes, Lisa Ress

P.O. Box 1272

Galesburg, IL 61402

Poetry, fiction, essays, translation, graphics.

A Midwestern magazine, publishing quality literary work by Midwestern authors and work by others that is reflective of Midwestern values and consciousness.

Michael McMahon, David Williams, Lloyd Zimpel, Mary Maddox, Kathleen Peirce, Joe

Survant, Gloria Regalbuto,
Thomas Fox Averill.
Payment: 1 copy.
Reporting time: 4–8 weeks.
Copyright held by author.
1982; 2/yr; 500
$8/yr; $4.50/ea; 40%
78 pp; 5½ x 8½
No ads
ISSN: 0748-6022

THE FEDERAL POET
Alicia deJoux
3707 Woodley Road N.W. #21
Washington, DC 20016

FELL SWOOP
X.J. Dailey
1521 N. Lopez St.
New Orleans, LA 70119
(504) 943-5198
Poetry, fiction, essay, drama, art,
    photographs.
The All Bohemian Revue, **FELL
    SWOOP** is a guerilla/gorilla
    venture exploring the edge of
    'acceptability' in contemporary
    writing. We like a good laugh
    at anyone's expense, especially
    our own.
Richard Martin, Elizabeth
    Thomas, Andrei Codrescu,
    Normandi Ellis, Clara Talley-
    Vincent, R. Speck.
Payment: in copies.

Reporting time: immediately.
Copyright reverts to author upon
    publication.
1983; 2–3/yr; 1,000
$6/yr; $3/ea
pp varies; 8½ x 11
ISSN: 1040-5607

FICTION INTERNATIONAL
Harold Jaffe, Larry McCaffery
Department of English
San Diego State University
San Diego, CA 92182
(619) 594-5443 or (619) 594-5469
Fiction, reviews, essays, visuals.
FICTION INTERNATIONAL's
    twin biases are toward postmod-
    ernism and progressive politics,
    either integrated or apart. We
    especially welcome writing
    from the "Third World" (both
    abroad and at home), and we
    favor writing that cuts through
    or fuses or ignores the canonical
    genres. Please note: we read
    manuscripts between 9/1–1/1 of
    each year.
Robert Coover, Claribel Alegria,
    Gerald Vizenor, Michel Serres,
    Marianne Hauser, Pierre Guyo-
    tat, Margaret Randall, Roque
    Dalton.
Payment: varies.
Reporting time: 1–3 months.
$12/yr ind; $24/yr inst; $6/ea;
    40%

McPherson, Blackwell North American, Faxon, Baker & Taylor

THE FIDDLEHEAD

Kent Thompson

Campus House, UNB P.O. Box 4400

Federicton NB, Canada E3B5A3

(506) 453-3501

Short fiction, poetry, book reviews. (Canadian Books Only) Canada's oldest continuing literary magazine, with a world-wide circulation. Any good writing, from any place, will be welcome here.

Fred Bonnie, Aryeh LeV Stollman, William Meyer, R. Cooperman.

Payment: $10 per published page

Reporting time: 2–3 months

Copyright 1st serial rights only, copyright remains with author.

1945; quarterly; 800

$16; $5.50; $1.00

120–128; 6 x 9

$100 per full page

ISBN: 015-0630

Canadian Magazine Publishers Association

FIELD

Stuart Friebert and David Young

Rice Hall

Oberlin College

Oberlin, OH 44074

(216) 775-8408

Poetry, criticism, essays, reviews, translation.

We look for the best in contemporary poetry, poetics and translations and emphasize essays by poets themselves on the craft.

Sandra McPherson, Charles Wright, William Stafford, Jean Valentine, Charles Simic, Dennis Schmitz, Judita Vaičiunaite.

Payment: $20–30/page.

Reporting time: 2 weeks.

Copyright held by Oberlin College; reverts to author upon publication.

1969; 2/yr; 2,500

$10/yr; $16/2 yrs; $5/ea; 30–40%

100 pp; 5½ x 8½

FINE MADNESS

Sean Bentley, Louis Bersagel, John Marshall, Christine Deavel, John Malek

P.O. Box 31138

Seattle, WA 98103

Poetry, fiction.

We look for poetry that shows wit, imagination, love of language, technical skill and individual style.

Andrei Codrescu; David Ignatow; David Young; Stacey Sollfrey;

Leslie Norris; Naomi Shihab Nye; Pattiann Rogers.
Payment: copies.
Reporting time: 3 months.
Copyright held by magazine; reverts to author upon publication.
1980 2/yr; 800
$9/yr; $5/ea
80 pp; 5½ x 8
ISSN: 0737-4704
Small Changes (Seattle); Ubiquity (New York); Homing Pigeon (Elgin, TX); Armadillo & Co. (Venice, CA); Don Olsen Dist. (Minneapolis).

FIVE FINGERS REVIEW

John High, Aleka Chase, Thoreau Lovell,
P.O. Box 15426
San Francisco, CA 94115
(415) 661-8052

Poetry, fiction, essays.

We publish poetry, fiction and essays from a diversity of perspectives and aesthetics, ranging from traditional to experimental. We also welcome work that crosses/falls between genres. Our goal is to present a wide variety of writing that expresses the complexity of the world we live in, in fresh, surprising ways. Although much of our work focuses on social or political concerns, we seek quality writing on any subject.

Philip Levine, Fanny Howe, Molly Giles, Ron Silliman, Juan Felipe Herrera, Marilyn Chin, Denise Levertov.
Payment: in copies.
Reporting time: 3 months. (Query for current deadlines.)
Copyright held by magazine; reverts to author upon publication.
1984; 1–2/yr; 1,000–1,500
$12/ind; $13/inst; $7/ea; 40%
150 pp; 6 x 9
$150/page/4½ x 7½; $100/½ page/4½ x 3½ or 2 x 7½; $75/¼ page/2 x 3½
Bookpeople, Inland, Bookslinger, Baker & Taylor; Small Press Distribution, Berkeley; L-S Distributors, San Francisco; Anton J. Mikofsky, New York

FLOATING ISLAND

Michael Sykes
P.O. Box 516
Point Reyes Station, CA 94956
(415) 663-1181

Poetry fiction, photography in folio format, graphics/artwork.

Expansive, eclectic, very wide-ranging with center on West coast of North America— special interest in photography and graphic arts, lyric poetry and experimental prose. Volumes I-IV, First Series is now complete. Second Series to begin in 1992.

Diane di Prima, Gary Snyder, Michael McClure, Robert Bly, Christina Zawadiwsky, Frank Stewart, Lawrence Ferlinghetti, Joanne Kyger, Sam Hamill, Cole Swensen, Arthur Sze

Payment: in copies.

Reporting time: 4 weeks.

Copyright held by publisher; reverts to author upon publication.

1976; irreg; 2,000

All issues $15/ea; 40% 5 or more copies, 20% 1–4 copies

160 pp; 8½ x 11

ISSN: 0147-1686

Small Press Distribution, Bookpeople, Bookslinger

THE FLORIDA REVIEW

Russell Kesler, Gail Regier

English Department

University of Central Florida

Orlando, FL 32816

(407) 823-2038

Poetry, fiction, essays, reviews.

We publish stories with heart that aren't afraid to take risks. Experimental fiction is welcome, so long as it doesn't make us feel stupid. We look for clear, strong poems filled with real things, real people, real emotions, poems that might conceivably advance our knowledge of the human heart.

Stephen Dixon, Jane Ruiter, Liz Rosenberg, Karen Fish, Michael Martone.

Payment: Small honoraria are awarded when possible.

Reporting time: 2–3 months.

Copyright held by University of Central Florida; reverts to author upon publication.

1972; 2/yr; 1,000

$7/yr ind; $11/2yrs ind; $9/yr inst; $13/2 yrs inst; $4.50/ea; 40%

128 pp; 5½ x 8½

Ad rates: Exchange ads only

ISSN: 0742-2466

FOLIO

Department of Literature

American University

Washington, DC 20016

(202) 885-2973

Poetry, fiction, reviews, translations, interviews, black & white art & photography.

FOLIO prints quality fiction and poetry by established writers as well as those just starting out. We like to comment on submissions when time permits. Prose limit: 4,500 words. SASE required. Manuscripts read Aug.–April.

Henry Taylor, Simon Perchik, Kermit Moyer, Myra Sklarew, Linda McFerrin, Linda Pastan, Anne Louise Kerr.

Payment: prizes of up to $75 awarded for best fiction and poem.

Copyright reverts to author upon publication.

1984; 2/yr; 400

$9/yr; $4.50/ea; 30%

70 pp; 6 x 10

The Bookstall, Common Concerns, Chapters, The Writers Center (Bethesda)

FOOTWORK: The Paterson Literary Review

Maria Mazziotti Gillan

Cultural Affairs Department

Passaic County Community College

College Boulevard

Paterson, NJ 07509

(201) 684-6555

Poetry, fiction, review, graphics/artwork.

FOOTWORK is a high quality literary quarterly.

Laura Boss, Ruth Stone, Sonia Sanchez, William Stafford, Marge Piercy.

Payment: in copies.

Copyright held by Passaic County College; reverts to author upon publication.

Reporting time: 3 months.

1979; 1/yr; 1,000

$5/yr ind; $6/yr inst; $5/ea; 40%

120 pp; 8½ x 11 perfect-bound

Ad rates: $200/page/8½ x 11; $100/½ page/8½ x 5; $50/¼ page/4 x 2½

FOR POETS ONLY

Lillian M. Walsh

P.O. Box 4855

Schenectady, NY 12304

Poetry.

Little "little" publishes sincere, serious poet—any subject—no pornography.

J. Bernier, C. Weirich, A.M. Swaim, G. Labocetta, J. Schernitz.

Payment: in copies, plus prize money.

Copyright held by magazine; reverts to author upon publication.

1985; 4/yr; 150

$3/ea

30 pp; 5½ x 8

ISSN: 0087-0896

FORMATIONS

Jonathan Brent, Frances Padorr Brent

Northwestern University Press

625 Colfax St.

Evanston, IL 60201-2807

(708) 491-5313

Fiction, essays, plays, translation, interviews, photographs, graphics/artwork.

FORMATIONS publishes new American fiction in the context of both work being done in other media (painting, music theater) and work being done in foreign countries. Each issue therefore will contain a variety of essays, American fiction, and translations. The aim of the magazine is to become international in focus and to relate current American fiction to broader concerns of world culture.

Raymond Federman, Angela Carter, Milan Kundera, Primo Levi, Edna O'Brien.

Payment: fiction: $100–$500; essays: $100–$300.

Reporting time: 1–3 months.

Copyright held by magazine; reverts to author upon publication.

1984; 3/yr; 1,500

$16/yr ind; $32/yr inst; $6.95/ea; 40%

120 pp; 7 x 10

Ad rates: $200/page/5½ x 8½; $125/½ page/5½ x 4

ISSN: 0741-5702

DeBoer, Ingram

FOUR QUARTERS

John J. Keenan, Editor; John P. Ross, Associate Editor

La Salle Univ.

20th & Olney Avenues

Philadelphia, PA 19141

(215) 951-1610

Poetry, fiction, nonfiction, short dramatic pieces.

A magazine of contemporary culture aimed at college-educated readers. Publishes nonspecialized articles, essays, fiction, and poetry.

Seamus Heaney, Joyce Carol Oates, James Merrill, John Lukacs, John Hollander, J.D. McClatchy.

Payment: on contribution.

Reporting time: 6 weeks.

Copyright held by La Salle Univ.; assignable to author.

1951; 2/yr

$8/yr; $4 each; 40%

64 pp; 7 x 10

$100/full page

ISSN: 0015-9107

La Salle University

FRANK: An International Journal of Contemporary Writing and Art

David Applefield, Editor/Publisher

B.P. 29

94301 Vincennes Cedex

FRANCE

or:

Box 51

Lincoln, MA 01773

Poetry, fiction, translations, interviews, graphics/artwork, essays, photographs.

FRANK is a highly eclectic journal open to both established and emerging talent which emphasizes internationalism. The journal encourages both literary and visual work that takes risks but does not ignore the value of intellectual traditions.

Italo Calvino, James Tate, Allen Ginsberg, Paul Bowles, Robert Coover, Raymond Carver, Rita Dove, Stephen Dixon, Mavis Gallant.

Contemporary Chinese, Turkish, Nordic, Philippino and Pakistani writing.

Payment: $10/page plus two copies.

Copyright held by author.

1983; 2/yr; 3,000

$25/4 issues ind; $40/4 issues inst; $7/ea; 33%–40%

224 pp; 5½ x 8½

Ad rates: $500/page/5 x 8; $250/½ page/4½ x 3½; $150/¼ page/2½ x 3½

ISSN: 0738-9299

FREE FOCUS
Patricia D. Coscia
224 82nd Street
Brooklyn, NY 11209
(718) 680-3899

Women's Poetry.

FREE FOCUS is a small-press magazine which focuses on the educated women of today and needs stories and poems. The poems can be as long as 2 pages or as short as 3 lines. No X-rated material. Poems should be single-spaced on individual sheets.

Mary Place, Larry Nicastro, Terry Naudzunas, Richard Murray.

Payment: 1 copy.

Reporting time: 6 months.

Copyright held by editor.

1985; 2/yr; 500

$4/yr; $2/ea

20 pp; 8 x 14

$1/column; $3/page

ISSN: 0447-5667

Thursday's Press

FREE LUNCH
Ron Offen
P.O. Box 7647
Laguna Niguel, CA 92677

Poetry.

Copyright held by **FREE LUNCH** Arts Alliance; reverts to author upon publication.

1989; 3/yr; 525

$10/yr; $4 ea

32 pp; 5½ x 8½

Ad rates: $100/page/4 x 8; $60/½ page/4 x 4; $35/¼ page/2 x 2

G

GALLERY WORKS

Peter Holland, Jeanne Lance
218 Appleton Dr.
Aptos, CA 95003
(408) 685-9518
Poetry, fiction, photographs, graphics/artwork, short experimental prose.
Solicits a wide range of styles of writing from around the U.S. (and occasionally Canada and England). The editors believe a literary magazine should raise the level of communication among writers and artists. Feminist and language writing.
David Bromige, Beverly Dahlen, Rosmarie Waldrop, Patrick McGrath.
Payment: two free copies.
Copyright held by magazine; reverts to author upon publication.
1973; 1/2 yrs; 500
$30/ind. issues 1–7; $40/inst. issues 1–7; $5/ea; 40%
64 pp; 5 x 7

THE GALLEY SAIL REVIEW

Stanley McNail
1630 University Avenue, #42
Berkeley, CA 94703

(415) 486-0187
Poetry, reviews.
GSR seeks excellence in contemporary poetry, without regard for schools, cliques, or "movements." It values sincerity and honors craftsmanship. It tries to encourage poetry that speaks to the human condition in this modern world, and to develop a wider appreciation of poetry as an essential art in society.
Martin Robbins, Michael Culross, Laurel Ann Bogen, Harold Witt, Carol Hamilton.
Payment: in copies.
Copyright held by magazine; reverts to author upon publication.
1958; 3/yr; 400
$8/yr ind; $15/2 yr ind; $15/2 yr inst; $3/ea; 40%
40 pp; 8½ x 5½
ISSN: 0016-4100

GANDHABBA

Tom Savage
622 East 11th Street
New York, NY 10009
(212) 533-3893
Poetry, translation (of poetry), graphics/artwork.
Language, New York School, postmodern and emerging poetry. Each issue has a theme.
Allen Ginsberg, John Godfrey,

Alan Davies, Norman MacAfee,
Bernadette Mayer.
Payment: none.
Reporting time: 1 year.
Copyright held by magazine; reverts to author upon publication.
1983; 1/yr; 350
$12/ind for 3 issues; $15/inst for 3
issues; $3.50/ea; 40%. Please
make all checks payable to
Thomas Savage.
100 pp; 8½ x 11
No ads

THE GEORGIA REVIEW

Stanley W. Lindberg
University of Georgia
Athens, GA 30602
(404) 542-3481

Poetry, fiction, essays, reviews,
graphics/artwork.

An international journal of arts
and letters with a special interest in current American literary
writing; seeking interdisciplinary thesis-oriented essays—not
scholarly articles—and engaging
book reviews, plus the best in
contemporary poetry and fiction; authors range from Nobel
laureates and Pulitzer Prize winners to the as-yet unknown and
previously unpublished.

Rita Dove, T.R. Hummer, Eudora
Welty, Fred Chappell, Seamus
Heaney, Mary Hood, Louise
Erdrich.
Payment; $2/line for poetry;
$25/printed page for prose.
Reporting time: 8–12 weeks.
No unsolicited mss. read during
June, July, or August.
Copyright held by University of
Georgia; reverts to author upon
publication.
1947; 4/yr; 5,500
$12/yr; $5/ea
224 pp; 6¾ x 7½
Ad rates: $275/page/4¾ x 7½;
$175/½ page/4¾ x 3⅝
ISSN: 0016-8386
Bernhard DeBoer

THE GETTYSBURG REVIEW

Peter Stitt
Gettysburg College
Gettysburg, PA 17325-1491
(717) 337-6770

Poetry, fiction, essays, graphics/
artwork.

THE GETTYSBURG REVIEW
is an interdisciplinary magazine
of arts and ideas, which features
the highest quality poetry, fiction, essays, essay-reviews,
and graphics by both beginning
and established writers and
artists. Two special interests
are the publication of serial
fiction and the inclusion of a

full-color graphics section in each issue. Essays are in a variety of disciplines, with a wide range of subject matter.

Frederick Busch, Paul West, Joyce Carol Oates, Ed Minus, Linda Pastan, Rita Dove, Charles Wright, Deborah Larsen, Donald Hall, Mary Hood.

Payment: $20/page prose; $2/line poetry; upon publication.

Copyright held by Gettysburg College; reverts to author upon publication.

1988; 4/yr; 2,000

$15/yr ind; $12/yr inst; $27/2 yr; $36/3 yr; $6/ea; 40%

184 pp; 6 x 10

Ad rates: $150/page/5 x 7½; $225/inside cover

ISSN: 0898-4557

GIANTS PLAY WELL IN THE DRIZZLE

Martha King
326-A 4th Street
Brooklyn, NY 11215
(718) 788-7927

Poetry, fiction, essays, reviews, graphics/artwork.

With a tip of my hat to *Migrant* and *Floating Bear*, I try to keep the **DRIZZLE** small, free, and delicate. I publish—side-by-side—works by writers of sometimes vastly different aesthetics. It's the energy I look for and hope to share with readers. Very small format. Please ask for a sample copy before submitting.

August Kleinzahler, Bob Vander-Molen, Kim Lyons, Sheila Murphy, David Rattray, Connie Deanovich.

Payment: none.

Copyright held by **GPWITD**; reverts to author upon publication.

1984; 4/yr; 450

No ads

GIORNO POETRY SYSTEMS

John Giorno
222 Bowery
New York, NY 10012
(212) 925-6372

Poetry.

Magazine in three formats: LP record, Compact Disc, and Cassette. Video Pak series is a magazine in video format.

Laurie Anderson, William Burroughs, Patti Smith, Diamanda Galas, Nick Cave.

Payment: $400 royalty advance, and 12% of the retail price of each record sold.

1972; 4/yr; 10,000

$8.98/single album; $12.98/double album; $8.98/casette; $13.98/

compact disc CD; $39.95 video cassette; 40%, 55% to distributors

GRAB-A-NICKEL

Barbara Smith
Alderson-Broaddus College
Philippi, WV 26416
(304) 457-1700

Poetry, fiction, reviews, photographs, graphics/artwork.

GRAB-A-NICKEL is a tabloid journal of poems, fiction, book reviews, photographs and drawings. Open submissions; priority given to Appalachian writers and subject matter. There is encouragement of new writers of any age or background. It is a product of a college community's writers' workshop.

Barbara Smith, Dawn Norman, Mark Rowh, T. Kilgore Splake, Llewellyn McKernan, Jim Wayne Miller.

Payment: in copies.
Copyright held by author.
1977; 2–3/yr; 1,000
25¢/ea
16 pp; 11½ x 14

GRADIVA

Luigi Fontanella
P.O. Box 831
Stony Brook, NY 11794-3359
(516) 632-7448 or (516) 632-7440

Poetry, essays, reviews, translation, interviews.

GRADIVA is an international journal of modern Italian literature that focuses on literary criticism and theory. All contributions are published in English or Italian. Creative works written in other languages are published with translation.

Umberto Eco, Edoardo Sanguineti, Philipe Souppault, Jan Kott, Andrea Zanzotto.

Payment: in issues, subscription.
Copyright held by Gradiva; reverts to author upon publication.
1986; 2/yr; 3,000
$20/yr ind; $20/yr inst
100 pp; 5½ x 8½
Ad rates: $100/page/5½ x 8½; $60/½ page/5½ x 4¼; $35/¼ page/2¾ x 4¼

GRAHAM HOUSE REVIEW

Peter Balakian, Bruce Smith
Box 500
Colgate University
Hamilton, NY 13346
(315) 824-100, ext. 262

Poetry, essays, translation, interviews.

We publish the best poetry and poetry in translation we can get. We have just begun an inter-

view series and will publish essays in the future. We pay scrupulous attention to production, and have an international interest in selecting material. Seamus Heaney, Derek Walcott, Madeline DeFrees, David Wagoner, Maxine Kumin, Carolyn Forché.
Payment: in copies.
Reporting time: 1–2 months.
Copyright held by magazine; reverts to author upon publication.
1976; 1/yr; 1,750
$7.50/yr ind; $7.50/inst; $7.50/ea; 20%
125 pp; 8½ x 5½

GRAND STREET
Jean Stein
135 Central Park West
New York, NY 10023
(212) 721-3325
Poetry, fiction, criticism, essays, reviews.
Sandra Cisneros, Joy Harjo, William T. Vollmann, Alexander Cockburn.
Payment: inquire.
Reporting time: 4–6 weeks.
Copyright held by magazine; reverts to author upon publication.
1981; 4/yr; 4,000

$24/yr ind; $34/yr foreign; $8.50/ea
240 pp; 7 x 9
Ad rates: $400/page
ISSN: 0734-5496-
W. W. Norton.

GREAT RIVER REVIEW
Orval Lund
211 West Seventh St.
Winona, MN 55987
(507) 454-6564
Poetry, fiction, criticism, reviews, graphics.
Dedicated to publishing the best in fiction, creative prose, and poetry, and to showcasing the work of new, emerging and established writers. Specially interested in Midwestern writers. Jack Myers, Lucille Clifton, Tom McGrath.
Payment: in copies.
Reporting time: 1–3 months.
Copyright reverts to author.
1977; 2/yr; 1,200
$9/yr; $4.50/ea
280 pp; 6 x 8
Ad rates: $100/page; $50/½ page; $25/¼ page
EBSCO Subscription Services, Faxon Services, Aquinas Subscription Services

GREAT STREAM REVIEW
Diane Z. Himes, Rick Sutliff
Lycoming College

Box 66
Williamsport, PA 17701
(717) 321-4114

Poetry, fiction, familiar essays,
novel excerpts, screen and stage
plays, reviews, interviews.

GSR provides a forum for writers
engaged in evaluating, confront-
ing and offering alternatives to
literary modernism and postmodernism; writers who find
the source of their imagination
in other than despair, disease
and alienation.

Will Baker, Scott Cairns, Pam
Houston, Deborah Monroe,
Janet Sylvester, Lee Upton.

Payment: $10/page.
Reporting time: 4 weeks.
Copyright held by GSR.
1989; 2/yr; 1,000
$7.50/yr; $4/ea; 40%
100 pp; 6 x 9
ISSN: 1042-8208

GREEN MOUNTAINS
REVIEW

Neil Shepard, Poetry; Tony Whe-
don, Fiction
Johnson State College
Johnson, VT 05656
(802) 635-2356

Poetry, fiction, essays, reviews,
interviews, translations, photographs.

GMR publishes work by promising newcomers and well-known
writers from across the country.
In addition, each issue features
the work of one regional
writer—either a suite of poems,
extended work of fiction, interview or literary essay.

Galway Kinnell, Denise Levertov,
Larry Levis, David St. John,
Ellen Lesser, David Wojahn.

Payment: in copies.
Reporting time: 1–3 months.
Copyright held by GMR; reverts
to author upon publication.
1987; 2/yr; 1,000
$8.50/yr; $4.50/ea; 40%
120+ pp; 6 x 9
$150/page; $75/½ page
ISSN: 0895-9307
Ubiquity

THE GREENSBORO REVIEW

Jim Clark
Department of English
Univ. North Carolina-Greensboro
Greensboro, NC 27412
(919) 334-5459

Poetry, fiction.

Contemporary and experimental.
We want to see the best being
written regardless of theme,
subject or style.

Robert Morgan, Kelly Cherry,
Larry Brown, Madison Smartt
Bell, Ellen Herman.

Payment: in copies.

Reporting time: 2–4 months.
Copyright held by TGR; reverts to
author.
1966; 2/yr; 5–600
$5/yr; $12/3 yrs; $2.50/ea
120 pp; 6 x 9
ISSN: 0017-4084

COAST; reverts to author upon
publication.
1981; 2/yr; 500+
$8/yr ind; $6/yr inst; $4/ea; 40%
96 pp; 9 x 6
No ads
ISSN: 0896-2251

GULF COAST

Gary McKay, Lisa Lewis, Roger
Mullins, Randall Watson, Stew-
art James
Department of English
University of Houston
4800 Calhoun Rd.
Houston, TX 77204-5641
(713) 749-3640

Poetry, fiction, essays, translation,
photographs, graphics/artwork.

GULF COAST encourages submission of high-quality, well-
crafted and energetic poetry and
fiction, with emphasis on subject matter. Contributors may be
students in the University of
Houston creative writing program, but submission is open to
others.

Lisa Zeidner, Charles Baxter,
Rosellen Brown, Amy Clampitt,
Richard Howard, Rich Bass,
Rodney Jones, John Hawkes,
Ann Beattie, Padget Powell,
Glen Blake.

Payment: copies.
Copyright held by GULF

GULF STREAM MAGAZINE

Lynne Barrett, Editor; Pamela
Gross, Assoc. Editor
FIU, North Miami Campus
North Miami, FL 33181
(305) 940-5599

Poetry, fiction, essays.

GSM publishes high quality fiction, poetry and essays. We are
open to experimental and mainstream work. No more than 5
poems. Limit prose to 25 pages.

Gerald Costanzo, Ann Hood, Stuart Dybek, Dara Wier.

Payment: in copies.
Reporting time: 2 weeks–2
months.
Copyright held by Gulf Stream—
1st North American.
1989; 2/yr; 200
$7.50; $4/ea; 40%
96 pp; 8½ x 5½

GYPSY

Belinda Subraman
10708 Gay Brewer Drive
El Paso, TX 79935

(915) 592-3701
Poetry, Fiction, Reviews, Graphics/
Artwork.
We are an international family of
independent literary and visual
artists. We seek to enlarge our
family and support. We favor
poetry appeal and lasting value.
Subscriptions are encouraged. It
is our ONLY means.
Gay Brower, Laurel Speer, James
Purdy, Albert Huffstickler, Gerald Locklin.
Reporting time: 6–12 weeks
Copyright: Vergin' Press
1984; 2/yr; 302
$10 individual; $14 institutional;
$5–$8 (editors issues vary);
40%
72; 8½ x 11
$100/page; $55/½ page; $30/¼
page
ISSN: 0176-3148

H

HAIGHT ASHBURY
LITERARY JOURNAL

Joanne Hotchkiss, Alice Rogoff,
Will Walker
558 Joost Avenue
San Francisco, CA 94127
(415) 584-8264

The magazine began with six editors of extremely diverse backgrounds. The magazine
encompasses diversity of viewpoint, racial, sexual as well as
style, tending to confront the
difficult and painful of human
experiences as well as the
higher reaches of emotional experiences.
Eugene Rugghes, Mona Lisa Sa-
loy, Peter Plate, Jack Hier-
schman, Panco Aquilla.
Payment: in copies.
Reporting time: 2–4 months.
Copyright held by author.
+1980; 1½/yr; 1,600
$25/lifetime subs; $1/ea; 50%
16 pp; 11 x 17¼
Ad rates: $150/page/10 x 17;
$75/½ page/7½ x 9; $50/¼
page/9 x 5

HAMBONE

Nathaniel Mackey
132 Clinton Street
Santa Cruz, CA 95062
(408) 426-3072
Poetry, fiction, criticism, reviews,
plays, translation, interviews,
photographs, graphics/artwork.
Cross-cultural work emphasizing
the centrifugal.
Edward Kamau Brathwaite, Beverly Dahlen, Kenneth Irby,
Leslie Scalapino, Jay Wright.

Payment: copies.
Reporting time: 1–4 months.
Copyright held by magazine; reverts to author upon publication.
1974; 1/yr; 600
$10/2 issues ind; $14/2 issues inst; $6/ea; 40%
170 pp; 5½ x 8½
ISSN: 0733-6616
Inland Book Company, Small Press Distribution

HAMMERS

Nat David
1718 Sherman #205
Evanston, IL 60201
(708) 328-7555
Poetry.
An end of the millennium irregular poetry magazine.
Marty Campbell, Victor diSuero, Michael Warr, Luis Rodriquez, Chris Stone.
Payment: one free copy
Reporting time: 1–2 months
1990; annual; 500
$3.00; 40%
8½ x 11

THE HAMPDEN-SYDNEY POETRY REVIEW

Tom O'Grady
P.O. Box 126
Hampden-Sydney, VA 23943

(804) 223-8209
Poetry.
A small, carefully-printed correspondence among poets which attempts to print the unknown with the known.
David Ignatow, Robert Pack, Patricia Goedicke, David Huddle, Lewis Turco.
Payment: in copies.
Copyright held by Tom O'Grady; reverts to author upon publication.
1975; 2/yr; 500
$5/yr ind; $5/yr, $12/3-yr inst; $5/ea; 1990 Anthology 328 pp. $12.95; 40%
60 pp; 5 x 9
No ads

HANGING LOOSE

Robert Hershon, Dick Lourie, Mark Pawlak, Ron Schreiber
231 Wyckoff Street
Brooklyn, NY 11217
(718) 643-9559
Poetry, fiction, translation, graphics/artwork.
Our interests continue to center on finding new writers and then staying with them, often to the point of book publication.
(Book mss by invitation only.)
Paul Violi, Kimiko Hahn, Steven Schrader, Donna Brook, Gary Lenhart.

Payment: some payment to contributors.
Reporting time: 2–3 months.
Copyright held by magazine; reverts to author upon publication.
1966; 3/yr; 1,500
$12.50/yr ind; $15.00/yr inst; $5/ea; 20%–40%
80–96 pp; 7 x 8½
ISSN: 0440-2316
Small Press Distribution, Bookslinger, Inland Book Co.

HANSON'S: A Magazine of Literary & Social Interest
Eric Hanson
113 Merryman Court
Annapolis, MD 21401
(301) 626-1643

Poetry, fiction, essays, humor, interviews, dialogues, and various features.
A magazine of general interest, we are striving to combine the traditionally separate aspects of literary and social journals into one magazine.
Payment: $30–$100, plus one copy.
Reporting time: 2 weeks.
Copyright held by CIRE Publishing; reverts to author.
1988; 2/yr; 1,500
$8/yr; $2/ea; 40%
80 pp; 8½ x 11

Classified advertisments free to subscribers, no other advertising accepted.
ISSN: 0251-4316
CIRE Publishing

HAPPINESS HOLDING TANK
Albert Drake
1790 Grand River
Okemos, MI 48864
(517) 349-0552

Poetry, very short fiction, essays, reviews, interviews, etc. . . .
HHT is an eclectic magazine, and publishes a wide variety of poetry—free verse, forms, narrative, lyric, found poetry, visual poetry, etc. . . .
Emphasis is on the well-made poem that expresses a sense of humanity.
Earle Birney, Vern Rutsala, William Stafford, William Matthews, Judith Goren, Lee Upton.
Payment: in copies.
Reporting time: 2 weeks–2 months.
Copyright held by author.
1970; 1/yr; 300
No subs; $2/ea
pages and size varies
Have never had paid ads.

HAWAII REVIEW
Galatea Maman, Editor-in-Chief
UH Manoa

Department of English
1733 Donagho Road
Honolulu, HI 96822
(808) 956-8548
Poetry, fiction, criticism, essays,
reviews, plays, translations,
interviews, photographs, graph-
ics/artwork.
Ursule Molinaro, Ian MacMillan,
Nell Altizer, John Unterecker,
Michael McPherson, William
Pitt Root, Frank Stewart.
Payment: $10–75, plus 2 copies;
more for cover art.
Reporting time: 30–90 days.
Copyright held by magazine; re-
verts to author upon publica-
tion.
1973; 3/yr; 2,000
$12/yr; $5/ea
100–180 pp; 5½ x 9
Ad rates: $75/page
ISSN: 0093-9625
Chaminade University, Hawaii
State Library Systems, North-
western University, Columbia
University

HAYDEN'S FERRY REVIEW
Salima Keegan
Matthews Center
Arizona State University
Tempe, AZ 85287-1502
(602) 965-1243
Poetry, fiction, interviews, pho-
tography, artwork.

HAYDEN'S FERRY REVIEW is
Arizona State University's na-
tional literary magazine featur-
ing the best solicited and
unsolicited works of well
known and new writers.
Bob Shacochis, Raymond Carver,
Joy Harjo, Rick Bass.
Interviews with Joseph Heller,
John Updike, T.C. Boyle,
Richard Ford, Gloria Naylor,
Ai.
Published bi-annually. Reporting
time 8–10 weeks after deadline.
Deadlines: Fall/Winter, Feb. 28.
Spring/Summer, Sept. 30
Payment: in copies.
Copyright held by the magazine;
reverts to author upon publica-
tion.
1986; 2/yr; 1,000
$5.00
125 pp; 6 x 9
ISSN: 0887-5170

HELICON NINE
Gloria Vando Hickok
P.O. Box 22412
Kansas City, MO 64113
(913) 722-2999
With Issue #20, in the fall of
1989, **HELICON NINE** con-
cluded its publication. The editor has embarked on a venture
called **THE READER**, which
is an Anthology of previously

published works from **HELI-CON NINE**.

HELICON NINE provided a literary forum for women past and present in literature, music, visual and performing arts. **THE READER** reiterates highpoints from **HELICON NINE'S** ten year history. Contact Gloria Vando Hickok for details.

HELLAS, A Journal of Poetry & the Humanities

Gerald Harnett

304 South Tyson Avenue

Glenside, PA 19038

(215) 884-1086

Poetry, classics, Renaissance & modern literary studies.

We provide a unique forum for the poetry, theory and criticism of poets working in meter–"The new formalism," or as Hellas Advertising describes that movement, "The new Classicism."

Timothy Steele, Richard Moore, Joseph Malone, Frederick Turner, David Slavitt.

Copyright **HELLAS**; First North American serial rights only

1990; semi-annual;700

$12; $6.50; 40

176; 6 x 9

$175/page/ 4 x 7; $100/½ page/ 4 x 3½

ISSN: 1044-5331

HERESIES: A Feminist Publication on Art and Politics

Heresies Collective, Inc.

P.O. Box 1306

Canal Street Station

New York, NY 10013

(212) 227-2108

Essays, experimental writing, short fiction, interviews, poetry; page art, photography, graphic art, all visual arts.

HERESIES is the longest-lived feminist art journal still publishing. Thematic, political focus. "We believe that what is commonly called art can have a political impact and that in the making of art and all cultural artifacts our identities as women play a distinct role . . . A place where diversity can be articulated."

Payment: $10.

Reporting time: 6–8 months.

Copyright reverts to author upon publication.

1977; 2/yr; 8,000

Four issues - $23/ind; $33/inst; $6.75/ea

96 pp; 8½ x 11

Ad rates: $250/½ page; $125/¼ page

Bookpeople, Inland, Small Changes, Homing Pigeon

HIGH PLAINS LITERARY REVIEW

Robert O. Greer, Jr.
180 Adams Street, Suite 250
Denver, CO 80206
(303) 320-6827

Fiction, essays, poetry, reviews, criticism, interviews.

Designed to bridge the gap between commercial magazines and an outstanding array of academic quarterlies. A handsomely produced literary magazine that is intended to be more broadly based than academia without being commercially "targeted." A journal designed to display the absolute best of craft. O. Henry award winning fiction appeared as early as Vol. 1, No. 1.

Richard Currey, Nancy Lord, Marilyn Krysl, Darrell Spencer, Tony Ardizzone, Julia Alvarez, Rita Dove.

Payment: $5 per page for prose; $10 per page for poetry.

Reporting time: 8 weeks.

Copyright held by High Plains Literary Review; reverts to author upon publicaton.

1986; 3/yr; 1,100
$20/yr; $7/ea; 40%
140 pp; 6 x 9
Ad rates: $100/page; $50/½ page;
ISSN: 0888-4153
Bernhard DeBoer, Inc. Ubiquity Distrib. Inc.

HIRAM POETRY REVIEW

Hale Chatfield and Carol Donley
Box 162
Hiram, OH 44234
(216) 569-3211

Poetry, criticism, essays, reviews, interviews. Photographs, graphics, and artwork by invitation only.

Reporting time: 8–12 weeks.

Copyright reverts to author upon publication.

1967; 2/yr; 500
$2/ea; 40%–60%
40 pp; 6 x 9
ISSN: 0018-2036

HOB-NOB

Mildred K. Henderson
994 Nissley Road
Lancaster, PA 17601
(717) 898-7807

Short fiction, non-fiction, poetry, reviews, letters, cartoons.

HOB-NOB is a small literary publication of 72 + pages with material from contributors from around the world, of all ages and levels.

Fulbright scholar Sanford Pinsker, other college professors

Payment: free copy on first appearance (at least)

Reporting time: A few weeks, especially for rejections—maybe

longer for acceptances (or return of material not sent during reading period)
Copyright: Yes—first rights only—all rights revert to author or poet after that
1969: semi-annual; 400+
$6.00; $3.50
72–76; 8½ x 11
Free to subscribers, exchangers, or purchasers of issue
Only by Mail

HOBO JUNGLE
Marc Erdrich & Ruth Boerger
33 Rucum Rd.
Roxbury, CT 06783
(203) 354-4359

Poetry, fiction, essays, serialized novels; also drawings and musical scores.

HOBO JUNGLE seeks poetry, fiction, essays, musical scores and line art. There are no limits on length or subject matter. Simultaneous submissions are acceptable. Manuscripts should be typed.
Payment: $10 and 2 copies.
Reporting time: 8–12 weeks.
Copyright reverts to author upon publication.
1987; 4/yr; 11,000
Free at dist. outlets; Subsc. $12/yr.; $3 by mail.
64 pp; 8 x 10½

$61/⅛ page; $115/¼ page
ISSN: 1045-2591
Query for lists

THE HOLLINS CRITIC
John Rees Moore
P.O. Box 9538
Hollins College, VA 24020
(703) 362-6317 or 362-8268

Poetry, critical essays, reviews, graphics/artwork.

A non-specialist periodical concentrating on the work of a single contemporary poet, fiction writer or dramatist in each issue. Cover picture, essay of about 5,000 words, brief account of author, check-list of publications, several poems and a section of brief book reviews.
Dawn Schauer, Rod Farmer, K. J. Burhanna, Mattie F. Quensenberry, Michael Cadnum.
Payment: essays/$200 by permission of editor only; $25/poems.
Copyright held by magazine.
1964; 5/yr; 850
$6/yr; $2/ea
20 pp; 7 x 10
ISSN: 0018-3644

HOME PLANET NEWS
Donald Lev and Enid Dame, Editors
P.O. Box 415

Stuyvesant Station
New York, NY 10009
(718) 769-2854
Poetry, fiction, criticism, reviews, translation, interviews, photographs, news.
We publish poetry, reviews of books, art exhibits, theater, news of the literary and small press scene, interviews and fiction. Occasional pull-out section of single poet's work.
Cornelius Eady, Norman Rosten, Steve Kowit, William Packard, Antler, Lyn Lifshin, Gerald Locklin, Richard Kostelanetz.
Payment: in copies and subscription.
Reporting time: 2–3 months.
Copyright held by magazine; reverts to author upon publication.
1979; 3–4/yr; 1,000
$8/yr ind; $8/yr inst, $15/2 yrs; $2/ea; 40%
24 pp; 10 x 15
Ad rates: $150/page/10 x 15; $75/½ page/10 x 7½; $37.50/¼ page/5 x 7½

HORNS OF PLENTY: Malcolm Cowley and his Generation
Patricia Koutouzos
P. O. Box 65
Crete, Illinois 60417
(708) 747-0533

Poetry, criticism, essays, interviews, reviews, graphics/artwork, photographs, memoirs.
Focuses on the work and influence of poet/critic/literary historian Malcolm Cowley (1898–1989) and his contemporaries who came of age in the 1920's. Also special issues devoted to selected writers such as Kenneth Burke, Lewis Mumford and Kay Boyle.
Gay Wilson Allen, Robert B. Heilman, Helga Sandburg, Philip L. Gerber, and Bernard Bergonzi.
Payment: in copies.
Reporting time: 6 weeks.
Copyright reverts to author upon publication.
1988; 4/yr; 200
$15/ind; $20/inst; $4/ea; 15%
60 pp; 5½ x 8½
No advertising
ISSN: 0896-9965
Faxon, Faxon Europe, Boley International

HOW(ever)
Myung Mi Kim
Meredith Stricker
1171 E. Jefferson
Iowa City, IA 52245
(319) 351-6361
Poetry, reviews.
HOW(ever) hopes to create a

place in which women poets can talk to scholars through poems and working notes on these poems, as well as through commentary on neglected women poets who were/are making textures and structures of poetry in the tentative region of the untried.

Barbara Guest, Daphne Marlatt, Maureen Owen, Gail Sher, Lisa Pater Faranda.

Payment: none.

Copyright reverts to author.

1983; 4/yr; 400

$10/4 issues ind; $12/4 issues inst

16 pp; 8½ x 11

HOWLING DOG

Mark Donovan

8419 Rhode

Utica, MI 48317

(313) 254-5334

Poetry, fiction, graphics/artwork.

Our purpose is to have an effect similar to the howl of a dog with its foot caught in a fence. We desire something that may not be pleasant or permanent, but will still be heard by everyone in the neighborhood.

Arthur Knight, Alan Catlin, John Sinclair, M. L. Liebler.

Payment: in copies.

Reporting time: 6 months or more.

Copyright held by authors.

1985; 2/yr; 500

$10/yr; $5/ea; 40%

64 pp; 6 x 9

Ad rates: $80/page/4 x 8; $40/½ page/4 x 4; $20/¼ page/2 x 4

ISSN: 0888-3521

THE HUDSON REVIEW

Paula Deitz, Frederick Morgan

684 Park Avenue

New York, NY 10021

(212) 650-0020

Poetry, fiction, criticism, essays, reviews.

We publish both new and established writers. We have no university affiliation, and we are not committed to any narrow academic aim or to any particular political perspective. We focus on the area where literature and poetry bear on the intellectual life of the time.

Payment: 2½¢/word for prose; 50¢/line for poetry.

Reporting time: 1–3 months.

Copyright held only on assigned reviews.

1948; 4/yr; 4,500

$20/yr; $6/ea

160 pp; 6 x 9¼

Ad rates: $300/page/4½ x 7½; $200/½ page/4½ x 3⅝; $150/¼ page/2⅛ x 3⅝

ISSN: 0018-702X

Eastern News Distributors

HUNGRY MIND REVIEW

Bart Schneider, Editor
1648 Grand Avenue
St. Paul, MN 55105
(612) 699-2610
Essays, reviews, interviews, photographs and woodcuts.
HUNGRY MIND REVIEW publishes book reviews, essays, and forums on particular focuses. **HUNGRY MIND REVIEW** reviews large, small, and university presses, focusing on mid- and backlist titles.
Clark Blaise, Robert Bly, Rosellen Brown, Doris Grumbach, Lewis Hyde, W.P. Kinsella, Herbert Kohl, Phillip Lopate, William Stafford, Bill McKibben, Gerald Early, Francis Phillips.
Payment: varies.
Copyright held by David Unowsky, dba **HUNGRY MIND REVIEW**.
1986; 4/yr; 30,000
$10/yr ind; $13/yr Canada and inst; free/ea
56 pp; 9¾ x 15
Ad rates: $1,195/page; $650/½ page; $350/¼ page; $215/⅛ page; $130/⅟₁₆ page
ISSN: 0887-5499
We distribute free of charge to 350 independent bookstores across the U.S. and Canada.

HURRICANE ALICE: A Feminist Quarterly

Martha Roth
Lind Hall
207 Church Street, S.E.
Minneapolis, MN 55455
(612) 625-1834
Reviews, essays, criticism, fiction, poetry, graphics/artwork.
HURRICANE ALICE provides a feminist review of culture. It prints reviews of books by and about women, critical essays having a feminist perspective— especially essays on literature, film, dance, and the visual arts—fiction, some poetry and graphics.
Alice Walker, Toni McNaron, Peter Erickson, Meridel Le Sueur, Susan Griffin.
Payment: in copies.
Reporting time: 1–3 months.
Copyright reverts to author upon publication.
1983; 4/yr; 700
$10/yr; $8/yr students/seniors; $2.50/ea
14 pp; 11 x 17
Ad rates: $45/3 x 4; $20/3 x 2; $75/⅟₆ page
Ubiquity, L-S Distributor, Don Olson Distributors

I

IKON

Susan Sherman
P.O. Box 1355
Stuyvesant Station
New York, NY 10009
Poetry, fiction, essays, translation, interviews, photographs, graphics/artwork.

IKON is a cultural, political, feminist magazine, showing the experiences of third world, lesbian, Jewish and working women, all women in the diversity of our experience. **IKON** is about making connections through the words and images of women themselves in their essays, articles, paintings, photographs, fiction, art, songs and poems.

Audre Lourde, Kimiko Hahn, Beth Brant, Grace Paley, Adrienne Rich.
Payment: subscription and two copies.
Reporting time: 90 days.
Copyright held by magazine; reverts to author upon publication.
1982; 2/yr; 1,750
$10/yr ind; $15/yr inst; $6/ea; 40%
140 pp; 7 x 9

ILLINOIS WRITERS REVIEW

Kevin Stein, Jim Elledge
P.O. Box 1087
Champaign, IL 61820
(309) 243-7441
Essays, reviews.
We publish reviews by and about Illinois writers, particularly those published by small presses. In addition we seek reviews about publications of national import and offer our readers essays of interest to fiction writers and poets.
Payment: $25–35.
Reporting time: 1 month.
Copyright held by author.
1981; 2/yr; 500
$15/yr ind; $20/yr inst; 40%
24 pp; 5 x 8
Ad rates: $100/page/4½ x 7; $50/½ page/4½ x 4
ISSN: 0733-9526
Illinois Literary Publishers' Association

INDIANA REVIEW

Jon Tribble, Renée Manfredi, Allison Joseph
316 North Jordan Avenue
Indiana University
Bloomington, IN 47405
(812) 855-3439
Fiction, poetry, essays.
We have no prejudices of style or content, but will publish only

those poems and short stories which demonstrate: 1) keen sense of craft; 2) insight into the human condition. Writers should send their best work only. We prefer stories of rich texture to those that depend on a gimmick.

Naomi Shihab Nye, Robert Lacy, Andrew Hudgins, Antonya Nelson, Christopher Gilbert, Charles Johnson, Eleanor Wilner.

Payment: $5 per page poetry; $25 per story.

Reporting time: 3 weeks–3 months.

Copyright held by magazine; reverts to author upon publication.

1976; 3/yr; 1,200

$12/yr ind; $15/yr inst; $5/ea

120 pp; 6 x 9

Ad rates: $100/page/6 x 9; $60/½ page/6 x 4½

ISSN: 0738-386X

Ingram Periodicals

INNISFREE

Rex Winn

P.O. Box 277

Manhattan Beach, CA 90266

(213) 545-2607; (213) 546-5862 (FAX)

Fiction, poetry, essays, graphics/artwork.

We provide an open medium for artists to express their thoughts and relate their experiences. Home grown magazine, professional quality.

Payment: awards.

Copyright held by author.

1981; 6/yr; 300

$18/yr ind; $2.50/ea

50 pp; 8½ x 11

INTERIM

A. Wilber Stevens, Editor; James Hazen, Joe McCullough, Associate Editors

Department of English

University of Nevada

Las Vegas, NV 89154

Poetry, fiction.

INTERIM prints the best poetry and short fiction we can find, plus occasional reviews. It is the revival, under its original editor, of the magazine published and edited in Seattle in 1944–55.

William Stafford, John Heath-Stubbs, X.J. Kennedy, Stephen Stepanchev, Gladys Swan.

Payment: contributor's copies plus a two-year subscription.

Copyright held by magazine; reverts to author upon publication.

1944; 2/yr; 750

$10/3 yrs; $5/yr ind; $8/yr inst;
$3/ea; 40%
48–64 pp; 9 x 6
ISSN: 0888-2452

INTERNATIONAL POETRY REVIEW

Evalyn P. Gill, Alice Rice, Clare
Rosen
Box 2047
Greensboro, NC 27402
(919) 273-1711

Unpublished translation with contemporary original language poem. Contemporary English language poetry, graphics.

Willis Barnstone, Catherine Savage Brosman, Charles Edward Eaton, Mary C. Snotherly, William Stafford.

Payment: in copies.
1975; 2/yr; 400
$4/ea; 40%
136 pp; 6 x 9
Ad rates: $100/page; $50/½ page

INTERSTATE

Loris Essary, Mark Loeffler
P.O. Box 7068
University Station
Austin, TX 78713
(512) 928-2911

Poetry, fiction, criticism, essays, reviews, plays, translations, interviews, photographs, graphics/artwork; experimental art in all genres and non-genres.

INTERSTATE has a special focus on non-traditional, experimental writing and art, particularly visual literature, mixed media and work for theatre. There is a strong non-U.S. content.

Charles Brownson, Robert Coover, Brian Eno, Karl Kempton, Dan Raphael.

Payment: in copies.
Reporting time: immediately, occasionally longer.
Copyright reverts to author upon publication.
1974; 1/2 yrs; 500
$10/2 issues; 40%
92 pp
ISSN: 0363-9991

INVISIBLE CITY

John McBride and Paul Vangelisti
P.O. Box 2853
San Francisco, CA 94126
(415) 527-1018

Poetry, criticism, translation, graphics/artwork, visual poetry.

A book series, formerly tabloid, of poetry, translation, visuals and statements published whenever enough good material is available: focusing on current U.S. writing, some concrete poetry and Italian writing—

focused on "the internal tension of language."

Adriano Spatola, Giulia Niccolai, Ernst Meister, John Thomas, Stanislaw Baranczak, Antonio Porta, Emilio Villa; and now DAYBOOK by Robert Crosson, with DIVISION appended, remarks, criticism & such.
Payment: copies and then some.
Reporting time: 2 months.
Copyright reverts to author upon publication.
1971; 1–2/yr; 1,000
$10/yr ind; $15/yr inst
80+ pp; 5 x 9
ISSN: 0034-2009

IO

Richard Grossinger, Lindy Hough
North Atlantic Books
2800 Woolsey St.
Berkeley, CA 94705
(415) 652-5309

Poetry, essays, translations, interviews, photographs, graphics/artworks, prose.

IO does special issues on subject matters ranging among geographical/ecological concerns, hermetic studies (alchemical symbolism), sports literature (baseball, basketball), literature (issues on Melville, Blake, contemporary poets), and psychological/anthropological issues (dreams, American Indian mythology).

Michael McClure, James Broughton, John Updike, Diane Di Prima, Joanne Kyger.
Payment: some payment to contributors.
Reporting time: immediately.
Copyright held by author.
1964; irreg; 2,000
$25/4 issues; $5–$12.95/ea; 20%–50%
300 pp; 6 x 9
ISSN: 0021-0331

THE IOWA REVIEW

David Hamilton
308 EPB
University of Iowa
Iowa City, IA 52242
(319) 335-0462

Poetry, fiction, criticism, essays, reviews, interviews.

We look for new as well as established writers and are usually pleased, on the whole, with what we are able to publish.
Payment: $1/line for poetry; $10/page for prose.
Reporting time: 2–3 months.
Copyright held by the University of Iowa; reverts to author upon publication.
1970; 3/yr; 1,500
$15/yr ind; $20/yr inst; $6.95/ea; 30%

180 pp; 6 x 9
Ad rates: $150/page/5½ x 8½
ISSN: 0021-065X
Ingram Periodicals

IOWA WOMAN
Marianne Abel; Sandra Witt, poetry
P.O. Box 680
Iowa City, IA 52244
(319) 987-2879
Fiction, essays, reviews, interviews, poetry, news briefs, features, ads, memoirs, graphics/artwork.
Rooted in the Midwest, **IOWA WOMAN** publishes award-winning women writers everywhere. National readership. Annual writing contest guidelines for SASE.
Judy Ruiz, Jane Ruiter, Ingrid Hill, Alice Friman, Natalie Kusz.
Payment: in copies and subscription.
Reporting time: 2 months.
Copyright held by magazine; reverts to author upon publication.
1980; quarterly; 2,500
15/yr; $17/yr Canada and Pan-Amer.; $20/other; $4/ea; 30%
48 pp; 8⅛ x 10⅞
ISSN: 0271-8227

THE ITHACA WOMEN'S ANTHOLOGY
Alicia Dowd, Joyce Gross
P.O. Box 582
Ithaca, NY 14851
Poetry, fiction, translation, photographs, graphics/artwork, criticism.
THE ITHACA WOMEN'S ANTHOLOGY was originally established as an annual collection of creative work, by, for and about women. The types of work we publish include essays, interviews, criticism, journal entries, translations, fiction, and poetry as well as graphics of all kinds. Our commitment is to provide a medium for women to creatively express their concerns, to coin varied and new voices, while emphasizing the highest in artistic quality.
Phyllis Janowitz, Alice Fulton, Lisa Ress, Carolyn Beard Whitlow, Beth French (Lorden).
Payment: none.
Copyright held by magazine; reverts to author upon publication.
1976; 1/yr; 350
$2.80/yr; $3/ea; 40%
Borealis Book Store, Smedley's Book Shop, Triangle Book Store

J

JACARANDA REVIEW

Katerine Swiggart
Department of English
2225 Rolfe Hall
University of California
Los Angeles, CA 90024
(213) 825-4173

Poetry, fiction, essays, reviews translation, interviews.

We try to publish the best fiction, poetry, and essays we can find. A potential contributor should read an issue or two to see what we mean by that. We feature in each issue an interview with a major writer and, usually, a supplement featuring work of special interest to us.

Jorge Luis Borges, Carolyn Forché, Alfred Corn, Ed Minus, Joscha Kessler.

Payment: three copies.

Copyright held by University of California; reverts to author upon publication.

1985; 2/yr; 1,000

$7/yr ind; $10/yr inst; $3.50/ea; 40%

120 pp; 5½ x 8

Ad rates: $75/page/5½ x 8; $50/½ page/5½ x 4; $25/¼ page/2¾ x 4

JAMES WHITE REVIEW

G. Baysans, P. Willkie
P.O. Box 3356
Traffic Station
Minneapolis, MN 55403
(612) 291-2913

Poetry, fiction, criticism, reviews, plays, photographs, graphics/ artwork.

We are a gay men's literary quarterly.

Robert Peters, Robert Gluck, James Broughton, Felice Picano, Harold Norse.

Payment: none.

Reporting time: 6–8 weeks.

Copyright held by magazine; reverts to author upon publication.

1983; 4/yr; 2,000

$12/yr ind; $12/yr inst; $2/ea; 40%

16 pp; 11 x 15

Ad rates: $400/page; $200/½ page; $120/¼ page

THE JOURNAL

Bill Endres, Associate Editor, Hillary Foote, Managing Editor
164 West 17th Avenue
Department of English
The Ohio State University
Columbus, OH 43210
(614) 292-4076

Poetry, Fiction, Reviews.

THE JOURNAL attempts to provide an outlet for good writing by Ohio writers and writers from around the country. We seek out good work and attempt to attract the best new writers. The editorial staff works to publish and distribute poetry, fiction, non-fiction, and reviews, the sole criterion for which is excellence.

Maurya Simon, J. R. Hummer, Jonathan Holden, Eric Pankey and Linda Bierds.

Reporting time: 4–6 weeks

Copyright: The Ohio State University

1972; Bi-annual; 1100

$8.00; $4.50; 40%

80-100; 6 x 9

ISSN: 1045-084X

JOURNAL OF IRISH LITERATURE

Robert Hogan, Kathleen Danaher

P.O. Box 361

Newark, DE 19711

(302) 764-8477

Poetry, fiction, criticism, reviews, graphics.

Irish literature past and present is of central interest, and new or previously unpublished creative material forms the majority of works published.

Mervyn Wall, Mary Rose Callaghan, Thomas Sheridan, Mary Manning, W.J. Lawrence, Ivy Bannister, James Douglas.

Payment: none.

Reporting time: about 2 months.

Copyright reverts to author.

1972; 3/yr; 600

$12/yr ind; $18/yr inst; $4.50/ea

60 pp; 5½ x 8½

Ad rates: $100/page; $50/½ page; $25/¼ page

ISSN: 0047-2514

K

KALEIDOSCOPE: International Magazine of Literature, Fine Arts, and Disability

Darshan C. Perusek, Ph.D., Editor-in-Chief; Gail Willmott, Senior Editor

United Cerebral Palsy and Services for the Handicapped

326 Locust Street

Akron, OH 44302

(216) 762-9755

Poetry, photographs, graphics/artwork, fiction, essays, reviews.

KALEIDOSCOPE addresses the experience of disability through literature and the fine arts by publishing unsentimental disability-related fiction, poetry, and visual art.

Irving K. Zola, Patricia Ranzoni, Lawrence D. Lynch, Kay Yasutome, Amber Coverdale Sumrall, Fritz Hamilton.

Payment: $25–$100 fiction, up to $25 for body of poetry.

Reporting time: 6–12 weeks.

Copyright held by Kaleidoscope; reverts to author upon publication.

1979; 2/yr; 1,500

$9/yr, $16/2 yrs ind; $12/yr, $20/2 yrs inst; $4.50/ea; 40%; agency discount 20% of price

64 pp; 8½ x 11

ISSN: 0748-8742

Ubiquity, Trinity News Co.

KALLIOPE: A Journal of Women's Art

Mary Sue Koeppel

Florida Community College

3939 Roosevelt Boulevard

Jacksonville, FL 32205

(904) 387-8211

Poetry, fiction, essays, reviews, interviews (3 annually), photographs, graphics/artwork.

Purpose of **KALLIOPE** is to offer support and encouragement to women in the arts. We are open to experimental forms of drama, fiction, poetry, prose and art as well as traditional formats. Editors like to see work that challenges the reader and addresses the complex relationships women have with each other, men, children and society.

Marge Piercy, Ruthann Robson, Roberta Allen, Sylvia Sleigh, Louise Fishman, Colette.

Payment: 3 copies or 1 yr subscription to writers and artists.

Reporting time: 2–3 months.

Copyright held by magazine; reverts to author upon request.

1978; 3/yr; 1,000

$10.50/yr ind; $18/yr inst; $7/ea last issues; $4/ea early issues; 40%

80 pp; 7¼ x 8½

No ads

ISSN: 0735-7885

Ingram Periodicals, DeBoer

KANSAS QUARTERLY

Harold Schneider, Ben Nyberg, W.R. Moses, John Rees, Paul McCarthy

Denison Hall 122

Kansas State University

Manhattan, KS 66506-0703

(913) 532-6716

Poetry, fiction, criticism, translation, interviews, photographs, graphics/artwork.

A cultural arts and literary magazine emphasizing but not restricted to the culture, history, art and writing of Mid-America but with international interests.

David Kirby, John Bovey, Stephen Dixon, Jonathan Holden, Peter LaSalle, Susan Fromberg Schaeffer, Jerry Bumpus, Lex Williford, Annabel Thomas.

Payment: 2 copies and two series of annual awards.

Reporting time: 2–6 months.

Copyright held by magazine; reverts to author upon request.

1968; 4/yr; 1,500

$20/yr; $6/ea; 10%–40%

152+ pp; 6 x 9

Ad rates: $100/page/4½ x 7½; $60/½ page/4½ x 3¾; $35/¼ page/2¼ x 3¾

ISSN: 0022-8745

Available to bookstores at 40% discount on consignment.

THE KENYON REVIEW

Marilyn Hacker, Editor; David Lynn, Assoc. Editor

Kenyon College

Gambier, OH 43022

(614) 427-3339

Poetry, fiction, essays, reviews, plays, translation, memoir.

THE KENYON REVIEW seeks excellent writing more than any particular kind or style; essays which combine actual analysis with aesthetic, philosophical, and cultural issues of significance; fiction that exploits "viewpoint" and the arts of storytelling; poetry of all kinds, though with a respect for the verse-line; we invite offers to review books.

Lee K. Abbott, Cynthia Huntington, Philip Levine, Lynne McMahon, Reginald McKnight, Reynolds Price.

Payment: $10/page, prose; $15/page, poetry.

Reporting time: 3 months.

Copyright reverts to author.

1979; 4/yr; 4,500

$20/yr ind; $23/yr inst; $7.00/ea; 25%

150 pp; 7 x 10

ISSN: 0163-075X

Inland

KEY WEST REVIEW

William J. Schlicht, Jr., Ph.D.

9 Avenue G

Key West, Florida 33040

(305) 296-1365

Poetry, fiction, essays, interviews, photographs, graphics/artwork, folktale, editorial.

We are a traditional literary magazine, but with important differences, including extraordinary emphasis on publishing prestigious writers along with excellent less well-established authors, aggressive marketing aimed at an audience beyond the usual scope of literary magazines, an interest in dialogue between authors and readers, and a particular focus on the Florida Keys.

Peter Taylor, Richard Eberhart, George Starbuck, Richard Wilbur, James Merrill, Alice Adams, Marge Piercy.

Payment: Author's copies.

Copyright held by magazine; reverts to author upon publication.

1988; 2/yr; 2,000
$17/yr ind & inst; $5/ea; 40% (sometimes 20%)
100 pp; 6 x 9
Ad rates: $100/page/5½ x 8; $50/½ page/5½ x 3¾; $300/inside front cover; $200/inside back cover
ISSN: 1041-5254

KIOSK

Stephanie Foote, Marten Clibbens
English Department
302 Clements Hall
SUNY at Buffalo
Buffalo, NY 14226
(716) 886-0533

Poetry, fiction, essays, interviews.

KIOSK is interested in publishing quirky, unconventional, experimental, polished and/or well-crafted fiction and poetry. We are looking also for essays and criticism, where appropriate.

Carol Berge, Ted Pelton, Fritz Bacher, Beverly Sanford, as well as Raymond Federman.

Payment: none.

Copyright held by KIOSK; reverts to author upon publication.

1986; 1/yr; 1,000
Free with large SASE
100 pp; 5½ x 8½
No ads

L

LA NUEZ

Rafael Bordao, Celeste Ewers
P.O. Box 1655
New York, NY 10276
(212) 260-3130

Poetry, fiction, criticism, essays, interviews, plays, reviews, photographs and artwork.

LA NUEZ is an international quarterly magazine of literature and art published entirely in Spanish. We publish established as well as new and emerging writers and artists.

Reinaldo Arenas, Clara Janes, José Triana, Antonio Benítez-Rojo, César Leante, Frank Dauster.

Payment: 2 copies.

Reporting time: 6–8 weeks.

Copyright reverts to author upon publication.

1988; 4/yr; 500

$12/ind; $15/inst; $18/foreign; $3/ ea; 40%

32 pp; 8½ x 11

$200/page; $115/½ page; plus smaller

ISSN: 0898-1140

verts to author upon publication.

1986; 3/yr; 500

$10/yr ind; $10/yr inst; $3.50/ea; 40% bookstores, 60% distributors

60 pp; 7 x 8½

Ad rates available. Contact CLMP for information.

LACTUCA

Michael Selender

P.O. Box 621

Suffern, NY 10901

Poetry, fiction, black and white art.

Our bias is toward work with a strong sense of place or experience. Writing with an honest emotional depth and writing that is dark or disturbing are preferred over safer material. Work with a quiet dignity is also desired. Subject matter is wide open and work can be rural or urban in character. We don't like poems that use the poem, the word, or the page as images or writing about being a poet/ writer (though work about dead poets/writers is o.k.).

David Cope, David Chorlton, Barbara Henning, Alan Catlin, Joe Cardillo.

Payment: in copies.

Copyright held by magazine; re-

LAKE EFFECT

Jean O'Connor Fuller

Lake County Writers Group

Oswego Civic Arts Center

P.O. Box 59

Oswego, NY 13126

Poetry, fiction, essays, reviews, translations, black and white art.

LAKE EFFECT, a regional quarterly of arts and comment, is published four times a year by Lake County Writers Group. It seeks to provide residents of the lake country region of Upstate New York with nonfiction, fiction, poetry, and art of interest to them and to publish the works of writers and artists who live in the area. The magazine also includes the works of artists in other parts of the country.

Katharyn Machan Aal, Zena Collier, Lewis Turco.

Payment: $25/review;

$25/essay; $25/fiction;
$5/poems; $5/incidental
photo/art.
Acquired First Serial Rights.
1986; 4/yr; 10,000
$5/yr ind; $5/yr inst; $2/ea
24–32 pp; 11½ x 17
Ad rates available. Contact CLMP
for information.
ISSN: 0887-4492
We distribute direct mail to 2,000
and 8,000 free in the region of
Lake Ontario.

**LAKE STREET REVIEW
PRESS**

Kevin Fitzpatrick
Box 7188
Powderhorn Station
Minneapolis, MN 55407

Poetry, fiction, essays, interviews,
graphics/artwork. Not consider-
ing manuscripts at this time.

**LATIN AMERICAN LITER-
ARY REVIEW**

Yvette E. Miller
University of Pittsburgh
Department of Hispanic Lan-
guages
2300 Palmer Street
Pittsburgh, PA 15218
(412) 351-1477
FAX #: (412) 351-6831
Poetry, fiction, plays, in transla-

tion. Criticism, essays, interviews, reviews.
The Journal in English devoted to
the literatures of Latin America.
It contains feature essays and
translations of poetry (Bilingual
format), plays, and short stories.
Gabriel Garcia Marquez, William
Gass, Margaret Sayers Peden,
Severo Sarduy, Mario Vargas
Llosa.
Payment: varies.
Reporting time: 3 months.
Copyright held by magazine.
1972; 2/yr + Special double issue;
1,200
$19/yr ind; $33/yr inst; $35/yr
foreign; $16/ea; 10%
150 pp; 250 pp special issue;
6 x 9
Ad rates: $200/page/4½x 7½;
$125/½ page/4½ x 3¾; $80/¼
page/4½ x 2¼
ISSN: 0047-4134
Ebsco, Faxon, McGregor, Turner

THE LAUREL REVIEW

Craig Goad, David Slater, William
Trowbridge
GreenTower Press
Department of English
Northwest Missouri State Univer-
sity
Maryville, MO 64468
(816) 562-1265

Poetry, fiction.

THE LAUREL REVIEW is national in scope and prints the best work received, regardless of style or author's reputation. Stephen Dunn, Sydney Lea, Katherine Soniat, Carol Bly, Albert Goldbarth.

Payment: two copies and subscription.

Reporting time: 1 week–4 months.

Copyright held by GreenTower Press; reverts to author upon request.

1960; 2/yr; 800

$8/yr; $14/2 yrs; $5/ea; 40%

124 pp; 6 x 9

Exchange ad rates: $80/page/6 x 9; $50/½ page/6 x 4½

ISSN: 0023-9003

THE LEDGE POETRY MAGA-ZINE

Timothy Monaghan

64-65 Cooper Ave.

Glendale, NY 11385

(718) 366-5169

Poetry.

THE LEDGE is meant to publish all types and forms of well-written poetry, by both established and young or little-known writers on the contemporary scene. We're independent and will make no move for compromise.

Steve Hartman, Les Bridges, Elizabeth Hansen, A. J. Pedevillano.

Payment: in copies.

Reporting time: 6 to 8 weeks.

Copyright reverts to author.

1988; 3x/yr; 450

$13.50/6 issues; $3/ea; 40%

70 pp; 5 x 7

$50/page; $30/½ page

ISSN: 1046-2724

LIPS

Laura Boss

P.O. Box 1345

Montclair, NJ 07042

(201) 662-1303

Poetry.

LIPS publishes the best contemporary poetry submitted. No biases.

Michael Benedikt, Gregory Corso, Maria Gillan, Allen Ginsberg, Robert Phillips, Marge Piercy, Ishmael Reed.

Payment: in copies.

Reporting time: 1 month.

Copyright held by magazine; reverts to author upon publication.

1981; 2/yr; 1,000

$10/yr ind; $13/yr inst; $5/ea; 40%

88 pp; 5½ x 8½

ISSN: 0278-0933

Anton Mikofsky

THE LITERARY CENTER QUARTERLY

Sarah Sarai, Neile Graham, Jim Gurley

P.O. Box 85116

Seattle, WA 98145

(206) 547-2503

Reviews, essays, poetry, interviews.

We are a small quarterly hoping to offer a voice for North West writers of all genres.

Denise Levertov, Marvin Bell, Gerald Gold.

Reporting time: We solicit manuscripts

Copyright: Reverts

Quarterly; 2,000

$15/yr

16–32; 8½ x 11

Write for rates and sizes

LITERARY MAGAZINE RE-VIEW

G. W. Clift, J. E. Roper, Mark Jarvis

Department of English

Kansas State University

Manhattan, KS 66506

(913) 532-6716

Reviews and essays concerning literary magazines.

LITERARY MAGAZINE RE-VIEW is devoted almost exclusively to objective reviews of the specific contents of issues of magazines which publish at least some short fiction or poetry.

David Kirby, Ben Nybers, J. B. Hall.

Payment: copies

Reporting time: Queries only, please

Copyright: Reverts

1982; quarterly; 600 +

$12.50; $4; 40%

60: 8½ x 5½

Ads not accepted

ISSN: 0732-6637

THE LITERARY REVIEW

Walter Cummins, Martin Green, Harry Keyishian, William Zander

Fairleigh Dickinson University

285 Madison Avenue

Madison, NJ 07940

(201) 593-8564

Poetry, fiction, criticism, essays, reviews, translation, interviews, graphics/artwork.

New writing in English and translation. We're looking for a unique blend of craft and insight.

George Looney, Kent Nelson, Jane Bradley, Talan Broughton.

Payment: 2 copies.

Reporting time: 8–12 weeks.

Copyright held by Fairleigh Dick-

inson University; reverts to author upon publication.
1957; 4/yr; 1,800
$18/yr; $5/ea; 40%
128 pp; 6 x 9
Exchange ads
ISSN: 0024-4589

LITERATI

Sharon Lonergan
P.O. Box 15245
East Providence, RI 02915

Poetry, fiction, essays, humorous commentary, cartoons, black and white art.

LITERATI seeks to publish work of innovative form and artistic quality. Well crafted submissions of any reasonable length, subject or style are welcome. Admittedly biased against rhyming poetry and trite sentiments. Committed to becoming a major voice in literary publishing and to keeping our sense of humor.

Dionisio D. Martinez, April Selley, Millie Mae Wicklund, John Grey, Ben Haes.
Payment: in copies.
Reporting time: 1–3 months.
Copyright reverts to author upon publication.
1989; 2/yr; 500
$10/yr; $5/ea; 40%
100 pp; 8½ x 11

$100/page; $50/½ page; $25/¼ page
ISSN: Pending

LONG POND REVIEW

Russell Steinke, William O'Brien, Anthony Di Franco
Suffolk Community College
533 College Road
Selden, NY 11784
(516) 451-4153

Poetry, fiction, essays, reviews, interviews, photographs, graphics/artwork.

LONG POND REVIEW publishes the finest work submitted by established, emergent, and beginning writers. **LPR** has been recognized as an outstanding small press in **The Pushcart Prize II** (1977–78), **IV** (1979–80), **V** (1980–81), **VI** (1981–82), **VII** (1982–83), and **IX** (1984–85).

Fred Chappell, David Citino, Colette Inez, Linda Pastan, Jim Barnes, William Stafford, Michael Blumenthal.
Payment: one contributor's copy.
Reporting time: 2–6 months.
Copyright held by author.
1975; 1/yr; 500
$3/ea ind; $5/ea inst
72–88 pp; 6 x 9
Ad rates: $75/page; $40/½ page

LONG SHOT

Jack Wiler, Jessica Chosid, Tom Pulhamus, Danny Shot

P.O. Box 6231

Hoboken, NJ 07030

Poetry, fiction, photographs, graphics/artwork.

"Writing From The Real World." Charles Bukowski, Allen Ginsberg, Amiri Baraka, June Jordan, Sean Penn.

Payment: in copies.

Reporting time: 6 weeks.

Copyright held by magazine; reverts to author upon publication.

1982; 2/yr; 1,000

$20/2 yrs; $5/ea; 40%

128 pp; 5 x 8½

Ad rates: $125/page/5 x 8½; $75/½ page/5 x 4¼

ISSN: 0895-9773

B. DeBoer & Co.; Ubiquity Distributors

THE LONG STORY

R. Peter Burnham

11 Kingston Street

North Andover, MA 01845

(508) 686-7638

Fiction.

We are interested strictly in long stories (8,000–20,000 words, or roughly 20–50 pages)—bias is left wing and concern for human struggle for dignity etc.; but quality is the main criterion.

Payment: 2 copies.

Reporting time: 2 weeks–2 months.

Copyright held by magazine; reverts to author upon publication.

1983; 1/yr; 500

$5/yr; $5/ea; 40%

160–200 pp; 5½ x 8½

ISSN: 0741-4242

Ingram

LOOK QUICK

Joel Scherzer, Robbie Rubinstein

P.O. Box 222

Pubelo, CO 81002

Poetry, fiction, reviews, photographs.

Emphasis is on free verse, blues lyrics and brief vignettes. We have also published material relating to the Beats. Not reading unsolicited manuscripts.

Payment: in copies.

Copyright held by Quick Books; reverts to author upon publication.

1975; irreg; 200

Single issue only, $3/ea

24–32 pp; 5½ x 8½

LOONFEATHER: A Magazine of Poetry, Short Prose & Graphics

Betty Rossi, Jeane Sliney

526 Bemidji Avenue

Bemidji, MN 56601

(218) 751-4869

Poetry, Fiction, Graphics.

LOONFEATHER is primarily but not exclusively a regional literary magazine publishing the works of both emerging and established writers. Our purpose is to promote good writing and encourage emerging artists by publishing their work; sponsoring readings, workshops, and exhibits; and supporting fellow artists/writers/organizations. Our regional focus is northern Minnesota, Minnesota, and the surrounding states and Canada.

Will Weaver, Susan Hauser, Gary Erickson, Gail Rixen, James Lenfestey.

Reporting time: Within three months following deadline for submissions.

Copyright: **LOONFEATHER** (reverts to author upon publication.)

1979; bi-annual;200–250

$7.50; $4.00; 40%

48; 6 x 9

$360/ page; $180/ ½ page; $45/ ¼ page

ISSN: 0734-0699

LOUISIANA LITERATURE:
Literature/Humanities Review

Tim Gautreaux, Editor; William Parrill, Associate Editor; Norman German, Assistant Editor

Box 792

Southeastern Louisiana University

Hammond, LA 70402

(504) 549-5022

Poetry, fiction, reviews of Louisiana-related books, articles on LA writing and culture.

We are interested in publishing essays and photo articles on Louisiana writing, history or art, but no college term papers or anything full of jargon. Creative work we will take from anywhere on any topic.

Lewis P. Simpson, Elton Glaser, Shirley Ann Grau, Sue Owen, Ann Dobie.

Payment: in copies.

Reporting time: 1 month.

Copyright held by author.

1984; 2/yr; 650

$10; $5/ea; 40%

100 pp; 6½ x 9½

Query for ad rates

ISSN: 0890-0477

LYNX

Terri Lee Grell

P.O. Box 169

Toutle, WA 98649

(206) 274-6663

Poetry, Criticism, Essays, Reviews, Translation, Interviews, Photographs, Graphics/Artwork, Features.

LYNX is a quarterly journal of

renga. It is the only renga magazine in the world. Renga (linked verse) started in Japan in the 12th century. It died out there after WWII, and was resurrected in the West in the last decade.

Marlene Mountain, Hiroaki Sato, Alexis Rotella, Francine Porad, Bernard Hewitt.

Payment: $1–$2 per column inch.
Reporting time: 3–6 weeks
Copyright: Contributors
1989; 4 times/yr;900
$15; $4; 40%
24; 5¾ x 14
$100/page; 450/½ page; $35/¼ page
ISSN: 1049-4502
Bulldog News (Seattle), City Lights (San Francisco)

LYRA

Lourdes Gil, Iraida Iturralde
P.O. Box 3188
Guttenberg, NJ 07093
(201) 861-1941 or (201) 869-2558

Poetry, fiction, criticism, interviews, essays, photographs, graphics/artwork.

We publish in English, French, Spanish, Italian, as we are committed to raising the level of communication among contemporary writers and artists in North America and other parts of the world.

Mario Benedetti, Elizabeth Macklin, Virgilio Piñera, Alan West, Tom Whalen.

Payment: in copies.
Copyright held by magazine; reverts to author upon publication.
1987; 4/yr; 700
$15/yr ind; $18/yr inst; $4/ea; 40%
32 pp; 8½ x 11
Ad rates: $200/page; $125/½ page; $70/¼ page. Also, on exchange.
ISSN: 0897-6716
Faxon, SLUSA, Giralt

THE LYRIC

Leslie Mellichamp
307 Dunton Drive SW
Blacksburg, VA 24060
(703) 552-3475

Poetry.

We use rhymed verse in traditional forms, for the most part, about 36 lines max. We print only poetry, no opinions, no reviews. Our themes are varied, ranging from religious ectasy to humor to raw grief, but we feel no compulsion to shock, embitter, or confound our readers.

John Robert Quinn, Gail White, Amy Jo Schoonover, Alfred

Dorn, Rhina P. Espaillat, Sarah Singer, Charles B. Dickson. $700 in prizes annually.

$10/yr; $3/ea

M

THE MACGUFFIN

Arthur J. Lindenberg
Schoolcraft College
18600 Haggerty Road
Livonia, MI 48152-2696
(313) 462-4400 ext 5292

Poetry, fiction, essays, photographs, graphics/artwork.

We publish poetry, fiction, and essays of the highest quality. We have no biases with regard to style, but we are committed to seeking excellence. Prose submissions should be less than 4,000 words.

Joe Schall, Tom Sheehan, Dan Dervin, David Sosnowski, Curtis Zahn.

Payment: 2 copies.

Reporting time: 8 weeks.

Copyright held by Schoolcraft College; reverts to author upon publication.

1984; 3/yr; 500

$10/yr ind; $8/yr inst; $3.75/ea; 40%

128 pp; 5½ x 8½
No ads

THE MALAHAT REVIEW

Constance Rooke, Assistant Editor, Marlene Cookshaw
Box 3045
University of Victoria
Victoria, British Columbia, Canada V8W3P4
(604) 721-8524

Fiction, Poetry.

A "generalist" literary magazine, open to new and celebrated writers. Meticulously edited, eclectic and elegant.

Tim Findley, Michael Ondaatje, Diane Williams.

Payment: $20 per magazine page

Reporting time: 3 months

Copyright reverts to author: we buy first rights in English.

1967; Quarterly; 2,000

$15 (US); $7 (US)

132; 6 x 9

ISSN: 0025-1216

Director

MANHATTAN POETRY REVIEW

Elaine Reiman-Fenton
36 Sutton Place South
New York, NY 10022
(212) 355-6634
Also:

FDR Box 8207
New York, NY 10150
Poetry.

MANHATTAN POETRY REVIEW is dedicated to a celebration of excellence in contemporary American poetry, welcomes unsolicited manuscripts, and presents a balance of new and established poets in each issue. It was founded as a community of poets and readers to demonstrate the diversity of fine poetry in America today.

Marge Piercy, Judith Farr, Theodore Weiss, Diane Wakoski, David Ignatow.
Payment: none.
Reporting time: 12–16 weeks.
Copyright reverts to author.
1982; 2/yr; 500–1,000
$12/yr; $7/ea (domestic, in U.S.$)
60–72 pp; 5½ x 8½
ISSN: 885-9205

THE MANHATTAN REVIEW
Philip Fried
440 Riverside Drive, #45
New York, NY 10027
(212) 932-1854

Poetry, interviews, photographs, reviews.

We try to compare and contrast American and foreign writers, and we focus on foreign writers with something to offer the current American scene. We like to think of poetry as a powerful discipline engaged with many other fields.

Peter Redgrove, Edmond Jabès, Christopher Bursk, A.R. Ammons, Stanislaw Baranczak, Bei Dao.
Payment: none.
Reporting time: 8–10 weeks.
Copyright held by Philip Fried.
1980; 1/yr; 500
$8 per volume (two issues)
64 pp; 5½ x 8½/page; 5½ x 4¼/½ page horizontal
ISSN: 0275-6889

MANOA: A Pacific Journal of International Writing
Robert Shapard, ed., Frank Stewart, assoc. ed.
English Department
University of Hawaii
Honolulu, HI 96822
(808) 956-3070

Fiction, poetry, essays, reviews, interviews, translations, art.

Primarily U.S. fiction and poetry, not limited to Pacific writers or themes; also features original translations of recent work from Pacific Rim nations.

W. S. Merwin, Kim Chiha, Ann Beattie, Tim O'Brien, Joyce Carol Oates, John Updike, Norman Dubie.

Payment: $20 per page prose;
more for poetry, reviews; copies
Reporting time: 6 weeks
Copyright reverts to author on
publication
1989; twice a year; 1,700
$12; $8; 50%
200+; 7 x 10
$150/page; $95/½ page
ISSN: 1045-7909
University of Hawaii Press

THE MASSACHUSETTS REVIEW

Mary Heath, Paul Jenkins, Jules
Chametzky
Memorial Hall
University of Massachusetts
Amherst, MA 01003
(413) 545-2689

Poetry, fiction, criticism, plays,
translation, interviews, photographs, graphics/artwork.
A quarterly of literature, the arts
and current affairs; special art
sections and special issues devoted to Feminism, Black literature, Ethnicity, Latin America,
contemporary Ireland, etc. oca-
sionally featured. S.A.S.E. with
all mss & inquire.
Ariel Dorfman, Marilyn Hacker,
Seamus Heaney, Joyce Carol
Oates, Octavio Paz.
Payment: $50 prose; 35¢/line po-
etry ($10 min.).

Reporting time: 3 months.
Copyright held by magazine; reverts to author upon publication
when requested.
1959; 4/yr; 1,700
$14/ind; $17/inst; $5.00/ea +
50¢/postage; 40%
172 pp; 6 x 9
Ad rates: $125/page 4⅛ x 7;
$75/½ page/4⅛ x 3½
Special university press rate:
$100/2 full pages
ISSN: 0025-4878
DeBoer

METAMORFOSIS

Erasmo Gamboa, Lauro Flores
Chicano Studies Program
American Ethnic Studies Dept.
B523 Padleford Hall, GN-80
University of Washington
Seattle, WA 98195
(206) 543-5401

Poetry, fiction, criticism, essays,
reviews, translation, interviews,
photographs, graphics/artwork.
METAMORFOSIS welcomes
submissions of poetry, drama,
critical articles, book reviews,
and artwork (black and white 8
x 10 photographs) with SASE.
Shifra Goldman, Pedro Rodriguez,
Alfredo Arreguin, Margaret
Randall, Bobby Paramo.
Payment: none.
Copyright held by the Center; re-

verts to author upon publication.

1977; 2/yr; 500
$10/yr ind; $15/yr inst; $5/ea
50 pp; 8 ½ x 10
ISSN: 0273-1606

MICKLE STREET REVIEW

Walt Whitman Association
326 Mickle Street
Camden, NJ 08103
(609) 757-6129

Poetry, essays, reviews, criticism, translations, interviews, photographs, graphics/artwork.

The **MICKLE STREET REVIEW** is published by the association whose offices are adjacent to Whitman's house on Mickle Street in Camden. Material reflecting Whitman's influence on American letters is welcome.

James Dickey, Stanley Kunitz, Richard Eberhart, Philip Dacey, Antler.

Copyright held by magazine; reverts to author upon publication.

1979; 1/yr; 800
$15 each (includes Association membership)
150 pp; 6 x 9
ISSN: 0194-1313

MID-AMERICAN REVIEW

Ken Letko
English Department
Bowling Green State University
Bowling Green, OH 43403
(419) 372-2725

Poetry, fiction, translations, essays, book reviews, interviews.

MAR publishes poetry using strong, evocative images and fresh language; fiction which is both character and language-oriented; translations of contemporary writers; essays and book reviews on contemporary authors.

Cid Corman, Eve Shelnutt, Lee Upton, Rolf Jacobsen, Margaret Gibson, Dan O'Brien.

Payment: copies and $7/page, up to $50.

Reporting time: 1–4 months.

Copyright held by MAR; reverts to author upon publication.

1979; 2/yr; 1,000
$6/yr, $10/2 yrs; $4.50/ea; 40%
200 pp; 5½ x 8½
Exchange ads, 5 x 8
ISSN: 0747-8895

MID COASTER

Peter Blewett
2750 North 45th St.
Milwaukee, WI 53210–2429
Poetry, fiction.
Payment: in copies.

Reporting time: up to 8 weeks
Copyright held by author.
1987; annual; 800
$3; 40%
36 pp; 8½ x 11
ISSN: 0892-970X

MILDRED

Ellen Biss, Kathryn Poppino
P.O. Box 9252
Schenectady, NY 12309
(518) 783-8849

Poetry, fiction, reviews, interviews, photographs, graphics/artwork.

MILDRED is a biannual magazine of poetry, fiction, art and photography with an emphasis on psychological realism.
MILDRED is not limited to female contributors.

Robert Bly, Christopher Bursk, James Freeman, Joseph Bruchac, Gary Fincke, Madeline Tiger, Louis Little, Coon Oliver, Rachel deVries.

Payment: in 2 copies.

Copyright held by Mildred Publishing: reverts to author upon publication.

1987; 2/yr; 500
$12/yr ind; $14/yr inst; $6/ea; 30%—1–4 copies; 40%—5–19 copies; 60%—20+ copies
100–150 pp; 6 x 9
No ads

ISSN 0892-5267

MINDPRINT REVIEW

Ron Pickup
P.O. Box 62
Soulsbyville, CA 95372
(209) 532-7045

Poetry, fiction, photographs, translations, graphics/artwork.

We publish quality prose, fiction, poetry, translations, B&W photography and graphics of both well-established and emerging writers, artists and photographers. Our submission base is Northern California, but our publication reflects a national/international cross section of work. Each issue forms a thematic focus pertaining to humanity or philosophy, but submissions are never limited to any subject, style or persuasion. Quality is our criteria for acceptance.

Rosalie Moore, John Oliver Simon, Lo Fu, Agusti Bartra, Jack Hirschman.

Payment: in copies only, upon publication.

Copyright held by Mindprint Review; reverts to author upon publication.

1983; 1/yr; 600
$7/yr ind; $7/yr inst; $6.50/ea;

$7.50 by mail; 40%; consign-
ment
128 pp; 6 x 9
Ad rates: $240/page/4 x 7¾;
$120/½ page/4½ x 4; $60/¼
page/4½ x 2½ or 2½ x 3¾
ISSN: 1040-2233
Bookpeople

THE MINNESOTA REVIEW
Helen Cooper, Michael Sprinker,
Susan Squier
SUNY Stony Brook
Department of English
Stony Brook, NY 11794
(516) 246-5080
Poetry, fiction, criticism, essays,
reviews, translation, interviews.
THE MINNESOTA REVIEW is
a journal of committed writing.
We are particularly interested in
new work that is progressive in
nature, with special commit-
ment to the areas of socialist
and feminist writing.
Jonathan Holden, Jean Franco,
Joan Joffe Halle, Marge Piercy,
Fredric Jameson.
Payment: in copies.
Reporting time: 60–90 days.
Copyright held by magazine; reverts to author upon publication.
1960; 2/yr; 1,000
$8/yr ind; $16/yr inst; $4.50/ea
160 pp; 5½ x 8 ½

Ad rates: $80/page/5 x 7; $50/½
page/5 x 3½ ; $30/¼ page/
2 x 3
ISSN: 0026-5667

MISSISSIPPI MUD
Joel Weinstein
1336 S.E. Marion Street
Portland, OR 97202
(503) 236-9962
Poetry, fiction, photographs,
graphics/artwork.
MISSISSIPPI MUD presents lu-
cid, elegant writing and art
from the *ne plus ultra* of the
American scene.
Katherine Dunn, Joyce Thompson,
Fred Pfeil, Todd Grimson,
Christina Zawadiwsky, Tom
Spanbauer.
Payment: cash, on publication,
depending on length or scale.
Reporting time: 3 months.
Copyright held by magazine; re-
verts to author upon publica-
tion.
1973; 2–3/yr; 1,500
$19/4 issues, $6 ea
48 pp, 11 x 17

MISSISSIPPI REVIEW
Frederick Barthelme
Southern Station, Box 5144
Hattiesburg, MS 39406
(601) 266-4321

Fiction, poetry, criticism, translation, interviews.

MISSISSIPPI REVIEW is a nonregional literary magazine published by the Center for Writers at the University of Southern Mississippi. The editors combine solicited and unsolicited works of well-known as well as new writers in an innovative format, producing three numbers a year. Although **MR** publishes mostly fiction and poetry, the editors are interested in literature in translation, interviews, and literary criticism.
Elizabeth Tallent, William Gibson, E.M. Cioran, Amy Hempel, Tama Janowitz.
Payment: in copies.
Reporting time: 8–12 weeks.
Copyright held by magazine; reverts to author upon publication.
1976; 2/yr; 2,000
$15/yr; $7.50/ea
120 pp; 5½ x 8½
Ad rates: $100/page; $50/½ page; exchange
ISSN: 0047-7559
Bernhard DeBoer

MISSISSIPPI VALLEY REVIEW

Forrest Robinson, Loren Logsdon, John Mann
Department of English
Western Illinois University
Macomb, IL 61455
(309) 298-1514
Although an expression of outgrowth of Midwest's commitment to literary art, **MVR**'s eclectic editorial philosophy makes possible a wide variety of styles and concerns.
The Fall-Winter number of our twentieth anniversary volume contains work donated by Ray Bradbury, Doris Lessing, Howard Nemerov, Gwendolyn Brooks, Issac Bashevis Singer, Jack Matthews, Wole Soyinka, Louis Erdrich, and Darcy O'Brien.
Payment: in copies.
Reporting time: 3 months.
Copyright held by author.
1971; 2/yr; 500
$10/yr; $5/ea
64 pp; 9 x 6
ISSN: 0270-3521

MISSOURI REVIEW

Speer Morgan, Greg Michalson
University of Missouri
1507 Hillcrest Hall
Columbia, MO 65211
(314) 882-4474
Poetry, fiction, essays, reviews, interviews, special features of literary interest, cartoons.

Payment: $20/page.
Reporting time: 10–12 weeks.
Copyright held by the University
  of Missouri; reverts to author
  upon request.
1978; 3/yr; 2,700
$12/yr; $5/ea; 30%
224 pp; 6 x 9
Ad rates: $50/page
ISSN: 0191-1961

MODERN HAIKU

Robert Spiess
P.O. Box 1752
Madison, WI 53701
(608) 233-2738

Haiku, essays, reviews.
We publish only quality haiku in
  which felt-depth, insight and
  intuition are evident. Good university and public library subscription list includes foreign.
Dr. Paul O. Williams, Geraldine
  Little, William J. Higginson,
  Cor Van den Heuvel, Wally
  Swist, Charles Dickson, Patricia
  Neubauer.
Payment: $1/haiku on acceptance;
  $5/page for articles.
Reporting time: 2 weeks.
Copyright held by Robert Spiess;
  reverts to author upon publication.
1969; 3/yr; 625
$12.35 yr; $4.35/ea
100 pp; 5½ x 8½

ISSN: 0026-7821

THE MONOCACY VALLEY REVIEW

c/o William Heath, Editor
Mt. St. Mary's College
Emmitsburg, MD 21727
(301) 447-6122 x4832

Fiction, poetry, photographs,
  graphics, artwork, criticism,
  interviews, essays.
Holly St. John Bergon, Roser
  Caminals, Mary Noel, John
  Grey, Robert Bevington, Barbara Petoskey, Maxine Combs.
Payment: $25 for each poem,
  story, or artwork accepted
  (funds permitting).
Submission deadlines: Sept. 15
  and March 15
$5/yr; $3/ea
Distributors: Frederick Arts Council; Square Corner Bookshop

MOTHEROOT JOURNAL

Anne Pride, Paulette J. Balogh
P.O. Box 8306
Pittsburgh, PA 15218
(412) 731-4453

Reviews, interviews.
Reviews of small press books of
  interest to women; interviews
  and essays.
Virginia Scott, Judy Hogan, Felice
  Newman, Doris Davenport.

Payment: none.
Reporting time: 6 weeks.
Copyright held by magazine; reverts to author upon publication.
1978; 3/yr; 1,000
$5/yr ind; $7/yr inst; $1.25/ea; 40%
8 pp; 9 x 16
Ad rates: $250/page; $125/½ page; $75/¼ page; column size: 2¼ x 16
ISSN: 0739-5272

MR. COGITO

John M. Gogol, Robert A. Davies
U.C. Box 627
Pacific University
Forest Grove, OR 97116
(503) 226-4135; 233-8131
Poetry, photographs, graphics/artwork.
Poetry in English, including translations; photographs, graphics. We like poems that surprise us with their language, sound and invention.
Dian Million, Elizabeth Woody, Tomasz Jastrun, Ann Chandonnet, W.D. Ehrhart.
Payment: 1 copy.
Reporting time: 1–3 months.
Copyright held by magazine; all but anthology rights revert to author upon publication.
1973; irregular; 500

$9/3 issues; $3/ea
24–28 pp; 4¼ x 11
ISSN: 0740-1205
EBSCO; Faxon; Acquinas

MUSCADINE

Lucille Cyphers
1940 Walnut St., #418
Boulder, CO 80302
(303) 443-3243
Poetry, fiction, essays, graphics/artwork.
Old (60 yrs) people celebrating all aspects of life.
Segmund Weiss, Grace Young, Mary Olson.
Payment: 1 copy and $1.
Reporting time: 3 weeks.
Copyright held by magazine; reverts to author upon publication.
1977; quarterly; 400
$6/yr ind; $1.50/ea
28 pp; 8½ x 11

N

NAHANT BAY

Kalo Clarke, Kim Alan Pederson
45 Puritan Road
Swampscott, MA 01907
(617) 595-3722

Essays, poetry, fiction, drawings, B&W photographs.
Literary magazine looking for unique voices and original style.
Lyn Lifshin, Michael Kramer, Jane Varley, Sue William Silverman, Stuart Peterfreund.
Payment: 1 copy
Reporting time: 2–4 months
Copyright: 1st Serial Rights
1990; 2 per year
$8; $4; 40%
50–60; half-sheet
Buddenbrooks, Trident Bookstore, Avenue Victor Hugo Bookstore (all in Boston)

NASSAU REVIEW

Paul A. Doyle
English Dept.
Nassau Community College
Garden City, NY 11530
(516) 222-7186

Poetry, fiction, criticism, essays.
Payment: none.
Reporting time: 3–4 months.
Copyright held by Nassau Community College; reverts to author upon publication.
1967; annual; 1,000
Free.
92–95 pp; 6½ x 9½

THE NEBRASKA REVIEW

Richard Duggin (fiction), Art Homer (poetry)

215 ASH
University of Nebraska–Omaha
Omaha, NE 68182-0326
(402) 554-2771

Poetry, fiction.
TNR publishes quality literary fiction and poetry, material that transcends mere technical proficiency.
Carolyne Wright, Stephen Dixon, Joan Joffe-Hall, Elizabeth Evans, David Hopes, Vern Rutsala.
Payment: 1 year subscription plus contributer's copies.
Reporting time: 3–4 months (longest for poetry.)
Copyright held by magazine; reverts to author upon publication.
1972; 2/yr; 500
$6/yr; $3.50/ea; 40%
65 pp; 5½ x 8½
Ad rates: $45/page/3⅝ x 6¼; $25/½ page/3⅝ x 3
ISSN: 8755-514X

NEGATIVE CAPABILITY

Sue Brannan Walker, Ron Walker
62 Ridgelawn Drive, East
Mobile, AL 36608
(205) 343-6163

Poetry, fiction, essays, reviews, interviews, photographs, graphics/artwork, original music, bagatelles.

NEGATIVE CAPABILITY is a creative journal whose emphasis is joy—not merely laughter, though we encourage humor, but the joy that arrives through insight into oneself and others, the world and our all too human condition.
Richard Eberhart, X.J. Kennedy, Denise Levertov, William Stafford, John Updike, Diane Wakoski.
Payment: in copies.
Reporting time: 8 weeks.
Copyright held by magazine; reverts to author upon publication.
1981; 3/yr; 1,000
$12/yr ind; $16/yr inst; $4/ea; 40%
180 pp; 5¼ x 8¼
Ad rates: $100/page/4½ x 8; $50/½ page/4 x 4; $25/¼ page/4 x 2½
ISSN: 0277-5166

NEW AMERICAN WRITING
Maxine Chernoff, Paul Hoover
2920 West Pratt
Chicago, IL 60645
(312) 764-1048
Poetry, fiction, essays, plays, graphics.
NAW is open to work that presents a progressive and lively point of view.

Ned Rorem, Lyn Hejinian, Charles Simic, Ron Padgett, Bob Perelman, Kenneth Koch, John Ashbery.
Payment: $5/page, when available.
Reporting time: 1–3 months.
Copyright held by OINK! Press, Inc.; reverts to author upon publication.
1971; 2/yr; 1,500
$12/yr; $6/ea; 40%
$16.00/yr; $8.00 ea. libraries and foreign orders.
120 pp; 5½ x 8½
Ad rates: $100/page/5 x 8; $50/½ page/2¼ x 4
ISSN: 0893-7842
DeBoer, Ingram Periodicals, SBD, Illinois Publishing Project

NEW DELTA REVIEW
Kathleen Fitzpatrick, Editor; Janet Wondra, Poetry; David Racine, Fiction
c/o Department of English
Louisiana State University
Baton Rouge, LA 70803
(504) 388-4079
Poetry, fiction, interviews.
The **NEW DELTA REVIEW** is a literary journal published by the creative writing program of the English Department of Louisiana State University. We at **NEW DELTA REVIEW** are most interested in promoting

"new" writers and exploring new directions in poetry and fiction. We offer The Eyster Prizes, given with each issue to the contributors of the "best" new pieces of fiction and poetry. The Eyster Prizes honor author and teacher Warren Eyster, who served for many years as advisor to **NEW DELTA REVIEW**'s predecessors, *Manchac* and *Delta*. Judges for these prizes last year were Moira Crone, Rodger Kamenetz, and Eve Shelnutt. Thomas E. Kennedy, Michael J. Rosen, Dinty Moore.

Payment: in copies, upon publication.

Copyright held by **NEW DELTA REVIEW**—First North American Serial Rights; reverts to author upon publication.

1984; 2/yr; 450

$7/2 issues; $4/ea; 40%

80 pp; 6 x 9

No ads

NEW ENGLAND REVIEW AND BREAD LOAF QUARTERLY

T.R. Hummer, Devon Jersild, assoc. ed.

Middlebury College

Middlebury, VT 05753

(802) 388-3711 ext 5075

Fiction, poetry, essays, reviews, translation, interviews—open to strong writing of all kinds. **NEW ENGLAND REVIEW** has been a mainstay of the American literary community for twelve years. Now located in Middlebury College, under new editorship, and newly affiliated with University Press of New England, *NER* is beginning a new series, *MIDDLEBURY SERIES,* to reflect its energy and direction, its recommitment to the art, craft, and politics of writing.

Arnost Lustig, Ann Beattie, Stephen Dunn, Bridget Pegeen Kelley, Edward Hirsch, W. D. Wetherell, Miroslav Holub, Samuel F. Pickering

Payment: $10/minimum.

Reporting time: 5–7 weeks.

Copyright held by author.

1978; 4/yr; 3,000

$18/yr ind; $30/yr inst; $6/ea; 40%

128 pp; 6 x 9

Ad rates: $300/page/7 x 10; $150/½ page/7 x 5; $100/¼ page 3½ x 5

ISSN: 0736-2579

NEW LAUREL REVIEW

Lee Meitzen Grue

828 Lesseps Street

New Orleans, LA 70117

(504) 947-6001

Poetry, fiction, criticism, essays, reviews, translation, interviews, graphics/artwork, whatever is interesting.

NEW LAUREL REVIEW publishes poetry, fiction, translation, articles; work of sound scholarship which is alive. We hope to continue showing the best writing by nationally accepted writers with that of fresh new talent not seen before.

Enid Shomer, Sue Walker, Martha McFerren, Dixie Partridge, Yevgeny Yevtushenko.

Reporting time: varies.

Copyright held by author.

1971; 500

$8/yr ind; $10/yr inst

85 pp; 6 x 9

ISSN: 0145-8388

NEW LETTERS

James McKinley, Editor; Robert Stewart, Managing Editor; Glenda McCrary, Administrative Assistant

University of Missouri—Kansas City

Kansas City, MO 64110

(816) 235-1168; 235-1120

Poetry, fiction, reviews, photographs, graphics/artwork.

NEW LETTERS, an international literary quarterly, publishes contemporary writing, including that of well-known writers and fresh, new talents. Also publishes photographs and graphics; notable discoveries of overlooked gems. e.g., Theodore Roethke interview, Countee Cullen memoir, Richard Wright and Jack Conroy, archival material.

Josephine Jacobsen, Jim Harrison, Jorie Graham, Theodore Roethke, Joyce Carol Oates, William Stafford, Thomas Berger, William Burroughs, Rosellen Brown, Lisel Mueller.

Payment: small honorarium and copies.

Reporting time: 6 weeks.

Copyright held by magazine; reverts to author upon publication.

1934; 4/yr; 2,500

$17/yr ind; $20/yr inst; $5/ea; 40%–50%

128 pp; 6 x 9

Ad rates: $150/page/4 x 6⅞; $100/½ page/4 x 3⅛

Ingram Periodicals Inc.

Ubiquity Periodicals.

Independent bookstores.

NEW MYTHS: MSS

Robert Mooney

SUNY Binghampton

Box 530
Binghampton, NY 13901
(607) 777-2168

Poetry, fiction, essays, photographs, graphics.

Special emphasis on publishing the best work of young and unestablished writers with the work of well-known writers.

Andrew Hudgins, Dianne Benedict, Gerald Stern, William Stafford, Linda Pastan.

Payment: whenever funds allow.

Reporting time: 2–8 weeks.

Copyright reverts to author upon publication.

1961; 2/yr; 1,000

$8.50/yr ind; $14/yr inst; $5.50/ea

$500/page; $250/½ page

NEW ORLEANS REVIEW

John Mosier, John Biguenet
Box 195
Loyola University
New Orleans, LA 70118
(504) 865-2294

Poetry, short fiction, translations, literary & film criticism, artwork.

Payment: Please Inquire

Reporting time: 3 months

1968; quarterly; 1,000

$25; $9

100; 8½ x 11

ISSN: 0028-6400

THE NEW PRESS

David Gerard (Editor), Bob Abramson (Publisher), Harry Ellison (Poetry Editor)
87-40 Francis Lewis Blvd #A44
Queens Village, NY 11427
(718) 217-1464

Poetry, short stories, essays, line drawings.

A literary quarterly that stresses poetic vision and voice. For the literate mind. Work should be accessible and enjoyable to an intelligent reader.

Joe Malone, Ken Di Maggio, Robert Parody, Bruce Isaacson.

Payment: 3 copies; $50 for best prose each issue. Poetry contest.

Reporting time: 2 months.

Copyright: First time/ reverts to author.

1984; quarterly; 1,000

$8; $2; 40%

28–32; 8½ x 11

$100/page; $60/½ page; $40/¼ page; $20/business card

ISSN: 0894-6078

De Boer

the new renaissance

Louise T. Reynolds, Harry Jackel, James E.A. Woodbury, Patricia Michaud
9 Heath Road
Arlington, MA 02174

Fiction, poetry, lead articles, stories & poetry in bilingual translations, reproduction of paintings, sculpture, mixed media, photographs, commentary, graphics, illustrations, essays, reviews.

We offer a forum for idea/opinion pieces on political/sociological pieces, and publish a wide variety of styles, statements, tones, & visions in our fiction & poetry sections. Since we take a classicist position, we avoid the trendy & the fashionable, for the most part, but our range is so broad it includes contradictory statements within a single issue. There is, however, an emphasis on the human condition.

Jeannette Bertles, Vitaliano Brancati (Jessie Bright trans.), Stewart O'Nan, Thomas Filbin; William Laufer, Leslie Tompkins, T. Hibbard, Paul Snoek (C. J. Stevens trans.)

Payment: After publication.

Reporting time: 8–20 weeks, poetry; 10–25 weeks, prose. One month queries. Overstocked through 1991 in poetry.

Copyright held by magazine.

1968; 2/yr; 1,500

$12.50/3 issues, US; $6.40/sample, US. (Add $2.00/3 issues, Europe, Mexico, Canada; 65¢ individual sample copies.)

144–192 pp; 6 x 9

ISSN: 0028-6575

NEW VIRGINIA REVIEW

1306 East Cary Street, 2A
Richmond, VA 23219
(804) 782-1043

Poetry, fiction, essays.

NEW VIRGINIA REVIEW: an annual collection of new poetry, fiction, and essays that strives to publish the best possible work being done by contemporary authors. Guest editors change yearly and accept material from unknown as well as widely recognized writers.

Richard Bausch, David Bradley, Mary Lee Settle, Roland Flint, Dave Smith.

Payment: $10 per printed page, $25 minimum for poems, upon publication.

Copyright held by **NVR**, editor, and individual writers; reverts to author upon publication.

1979; 1/yr; 1,800

$13.50/ea; 50% w/no return; 40% w/12 mo. return; discount on back issues w/ current volume

300 pp; 6½ x 10

No ads

ISSN: 0-939233-00-2

THE NEWPORT REVIEW

Michele F. Cooper
68 Benevolent Street
Providence, RI 02906
(401) 849-3278

Poetry, fiction, essays, plays, photographs, graphics/artwork, original music.

A journal of art, literature, and ideas which provides an outlet for gifted writers and artists of all backgrounds from Newport and other areas of Rhode Island.

Ruth Whitman, Charles Norman, Edwin Honig, Alan Pryce-Jones, Fritz Eichenberg.
Payment: $5 per contributor.
Reporting time: 3 months.
Copyright held by magazine; reverts to author upon publication.
1979; 1/yr; 1,000
$10/2 issues; $5/ea
88 pp; 8¼ x 10¼
Ad rates: $400/page; $200/½ page; $100/¼ page
ISSN: 0276-5241

NEXT EXIT

Eric Folsom
92 Helen Street
Kingston, Ontario, Canada
  K7L4P3
(613) 549-6790
Poetry.

Individual, eclectic, raw, quality, grunge, soup, visual, alternative, falling, dream, revealing, edge, tomorrow, break, come, wash, stay, home, after, night.

Sheila E. Murphy, Stan Rogal, Hillary Mellon, Greg Evanson.
Payment: copies
Reporting time: 3–6 months
Copyright belongs to authors
1980; 2/yr; 150
$6 for 2; $12 for 4; $3
32–36; 8¼ x 5½
ISSN: 0828-8496

NIGHT ROSES

Allen T. Billy, Sandra Taylor
P.O. Box 393
Prospect Heights, IL 60060
(708) 392-2435

Poetry (some Art).

We like to publish romance poetry, flower poetry, ghost images of past or future and odds and ends of interest.

Genoa, Mary R. De Maine, Ken Stone, Jane Camron.
Payment: copy of issue
Reporting time: 4–12 weeks
Copyright belongs to authors
1986; 2–4 times/yr; 250
$8 for 3 issues; $3
44–56; 5⅜ x 8½
By mail from **NIGHT ROSES** only

NIMROD: International Journal of Fiction & Poetry

Francine Ringold
Arts and Humanities Council of Tulsa
2210 South Main
Tulsa, OK 74114
(918) 584-3333

Poetry, fiction, translation, photographs, graphics/artwork, interviews.

NIMROD seeks vigorous writing that is neither wholly of the academy nor of the streets. Fall issues feature the winners and finalists of the Nimrod Literary Awards Competition and spring issues are thematic. Past thematic issues include "Arabic Literature," "China Today," "India: A Wealth of Diversity," "from the Soviets," "Oklahoma Indian Markings" "Clap Hands and Sing: Writers of Age" is slated for 1991.

Wendy Stevens, Tess Gallagher, Denise Levertov, Gish Jen, Sharon Sakson, Alvin Greenberg.

Payment: in copies; also $1,000 to first place winners in our fiction and poetry competition, $500 for second place.

Reporting time: 3 weeks–3 months.

Copyright of entire magazine held by the Arts & Humanities Council of Tulsa. Rights to individual stories revert to authors.

1956; semi-annual; 1,500–2,500
$11.50/yr; $6.90/ea
160 pp; 6 x 9
Ad rates: $150/page; $75/½ page
ISSN: 0029-053X

NIT & WIT

Harrison McCormick, Marie Aguirre
P.O. Box 627
Geneva, IL 60134
(312) 232-9496

Poetry, fiction, essays, reviews, interviews, photographs, graphics/artwork.

NIT & WIT is a full-spectrum cultural arts magazine with regular features on art, music, dance, theatre, film, architecture, photography, reviews, essays, fiction and poetry.

Philip Graham, June Brinder, Gordon Lish, Sharon Sheehe Stark.
Payment: none.
Reporting time: 2–3 weeks.
Copyright held by author.
1977; 6/yr; 6,000
$12/yr; $2/ea; 40%–50%
68 pp; 8½ x 11
Ad rates: $750/page/7⅛ x 10;
$390/½ page/4¹¹⁄₁₆ x 7⅜;
$210/¼ page/3½ x 4¹⁵⁄₁₆

THE NORTH AMERICAN REVIEW

Robley Wilson
University of Northern Iowa
Cedar Falls, IA 50614
(319) 273-6455
Poetry, fiction, criticism, essays, reviews, graphics/artwork.
Oldest magazine in North America, publishing fiction and non-fiction, poetry and reviews. Winner in 1981 and 1983 of National Magazine Award for fiction. Non-fiction frequently has ecological/environmental slant.
Payment: $10/published page; 50¢/line for poetry.
Reporting time: 1–3 months.
Copyright held by University of Northern Iowa; reverts to author upon publication.
1815; 4/yr; 4,700
$14/yr; $4/ea
72 pp; 8⅛ x 10⅞
Ad rates: $500/page/7 x 10; $200/⅓ page/2¼ x 10
ISSN: 0029-2397
Eastern News

NORTH ATLANTIC REVIEW

John Gill
15 Arbutus Lane
Stony Brook, NY 11790-1408
(516) 751-7886
Poetry, Fiction, Essays.

General fiction and poetry, with a special section in each issue devoted to prose and poetry about the sixties.
Lewis Tureo, Burton Raffel, Walter Cammius, Richard Eberhart, David Ignatow.
Reporting time: 4–5 months
Copyright: Author
1989; 2/yr; 500
$13/yr; $7; 40%
175; 7 x 9½
$200/page; $125/½ page; $75/¼ page
ISSN: 1040-7324

NORTH DAKOTA QUARTERLY

Robert W. Lewis, Editor; William Borden, Fiction Editor; Jay Meek, Poetry Editor
University of North Dakota, Box 8237
Grand Forks, ND 58202
(701) 777-3321
Poetry, fiction, criticism, essays, reviews, graphics.
An interdisciplinary journal in the arts and humanities. Recent and forthcoming special issues on Columbus' quincentenary, nature writing/writers, culture: International Bridge or Barrier?
Sherman Paul, Peter Nabokov, Kathleen Woodward, Denise

Duhamel, John Allman, Eugenio Montale.
Payment: in copies.
Reporting time: 1–3 months.
Copyright by University of North Dakota.
1909; 4/yr; 1,000
$15/yr; $5/ea; 20%
200 pp; 6 x 9
ISSN: 0029-277X

THE NORTHERN REVIEW
018 LRC
University of Wisconsin/Stevens Point
Stevens Point, WI 54481
(715) 346-3568
Essays, poetry, fiction, interviews, reviews, graphics/artwork.
William Kloefkorn, Lowell Jaeger, Layle Silbert, Donald Murry, Bret Lott.
$8/yr; $15/2 yrs; $21/3 yrs; $4/ea; 40%

THE NORTHLAND QUARTERLY
J. Namio
Published by Rio Salado Books
1522 E. Southern Ave.
Box 2161
Tempe, AZ 85282
Poetry, fiction, criticism, essays, reviews, plays, interviews, photographs, graphics/artwork.

Jennifer Lagier, Mark Vinz, Mitchell Tomfohrde, Tom Padgett, Mark Maire.
Payment: in copies, upon publication.
Reporting time: 8–10 weeks.
Copyright held by magazine; reverts to author upon publication.
1988; 4/yr; 500
$20/yr ind & inst; $4.95/ea; 40%; 20% to college bookstores; 30% on ind. orders over 100
Ad rates: $300/page/5½ x 8½; $150/½ page/5½ x 4¼; $75/¼ page/2¾ x 4¼; advertising accepted on barter system
ISSN: 0899-708X

NORTHWEST REVIEW
John Witte, Cecelia Hagen
369 PLC
University of Oregon
Eugene, OR 97403
(503) 686-3957
Poetry, fiction, criticism, essays, reviews, translation, interviews, graphics/artwork.
NORTHWEST REVIEW is a tri-annual publishing poetry, fiction, artwork, interviews, book reviews and comment. We have no other criterion for acceptance than that of excellence. We are devoted to representing the widest possible

variety of styles and perspectives (experimental, feminist, political, etc.), unified within a humanist framework. "A publication to which the wise and honest, and literate, may repair!"—William Stafford.

Joyce Carol Oates, Madeline DeFrees, Alan Dugan, Morris Graves, Raymond Carver.

Payment: in copies.

Reporting time: 8–10 weeks.

Copyright held by magazine; reverts to author upon request.

1957; 3/yr; 1,100

$11/yr; $4/ea; 20%–40%

160 pp; 6 x 9

Ad rates: $160/page/6 x 9

ISSN: 0029-3423

NOTEBOOK/CUADERNO: A Literary Journal

Ms. Y. Zentella

P.O. Box 170

Barstow, CA 92312-170

Fiction, poetry, essays, reviews, graphics/artwork, editorial columns, environment, unionism, art, music reviews, food column, crossword puzzle.

Literary journal with focus on humanist literature by all writers, especially Asian Americans, Arab Americans; Black Americans, very special emphasis on Latino-Americans.

Pedro Pérez Sarduy; Aisha Eshe, Joan Leslie Woodruff, Walt Phillips, Arthur W. Knight.

Payment: 1 copy.

Reporting time: 6–12 weeks.

Copyright held by magazine; reverts to author upon publication.

1985; 1/yr; 200

$8/yr ind; $10/yr inst; $6/ea ind; $8/ea inst; 30%

100 pp; 5½ x 8½

Query for ad rates

ISSN: 0883-6337

Read More, Faxon, ZVF International, Subs

NOTUS new writing

Pat Smith

2420 Walter Dr.

Ann Arbor, MI 48103

(313) 747-1680

Poetry, fiction, reviews, translations.

NOTUS is a semi-annual magazine focusing on experimental and non-traditional writing. Its emphasis is two-fold: to publish new work from writers who already have an audience and to help introduce the work of younger writers. We also have a special interest in publishing translations.

Ed Sanders, Robert Kelly,

Nathanial Tarn, Clayton Eshle-
man, Leslie Scalapino.
Payment: none.
Copyright held by OtherWind
Press, Inc.; reverts to author
upon publication.
1986; 2/yr; 300
$10/yr ind; $20/yr inst; $5/ea;
40%
96 pp; 8½ x 11
No ads
ISSN: 0889-0803
Small Press Distribution, Segue
Foundation, Small Press Traffic

O

O-BLEK, a journal of language arts

Connell McGrath & Peter Gizzi
P.O. Box 1242
Stockbridge, MA 01262

Poetry, art, translation.

O-BLEK publishes formally innovative poetry and large art portfolios. Fiction is published
infrequently. O-BLEK prides
itself on its informative representations of contemporary
French poetics.

Robert Creeley, Rosmarie Waldrop, Michael Gizzi, Bernadette
Mayer, Emmanuel Hocquard.

Payment: $25 (when available).
Reporting time: 1–3 months.
Copyright reverts to author upon
publication
1987; twice yearly; 1,000
$18/4 issues; $5.50; varies
200; 5½ x 7
ISSN: 0896-303
Segue, SPD, DeBoer

OBSIDIAN II: Black Literature In Review

Gerald Barrax, Karla Holloway
Box 8105
Department of English
North Carolina State University
Raleigh, NC 27695-8105
(919) 737-3870

Poetry, fiction, criticism, essays,
reviews.

OBSIDIAN II is a tri-annual review for the study and cultiva-
tion of creative works in
English by Black writers world-
wide, with scholarly critical
studies by all writers on all aspects of Black literature, book
reviews, poetry, short fiction,
interviews, bibliographies, bibliographical essays, and very
short plays in English.

Houston A. Baker, Jr., Gayl
Jones, Wanda Coleman, Ray-
mond R. Patterson, Gerald
Early.

Payment: none.

Copyright held by Department of English, North Carolina State University; reverts to author upon publication.

1986; 3/yr; 500

$12/yr ind; $12/yr inst; $5/ea; 40%

130 pp; 6 x 9

Ad rates: $200/page/4½ x 7⅛; $100/½ page/4½ x 3½

ISSN: 0888-4412

ODESSA POETRY REVIEW

Jim Wyzard

RR 1, Box 39

Odessa, MO 64076

Poetry.

Ester Leipen, Rod Kessler, Rochelle Lynn Holt, Marian Park.

Payment: varies with quality of work.

Copyright held by Jim Wyzard; reverts to author upon publication.

1984; 4/yr; 500–700

$16/yr; $4/ea; 40%

150 pp; 5½ x 8½

No ads

THE OHIO REVIEW

Wayne Dodd

209 C Ellis Hall

Ohio University

Athens, OH 45701-2979

(614) 593-1900

Poetry, fiction, essays, reviews.

THE OHIO REVIEW publishes the best in contemporary American poetry, fiction, book reviews, and essays.

Galway Kinnell, Jane Miller, John Haines, Gladys Swan, William Matthews.

Payment: $1/line (poetry), $5/page (prose).

Reporting time: 90 days.

Copyright held by magazine; reverts to author upon request.

1971; 3/yr; 2,000

$12/yr; $30/3yrs; $4.25/ea; 40%

144 pp; 6 x 9

Ad rates: $175/page/4¼ x 7¼; $100/½ page/4¼ x 3¼

ISSN: 0360-1013

Ingram Periodicals, DeBoer, L.S. Distributors, Small Press Traffic

ONTARIO REVIEW

Raymond J. Smith, Joyce Carol Oates

9 Honey Brook Drive

Princeton, NJ 08540

Poetry, fiction, criticism, essays, translation, interviews, photographs, graphics.

Maxine Kumin, Albert Goldbarth, Russell Banks, Alicia Ostriker, Tom Wayman.

Payment: $10/page.

Reporting time: 6 weeks.

Copyright held by magazine; re-

verts to author upon publication.
1974; 2/yr; 1,100
$10/yr; $4.95/ea; 40%
112 pp; 6 x 9
Ad rates: $125/page/4¼ x 7;
$75/½ page/4¼ x 3¼; $50/¼
page/2 x 3¼
ISSN: 0316-4055
Ingram Periodicals, Ubiquity Distributors

OPEN MAGAZINE
Greg Ruggiero, Paul Pinkman
P. O. Box 2726
Westfield, NJ 07091
Fiction, poetry, essays, photographs, graphics/artwork, plays, interviews.
OPEN works with uninhibited forms of writing and art that inspire change—be they targeted at social processes or the consciousness of the individual. We are fast to accept work that pioneers form, questions the given, risks discussing the intimate or proposing the radical. New emphasis on essays. Special interest in dissident writing, women's issues, media, information & culture.
Margaret Randall, Noam Chomsky, Sylvia Plachy, John Cage, Claribel Alegria, Sesshu Foster.
Payment: copies and up to $50,

depending upon presence of grant money.
Reporting time: 1 month.
Copyright held by magazine; reverts to author upon publication.
1985; 2/yr; 1,000
$15/3 issues/ind; $20/3 issues/inst; $5/ea; 40%
60 pp; 8½ x 11
Ad rates: $400/page/8½ x 11;
$200/½ page/7½ x 5; $100/¼
page/3¾ x 5
Ad & Issue Swaps with other CLMP publications.
ISSN: 0894-265X
DeBoer, Inc.

ORO MADRE
Loss Glazier, Jan Glazier
4429 Gibraltar Drive
Fremont, CA 94536
Poetry, fiction, criticism, reviews, graphics.
ORO MADRE seeks to present fine poetry and fiction with attention to social and international themes, and also focuses on non-fiction coverage of the small press world through numerous reviews, interviews, and articles on literary bookstores, the art of small press, activities and trends.
Charles Bukowski, A.D. Winans,

Alejandro Muguia, Luke Breit, Jack Hirschman.
Payment: in copies.
Reporting time: 2 months.
Copyright held by author.
1981; irreg; 500
$12/yr ind; $16/yr inst; $3.50/ea; 40%
48 pp; 5½ x 8
Ad rates: $40/page/5 x 7½; $25/½ page/5 x 3¾

OSIRIS

Andrea and Robert Moorhead
Box 297
Deerfield, MA 01342
(413) 774-4027

Poetry, photographs, graphics/artwork.
OSIRIS is a multi-lingual poetry journal publishing contemporary work in English, French, Italian and Spanish. Poetry in other languages such as Polish, Latvian and Danish appears in a bilingual format.
Robert Marteau, Hélène Dorion, Simon Perchik, Gyula Illyés, Wally Swist.
Payment: in copies.
Reporting time: 4 weeks.
Copyright reverts to author upon publication.
1972; 2/yr; 500
$8/yr; $4/ea
32–40 pp; 6 x 9

Ad rates: $75/page/5½ x 8½; $50/½ page/5½ x 4¼
ISSN: 0095-019X

OTHER VOICES

Dolores Weinberg, Founding Editor/Publisher; Lois Hauselman, Sharon Fiffer
820 Ridge Road
Highland Park, IL 60035
(708) 831-4684

Fiction, interviews.
A Prize-winning (IAC), independent market for quality fiction, we are dedicated to original, fresh, diverse stories and novel excerpts. We've won 12 IAC awards in 6 years, plus a CCLM/GE Younger Writers Award in 1988.
David Evanier, Rolaine Hochstein, Edith Pearlman, Stephen Dixon, Karen Karbo.
Payment: gratuity plus copies.
Reporting time: 10–12 weeks.
Copyright held by magazine; reverts to author upon publication.
1985; 2/yr; 1,500
$16/ind; $18/inst; $4.95/ea; 40%, 50% to distributors
225 pp; 7 x 9
Ad rates: $100/page/7 x 9; $75/½ page/3½ x 4½
ISSN: 87565-4696

OUTERBRIDGE

Charlotte Alexander
112 E. 10th Street
New York, NY 10003
Poetry, fiction.
Craft first. Regular special themes, i.e., urban, rural, Southern. Slight bias to new voices and less published writers. Personal replies. Anti pure polemic. Theme projects: interdisciplinary (biology, physics, music, astronomy, etc.); the city, immigrant, migrant experience, best humor, wit nature, children's stories.
John Woodruff, Walter McDonald, Candida Lawrence, Linda Bierds, Susan Astor.
Payment: 2 copies.
Reporting time: 2–2½ months, except July–Aug.
Copyright held by magazine; reverts to author upon publication.
1975; annual issue; 800
$5/yr; $5/ea
120 pp; 8½ x 5
ISSN: 0739-4969

OYEZ REVIEW

Angela Lewis
Roosevelt University
430 South Michigan Avenue
Chicago, IL 60605
(312) 341-2017

Poetry, fiction, photographs.
OYEZ REVIEW is an award-winning, university-based magazine in its 23rd year of publication. Each issue contains a number of poems and short stories written by people from various parts of the country and many different walks of life. The writings are diverse in content; all have universal appeal.
Ronald Wallace, David Martin, Barry Silesky, John Jacob, Brooke Bergen.
Payment: none.
Reporting time: 6 months.
Copyright held by magazine; reverts to author upon publication.
1967; annual; 400
$4/ea; 40%
96 pp; 5½ x 8½
No ads

P

THE PACIFIC REVIEW

James Brown, (Faculty Editor)
Department of English
California State University
5500 University Pkwy.
San Bernardino, CA 92407-2397
(714) 880-5824; (714) 880-5894

Poetry, fiction, criticism, essays, reviews, plays, translation, interviews, photographs, graphics/artwork.

THE PACIFIC REVIEW is an academic-based journal of the verbal and visual arts, edited by graduate and undergraduate students at CSUSB. An annual publication now in its eighth year, **THE PACIFIC REVIEW** attempts to reflect aspects of its unique position in Southern California whenever possible, but without compromising its goal to serve as a vehicle for both emerging and established creative voices—from and about any area. February 1st deadline.

Payment: in copies, upon publication.

Copyright held by magazine; reverts to author upon publication.

1983; 1/yr; 750

$4/yr ind; $6.50/inst; $4/ea; 40%

102 pp; 6 x 9

Ad rates: $150/page/5 x 7½; $100/½ page/5 x 3¾; $50/¼ page/2½ x 3¾

PAINTBRUSH: A Journal of Poetry, Translations, and Letters

Ben Bennani

Division of Language and Literature

Northeast Missouri St. University

Kirksville, MO 63501

(816) 785-4185

Poetry, criticism, essays, reviews, interviews, translation, photographs, graphics/artwork.

Publishes serious but innovative poetry, translations from any language—especially neglected ones—and interviews, book reviews, and other readable stuff. The focus is always on quality and novelty.

William Stafford, Richard Eberhart, Colette Inez, Kathleen Spivack, Charles Edward Eaton.

Payment: in copies or $10/page when available.

Reporting time: 4–6 weeks.

Copyright held by magazine; reverts to author upon publication.

1974; 2/yr; 500

$9/yr ind; $12/yr inst; $7/ea; 40%

65 pp; 5½ x 8½

Ad rates: $150/page

ISSN: 0094-1964

PAINTED BRIDE QUARTERLY

Louis Camp and Joanna Di Paolo

230 Vine Street

Philadelphia, PA 19106

(215) 925-9914

Poetry, fiction, criticism, essays,

reviews, plays, photographs, graphics/artwork.

PAINTED BRIDE QUARTERLY
is a journal of literary and visual arts associated with the Painted Bride Art Center in Philadelphia. We publish both local and national writers and artists; the emphasis is on quality. We like crafted, articulate writing in any genre.

Naomi Shibab Nye, Eugene Howard, Etheridge Knight, Tina Barr, Robert Bly, Marnie Mueller.

Payment: in copies and 1 year subscription.

Reporting time: 2 weeks–2 months.

Copyright reverts to author.

1973; 4/yr; 1,000

$12/yr ind; $16/yr inst; $5/ea; 50%

80 pp; 5 x 8½

Ad rates: $75/page; $50/½ page; $25/¼ page

PANDORA

Meg MacDonald, Editor

2844 Grayson

Ferndale, MI 48220

Poetry, fiction, essays, reviews, graphics/artwork.

Character-oriented science fiction and fantasy by new and established writers. We emphasize role-expanding plots & characters and do not consider work that is racist, sexist, or x-rated. *No horror* or glorification of violence. Give us work about characters we can care about!

T. Jackson King, Ardath Mayhar, Deborah Wheeler, Wade Tarzia, Heather Gladney

Payment: 1¢-2¢/word; $7 and up on illos; $3.50 and up on cartoons and fillers.

Guidelines available for SASE.

Reporting time: 4–6 weeks.

Copyright held by author. Buy 1st NA Serial Rights usually.

1978; 2/yr; 800

$10/2 anthologies; $5/each (US); $15/2, $7 each CANADA; $20/2 $10 each overseas

72 pp; 5½ x 8½

Display ad rates: $40/page/4½ x 7½; $25/½ page/4½ x 3¾; $16.50/¼ page/2¼ x 3¾; $11/⅛ page; ($10 per 25 words non-display)

ISSN: 0275-519X

Faxon

PANHANDLER

Michael Yots, Stanton Millet

English Department

University of West Florida

Pensacola, FL 32514

(904) 474-2923

Poetry and short fiction.

THE PANHANDLER is a magazine of contemporary poetry and fiction. We want poetry and stories rooted in real experience in language with a strong colloquial flavor. Works that are engaging and readable stand a better chance with us than works that are self-consciously literary.

Walter McDonald, Malcolm Glass, Enid Shomer, David Kirby, Joan Colby.

Payment: in copies

Reporting time: 2–3 months.

Copyright held by University; reverts to author upon publication.

1976; 2/yr; 500

$5/yr; $8/2 yr; 40%

64 pp; 6 x 9

ISSN: 0738-8705

EBSCO Subscription Services (Birmingham, AL)

PARABOLA: The Magazine of Myth & Tradition

Rob Baker

656 Broadway

New York, NY 10012

(212) 505-6200

Essays, reviews, interviews, photographs, graphics/artwork.

PARABOLA's focus is on myth and the world's cultural and spiritual traditions. Accordingly, **PARABOLA**'s approach to literature involves an emphasis on myths, legends, folktales, and oral transmission. **PARABOLA** primarily publishes articles and interviews which deal with mythology, comparative religion, and contemporary spirituality. Each issue focuses on a central theme.

P.L. Travers, Peter Brook, Eknath Easwaran, Frederick Franck, Amadou Hampâté Bâ, Laurence Rosenthal, Edwin Birnbaum.

Payment: $250 for articles; $75 for reviews; $50 for retelling of traditional stories.

Reporting time: 6 weeks.

Copyright held by author.

1976; 4/yr; 35,000

$18/yr; $5.50/ea; 40%

128 pp; 6¾ x 10

Ad rates: $735/page/5¹⁄₁₆ x 8⁵⁄₁₆; $495/½ page/5¹⁄₁₆ x 4⅛; $285/¼ page/2⁷⁄₁₆ x 4⅛

ISSN: 0362-1596

PARAGRAPH

Walker Rumble, Karen Donovan

1423 Northampton Street

Holyoke, MA 01040

(413) 533-8767

Prose paragraphs only.

We publish paragraphs of 200 words or less on any subject. We are very selective and tend to like paragraphs that have an innovative topic and an arresting tone. Both fiction and nonfiction welcome.

Joel Dailey, Wanda Coleman, John Gilgun, Laurel Speer, Gary Fincke, Jessica Treat, Conger Beasley Jr.

Payment: in contributors copies.

Copyright held by Oat City Press; reverts to author upon publication.

1985; 3/yr; 500

$8/3 issues; $3/sample; 40%

Ad rates: negotiable

THE PARIS REVIEW

George Plimpton, James Linville, Patricia Storace

541 East 72nd Street

New York, NY 10021

Fiction, poetry, interviews, graphics/artwork and literary features (art portfolios solicited only).

Focus on best of emerging and established poets, writers and artists. Always on the look-out for lively newcomers.

Joseph Brodsky, Carolyn Kizer, Rick Bass, E.L. Doctorow, Alice Munro, Keith Haring.

Payment: varies.

Reporting time: 8–10 weeks.

Copyright held by Paris Review Inc.; reverts to author upon publication.

1953; 4/yr; 9,700

$20/yr; $6/ea

240 pp; 4 x 7½

Ad rates: $500/page/4 x 7½

ISSN: 0031-2037

Eastern News Distributors, Inc.

PARNASSUS

Herbert Leibowitz

41 Union Square West, Room 804

New York, NY 10003

(212) 463-0889

Criticism, essays, reviews, photographs, graphics/artwork.

Devoted to the in-depth analysis of contemporary books of poetry. **PARNASSUS** seeks essays and reviews that are themselves works of art. The ideal reviewer is a poet with his or her own particular point of view. **PARNASSUS** publishes special issues on music, poetry in translation, the long poem; includes paintings, illustrations and photographs.

Seamus Heaney, Ross Feld, Alice Fulton, William Logan, Helen Vendler.

Payment: $25–$250.

Reporting time: varies.

Copyright held by Poetry in Review Foundation; reverts to author upon request.

1972; 2/yr; 2,500

$18/yr ind; $36/yr inst; $10/ea

350 pp; 6 x 9¼
Ad rates: $250/page/6 x 9¼;
  $150/½ page/5 x 4
ISSN: 0048-3028
Spectacular Diseases (England)

PARTING GIFTS

Robert Bixby
3006 Stonecutter Terrace
Greensboro, NC 27405
(919) 282-3914
Poetry, fiction.
Payment: 2 copies.
Copyright held by March Street
  Press; reverts to author upon
  publication.
1988; 2/yr; 100
$6/yr; $3/ea; 40%
30 pp; 5½ s 8½
ISSN: 1043-3325

PARTISAN REVIEW

William Phillips
236 Bay State Road
Boston, MA 02215
(617) 353-4260
Poetry, fiction, criticism, essays,
  reviews, translation, interviews.
PARTISAN REVIEW examines
  the central issues of contemporary culture and social thought.
  It publishes critical essays on
  the arts and politics, new fiction
  and poetry, and book reviews.
Joseph Brodsky, Eugene Good-
heart, Pearl K. Bell, Elisabeth
Young-Bruehl, Jed Perl.
Payment: varies.
Reporting time: 3 months.
Copyright held by Partisan Review, Inc; reverts to author
  upon publication.
1937; 4/yr; 8,150
$18/yr ind; $28/yr inst; $5/ea;
  15%
160 pp; 6 x 9
Ad rates: $200–$250/page/4¼ x
  7⅜; $120/½ page/4¼ x 3½;
  $75/¼ page/2 x 3½
ISSN: 0031-2525
DeBoer, Nutley, NJ; Capitol
  News, Boston, MA; L-S Distribution, San Francisco, CA; Ingram Periodicals, Nashville, TN

PASSAGES NORTH

Ben Mitchell
Kalamazoo College
1200 Academy
Kalamazoo, MI 49007
Poetry, fiction, essays, interviews,
  photographs, graphics/artwork.
PASSAGES NORTH publishes
  high quality poetry and fiction,
  along with graphic arts, twice
  yearly in tabloid size. The magazine not only publishes established writers, but also
  encourages students in writing
  programs. It fosters interchange

between the Upper Midwest and other parts of the nation.
Jack Driscoll, Gary Gildner, Judith Minty, Gloria Whelan, Alice Fulton.
Payment: $20/poem, $50/short story, frequent prizes.
Reporting time: 3 weeks–3 months.
Copyright held by magazine; reverts to author upon publication.
1979; 2/yr; 2,000
$2/yr; $5/3 yrs; $1.50/ea; 50%
24 pp; 11½ x 14½
Ad rates: $200/page/9¾ x 12¼; $100/½ page/9¾ x 6¼; $50/¼ page/4¾ x 6¼
ISSN: 0278-0828

PASSAIC REVIEW

Richard Quatrone
Forstmann Library
195 Gregory Avenue
Passaic, NJ 07055
Poetry, fiction, plays, photographs, graphics/artwork.
PASSAIC REVIEW is an independent magazine that publishes the best work submitted to it. Emphasis is on strong, clear, direct writing.
Antler, Ronald Baatz, Amiri Baraka, Allen Ginsberg, Eliot Katz, Wanda Phipps.
Payment: none.

Reporting time: 1–52 weeks.
Copyright held by magazine; reverts to author upon publication.
1979; 2/yr; 500
$6/yr ind; $10/yr inst; $3.75/ea; 40%
48–54 pp; 5 x 8½
Ad rates: $80/page/5 x 8½; $40/½ page/2¾ x 4¼; $20/¼ page/1⅜ x 2⅛
ISSN: 0731-4663

PEMBROKE MAGAZINE

Shelby Stephenson
Box 60, PSU
Pembroke, NC 28372
(919) 521-4214, ext. 433
Poetry, fiction, criticism, reviews, plays, interviews, graphics/artwork.
Open to poetry, fiction, essays, interviews, and artwork.
A.R. Ammons, Fred Chappell, Carson McCullers, Robert Morgan, Betty Adcock.
Payment: none
Reporting time: up to 3 months.
Copyright held by magazine; reverts to author upon publication.
1969; 1/yr; 500–800
$5/yr; $5/ea; surface mail $5.50/yr; $5.50/ea; 40%
250 pp; 6 x 9
Ad rates: $40/page; $25/½ page

THE PENNSYLVANIA RE-VIEW

Lori Jakiela
English Department, 526 CL
University of Pittsburgh
Pittsbury, PA 15260
(412) 624-6506

Poetry, fiction, criticism, essays, reviews, translations, interviews, graphics/artwork, photos (b&w).

Publishing the finest contemporary fiction, poetry, non-fiction and illustrations. *Choice* calls **THE PENNSYLVANIA REVIEW** a "fine small literary magazine . . . highly recommended".

Gordon Lish, Edward Abbey, Linda Pastan, Maxine Kumin, Paul West.

Payment: in copies.
Reporting time: 6–10 weeks.
Copyright held by Univ. of Pittsburgh; reverts to author upon publication.
1990; 2/yr; 500
$10/yr; $5/ea; 40%
100 pp; 7 x 10
Ad rates: $120/page/6 x 9; $70 ½ page/6 x 4
ISSN: 8756-5668

PEQUOD

Mark Rudman
N.Y.U. English Dept., 2nd floor
19 University Place
New York, NY 10003

Poetry, fiction, criticism, essays, translation.

Past issues of **PEQUOD** have featured Irish, Scandinavian, Russian, Israeli, and Ukranian poetry. Recent issues have included a special issue on literature and the visual arts, a selection of recent British poetry, and a focus on the long poem.

Paul Auster, Thomas Bernhard, Eavan Boland, Louise Gluck, Charlie Smith.

Payment: some payment to contributors.
Copyright held by PEQUOD.
1974; 2/yr; 1,000–2,000
$10/yr ind; $18/2 yrs ind; $17/yr inst; $30/2 yrs inst; $100/lifetime; $5/ea; $10/double issues
128 pp; 5½ x 8½
Ad rates: $150/page/5½ x 8½; $200/2 pp
ISSN: 0149-0516
DeBoer

PEREGRINE: The Journal of Amherst Writers & Artists

Kate Gleason, 1989 Editor
Pat Schneider, Contact at Amherst Writers & Artists
P.O. Box 1076
Amherst MA 01004
(413) 253-3307; (413) 253-7764

Poetry, fiction, cover graphics/artwork.

PEREGRINE is the journal of Amherst Writers & Artists, an organization dedicated to the belief that good writing is honest and unpretentious. We believe literature is related to the speech of home and workplace, and to the meanings discovered in ordinary lives without the bias of sex, race or class.

Katharyn Machan Aal, A.D. Winans, Jane Yolen, William Packard, Noemi Escandell.

Payment: in copies, and occasional prizes, upon publication.

Copyright held by Amherst Writers & Artists Press, Inc.; reverts to author upon publication.

1983; 1/yr; 500

$4.50/ea; 40%

64 pp; 5½ x 8¼

Ad rates: contact magazine for information

ISSN: 0890-662X

PERMAFROST

Department of English
University of Alaska
Fairbanks, AK 99775
(907) 474-5247

Poetry, fiction, essays, photographs, graphics/artwork.

PERMAFROST seeks to promote excellence in contemporary literature and welcomes submissions in this vein.

Payment: 2 copies.

Reporting time: 4 months.

Copyright held by author.

1975; 2/yr; 250

$7/yr; $4/ea; 30%

80 pp; 5 x 8

No ads

PHOENIX

Joan S. Isom
College of Arts & Letters
Northeastern State University
Tahlequah, OK 74464
(918) 456-5511, ext. 3616

Poetry, fiction, essays, criticism.

We focus on contemporary poetry, fiction, and essays. Please query first. We do thematic issues occasionally.

William Stafford, Maurice Kenny, Louis Phillips, Ruth Schechter.

Payment: in copies.

Copyright held by Northeastern State University; reverts to author upon publication.

1964; 1/yr; 300

$7/yr

No ads

ISSN: 0-9615355

PIEDMONT LITERARY REVIEW

Gail White
Piedmont Literary Society

Route 1, Box 512
Forest, VA 24551
(804) 384-2027

Poetry, fiction, reviews, graphics/
artwork, newsletter.

We publish mainly poetry, short
stories; approximately 60 poems, 2 short stories. We need
short stories of around 1,500 to
2,000 words. Traditional to
avant-garde poetry—we publish
established poets and many first
timers.

William Matthews, Robert Wrigley, John Timmerman, Kurt
Rheinheimer, Judson Jerome.

Payment: in copies.

Reporting time: 2 days–3 months.

Copyright held by magazine; reverts to author upon publication.

1976; 4/yr; 300
$12/yr; $3/ea
50 pp; 5½ x 8½
ISSN: 0257-357X

PIG IRON

Jim Villani, Naton Leslie, Rose
Sayre
P.O. Box 237
Youngstown, OH 44501
(216) 783-1269

Poetry, fiction, essays, translation,
interviews, photographs, graph-
ics/artwork.

Special emphasis on popular culture, genres, and new literature
in a highly visual and cerebral
format. Publishes issues around
special themes: recent issues
have featured Third World, Humor, Psychological Literature,
Viet Nam Era, Surrealism, Science Fiction, and Baseball.
Forthcoming issues include
"Labor in the Post-Industrial
Age" and "Epistolary Fiction
and the Letter as Artifact."
Back issues available.

Joe Bruchac, Terry Stokes, Dallas
Wiebe, Lowell Jaeger, Miguel
Ángel Asturias, Lamia Abbas
Amara, Margot Treital, Soleida
Ríos, Carlos Cumpían.

Payment: $2 per published page.

Reporting time: 3 months.

Copyright held by editors; reverts
to author upon publication.

1975; 1/yr; 1,000
$5/1 issue; $9/2 issues; $12/3 is-
sues.
$7.95/ea; 40%
96 pp; 8½ x 11
ISSN: 0362-5214

Available through publisher only;
distributor queries accepted.

THE PIKESTAFF FORUM

Robert D. Sutherland, James R.
Scrimgeour, James McGowan,
Curtis White
P.O. Box 127

Normal, IL 61761

(309) 452-4831

Black and white photographs; line-drawings; small-press book reviews. Poetry, fiction, commentary on contemporary literature and the small-press scene.

A literary magazine eclectic in its tastes, publishing the best poetry and fiction that comes its way; sets a standard in tabloid design and format.

Gayl Teller, Jeff Gundy, Enid Dame, J. W. Rivers, R. Cooperman.

Payment: 3 free copies of issue in which work appears; 50 discount on extras.

Reporting time: 3 months.

Copyright remains with authors and artists.

1978; annual; 1,000

$10/6 issues; $2/ea

40; tabloid

ISSN: 0192-8716

ILPA

PIVOT

Martin Mitchell

250 Riverside Drive #23

New York, NY 10025

(212) 222-1408

Poetry.

Now in its 39th year, **PIVOT** publishes the work of both seasoned and new poets. It has a reputation for "firsts" of admirable performance. Mss. read Jan. 1 to June 1.

Philip Appleman, David Ignatow, Eugene J. McCarthy, Willliam Matthews, Craig Raine, W. D. Snodgrass.

Payment: in copies.

Reporting time: 2–4 weeks.

Copyright held by Sibyl Barsky Grucci; reverts to author upon publication.

1951; 1/yr; 1,500–3,000

$5/ea

76 pp; 6 x 9

Ad rates: $125/page; $70/½ page; $40/¼ page

PLAINS POETRY JOURNAL

Jane Greer

P.O. Box 2337

Bismarck, ND 58502

Poetry, criticism, essays.

PLAINS POETRY JOURNAL is a forum for poetry using traditional poetic conventions: meter, rhyme, alliteration, assonance, painstaking attention to sound. No prosaic, conversational "free verse." No Hallmark verse. Will publish one essay per issue: serious criticism, or humorous or serious essays on poetry. Widely published and unpublished poets receive same consideration.

Rhina Espaillat, Jack Butler, Johnny Wink, Gail White, R.S. Gwynn, Geoffrey Wagner.

Payment: none.

Reporting time: 1 month.

Copyright held by magazine; reverts to author upon publication.

1982; 4/yr; 500

$18/yr; $32/2 yrs; $4.50/ea; negotiable

44 pp; 5½ x 8½

ISSN: 0730-6172

PLAINSWOMAN

Elizabeth Hampsten

P.O. Box 8027

Grand Forks, ND 58202

(701) 777-8043

Essays, fiction, reviews, interviews, poetry, photographs, graphics/artwork.

PLAINSWOMAN publishes articles, interviews, fiction, poetry and graphics. We encourage clear writing by both academic and unpracticed writers, and we work with prospective contributors.

Emily Rhoads Johnson, Enid Shomer, Susan Strayer Deal.

Publication has been temporarily suspended, with Jan. 1991 as the anticipated date of resumption.

Payment: $5 to $50, or more if funds allow.

Reporting time: 1 week–1 month

Copyright held by magazine; reverts to author upon publication.

1977; 10/yr; 600

$20/yr; $2/ea; 40%

20 pp; 8 x 11

ISSN: 0146-902X

PLOUGHSHARES

DeWitt Henry, Don Lee, Joyce Peseroff, David Daniel

Emerson College

100 Beacon St.

Boston, MA 02116

(617) 926-9875

Poetry, fiction, criticism, essays, reviews, translation, interviews.

A magazine of new writing edited on a revolving basis by professional poets and writers to reflect different and contrasting points of view.

Rita Dove, Sven Birkerts, Mona Simpson, Seamus Heaney, Joseph Brodsky.

Reporting time: 5 months.

Copyright held by magazine; reverts to author upon request.

1971; 3/yr; 3,800

$15/yr ind; $18/yr inst; $5/ea; 20%–40%

200 pp; 5½ x 8½

Ad rates: $225/page/4½ x 7;
$125/½ page/4½ x 3¼; $80/¼
page/2¼ x 3¼

ISSN: 0048-4474

Bernhard DeBoer; L-S Distributors

POEM

Nancy Frey Dillard

English Department

University of Alabama in Huntsville

Huntsville, AL 35899

(205) 895-6320

Poetry.

High quality mature poetry. No bias as to form or theme. Particular regard given to less well known poets.

Charles Edward Eaton, John Ditsky, Stephen Lang, R.T. Smith, Alison Reed.

Payment: in copy.

Reporting time: 1 month.

Copyright held by Huntsville Literary Association.

1967; 2/yr; 400

$10/yr; $5/ea

70 pp; 4½ x 7½

No ads

POET AND CRITIC

Neal Bowers

203 Ross Hall

Iowa State University

Ames, IA 50011

(515) 294-2180

Poetry, criticism, reviews.

POET AND CRITIC publishes poems, essays on contemporary poetry and/or poetics (3,000 words or less), and reviews of current poetry books. We try to be receptive to all types of poetry, asking only that the work display a sense of language.

Brendan Galvin, Barry Sparks, Edward Kleinschmidt, Ann Struthers, Malcolm Glass, Ron Offen.

Payment: 1 copy.

Reporting time: 3 days–2 weeks.

Copyright held by Iowa State University; reverts to author upon publication.

1964; 3/yr; 400

$16/yr ind; $20/yr inst; $6/ea; 40%

48 pp; 6 x 9

Ad rates: exchanges with other magazines

ISSN: 0032-1958

POET LORE

Sunil Freeman, Managing Editor

7815 Old Georgetown Road

Bethesda, MD 20814

(301) 654-8664

Poetry, criticism, essays, reviews, translation, graphics/artwork.

POET LORE publishes original

poems of all kinds. The editors continue to welcome narrative poetry and original translations of contemporary world poets.

POET LORE publishes reviews of poetry collections and critical essays of contemporary poetry.

Walter McDonald, Robert Peters, Leonard Nathan, Susan Astor, Albert Goldbarth.

Payment: 2 copies.

Reporting time: 3 months.

Copyright held by The Writer's Center; reverts to author upon publication.

1889; 4/yr; 600

$12/yr ind; $20/yr inst; $4.50/ea; 40%

64 pp; 6 x 9

Ad rates: $100/page/5½ x 8; $55/½ page/5½ x 4

ISSN: 0032-1966

The Faxon Co., Inc.; EBSCO; McGregor Subscription Service, Inc.; Boley Subscription Agency, Inc.

POETIC SPACE: POETRY AND FICTION

Don Hildenbrand

P.O. Box 11157

Eugene, OR 97440

(503) 485-2278

Poetry, fiction, reviews, interviews, graphics/artwork.

Maia Peufold, Tom Strand, Patty McDonald, Lyn Lifshin, Sesshu Foster, Barbara Henning.

$15/yr; $2 ea

Fiction: 1,500 word limit

POETICS JOURNAL

Lyn Hejinian, Barrett Watten

2639 Russell Street

Berkeley, CA 94705

(415) 548-1817

Criticism, essays, reviews.

POETICS JOURNAL is an irregularly published journal of contemporary poetics by poets and prose writers as well as by other artists, critics, linguists, and political theorists. It features essays, articles, and investigatory reviews. Individual issues focus on topics including "close reading", "poetry and philosophy", "women and modernism", "non-narrative", etc.

Ron Silliman, George Lakoff, Rae Armantrout, Ted Pearson, Jackson MacLow.

Payment: in copies.

Reporting time: 2–4 weeks.

Copyright held by author.

1982; irreg.; 600

$20/yr; $8.00/ea; 25%–40%

144 pp; 6 x 9

ISSN: 0731-5236

Small Press Distribution; Segue

POETPOURRI

Comstock Writer's Group; Kathleen Bryce Niles, Coordinator; Jennifer B. MacPherson, President

P.O. Box 3737 Taft Rd

Syracuse, NY 13220

(315) 451-1406

Poetry only.

Perfect-bound 75–100 pp, put out twice yearly. We accept poetry on the basis of quality, not reputation. We do not accept porno, sentimental, greeting card verse and very few haikus or religious verse. Well crafted poetry, free or formal, written in understandable, grammatically correct English— metaphor, fresh, vivid imagery enjoyed.

Joseph Bruchac, Kathryn Machan Aal, Robt. Cooperman, A.D. Winans, Scott Sanders, Gayle Elen Harvey.

Payment: copy, prize $.

Reporting time: usually 2–4 weeks, with comments.

Copyright reverts to author.

1986; 2/yr; 500

$8/yr; $15/2 yrs; $4/ea

75–100 pp; 5½ x 8½

POETRY

Joseph Parisi

60 West Walton Street

Chicago, IL 60610

(312) 280-4870

Poetry, reviews, essays.

For 75 years **POETRY** has been the most widely read monthly of verse. From Auden to Ashbery, Pound to Pinsky, Stevens to Soto—voices famous and new.

David Wagoner, James Merrill, Linda Pastan, Amy Clampitt, Raymond Carver.

Payment: $2/line for verse; $20/page of prose.

Reporting time: 8–10 weeks.

Copyright held by Modern Poetry Association; reverts to author upon request.

1912; 12/yr; 7,300

$25/yr ind; $27/yr inst; $2.50/ea

64 pp; 5½ x 9

Ad rates: $280/page/3¾ x 7; $174/½ page/3¾ x 3½; $111/¼ page/1¾ x 3½

ISSN: 0032-2032

B. DeBoer, Inc.; Ingram Periodicals

POETRY CANADA

Barry Dempster (Poetry), Bob Hilderley (Prose)

P.O. Box 1061, 221 King Street E.

Kingston, Ontario, Canada U7L4Y5

(613) 548-8429

Poetry essays on poetry, reviews
of poetry books.
Bill Bissett, Maggie Helwig,
Daniel David Roses.
Payment: upon request
Reporting time: 3 months
Copyright for authors—first North
American Serial Rights.
1980; quarterly; 700
$15/4; $3.95
36; tabloid
Upon request
ISSN: 0709-3373
Quarry Press

POETRY EAST

Richard Jones
802 W. Belden
English Department
DePaul University
Chicago, IL 60614
(312) 362-5114

Poetry, translations, fiction, art,
interviews, reviews.
POETRY EAST publishes issues
dedicated to particular poets or
topics. We are also interested in
reading essays on poetics, the
relationship between art and the
world. We are also looking for
translations and ideas for feature/
symposia.
Marge Piercy, Sam Hamill, David
Ignatow, David Lee.
Payment: in copies, honoraria.
Reporting time: 3 months.

Copyright reverts, but reserve
right to include in anthology.
1980; bi-annually; 1,500
$12; $8
200; 5½ x 8½
$100/page; $50/½ page
ISSN: 0197-4009
DeBoer and Fine Print

POETRY FLASH

Joyce Jenkins; Richard Silberg,
Associate Editor
P.O. Box 4172
Berkeley, CA 94704
(415) 525-5476

Criticism, essays, reviews, interviews, photographs, poetry.
POETRY FLASH, A Poetry Review and Literary Calendar,
publishes the most complete
literary calendar of the West
available. Also reviews of
books, magazines, readings,
and events, as well as interviews, occasional essays, photos, general commentary and
information on submissions and
publications for poets.
Steve Kowit, Anselm Hollo, Marilyn Chin, Ivan Arguelles, Jack
Marshall.
Payment: subscription to $25; $50
to $100 maximum.
Reporting time: 3 months.
Copyright held by author.

1972; 12/yr; 17,000; free to public places
$10/yr ind; $12/yr inst
16–28 pp; 11½ x 15
Ad rates: $400/page/10 x 13¾; $200/½ page/10 x 7; $100/¼ page/6½ x 5 or 5 x 7 ($105)
ISSN: 0737-4747

POETRY/LA

Helen Friedland, Barbara Strauss
P.O. Box 84271
Los Angeles, CA 90073
(213) 472-6171

Poetry.

POETRY/LA is a semiannual anthology of poems by Los Angeles-area poets. We publish poetry by both well-known and previously unpublished poets, and will consider poems of every length, style and subject matter.

Charles Bukowski, Mark McCloskey, Kate Braverman, Gerald Locklin, Amy Uyematsu.

Payment: 1–5 copies.
Reporting time: 2 weeks–6 months.
Copyright held by magazine; reverts to author upon request.
1980; 2/yr; 500
$8/yr; $4.25/ea; 40%
128 pp; 5½ x 8½
No ads
ISSN: 0275-1739

THE POETRY MISCELLANY

Richard Jackson, Michael Panori
University of Tennessee at Chattanooga
Department of English
Chattanooga, TN 37402
(615) 624-7279 or 755-4629

Poetry, essays, reviews, translation, interviews.

We are very much a miscellany in the traditional sense of that word; we publish a variety of "types" of poetry.

John Ashbery, Marvin Bell, Carolyn Forche, William Stafford, Mark Strand.

Payment: none.
Reporting time: 6 weeks.
Copyright held by magazine; reverts to author upon publication.
1971; 2/yr; 1,100
$3/yr ind; $2/yr inst; $3/ea
130 pp; 6 x 9
Ad rates: $100/page/5 x 8; $65/½ page/5 x 4½; $40/¼ page/5 x 2

POETRY PROJECT NEWSLETTER

Jerome Sala
The Poetry Project
St. Mark's Church
131 E. 10th Street
New York, NY 10211-0494
(212) 674-0910

Poetry, criticism, essays, reviews, listings.

Bernadette Mayer, Anselm Hollo, Robert Creeley, Paul Violi, James Schuyler.

Payment: none.
Reporting time: 4 weeks.
Copyright held by author.
1967; 4/yr; 3,000
$20/yr
24 pp; 8½ x 11
Ad rates: $205/page/7 x 10; $130/½ page/7 x 5 or 3½ x 10; $90/¼ page/3½ x 5 or 7 x 2½; $6/⅛ page, 3½ x 2½; Discounts for nonprofits.

POETS ON

Ruth Daigon
29 Loring Avenue
Mill Valley, CA 94941
(415) 381-2824
Poetry.

POETS ON is a semi-annual poetry magazine. Theme-oriented, exploring basic human concerns through insightful, significant, well-crafted poetry. We publish recognized poets as well as unknown poets.

Linda Pastan, Charles Edward Eaton, Seamus Heaney, Joseph Bruchac, Marge Piercy, Philip Booth.

Payment: in copies.
Reporting time: 2–3 months.

Copyright reverts to author.
1977; 2/yr; 500
$6/yr; $3.50/ea
48 pp; 5½ x 8½

THE PORTABLE LOWER EAST SIDE

Kurt Hollander
Arthur Nersesian
P. O. Box 30323
New York, NY 10011

Fiction, poetry, photography, essays.

PORTABLE LOWER EAST SIDE is a literary magazine involved with New York City. Strong emphasis on ethnic and cultural diversity, and on social issues. Latest issue: "Crimes of the City". Forthcoming: Asian-New York.

Hubert Selby, Margaret Randall, Luisa Valenzuela, Willie Colon, Edward Limonov.

Payment: in copies and small sums.
Reporting time: 2 months.
Copyright reverts to author.
1984; 2/yr; 2,000.
$11/yr ind; $20/yr inst; $7/ea; 40%
175 pp; 5½ x 7
Ad rates: $100/page; $75/½ page
Inland Books, DeBoer

PORTLAND REVIEW

Nancy Row, Ken Angelo
P.O. Box 751
Portland, OR 97207
(503) 725-4468

Fiction, poetry, essays, plays,
photographs, graphics/artwork.

The **PORTLAND REVIEW** is
the annual Arts and Literature
Magazine of Portland State University. It draws material mainly
from the Pacific Northwest, but
is open to submissions from
outside the region.

Payment: 1 copy.
Reporting time: 1–2 months.
Copyright held by author.
1953; 3/yr; 1,000
$15/subscription; $4.00/ea +
$1.00 postage
80 pp; 9 x 12
Ads

POTATO EYES

Roy Zarucchi, Carolyn Page
Nightshade Press, P.O. Box 76
Troy, Maine 04987
(207) 948-3427

Canadian and US poetry, short
stories, reviews of poetry, black
and white art.

A semi-annual literary arts journal
focusing on poetry, short fiction
and art work from/about the
Appalachians from Alabama to
Quebec. This is a primary, but
not exclusive focus.

William Doveski, Shelby Stephenson, Alice Sink, Lynn Taetsch,
Robert Chute.

Payment: paid in copies
Reporting time: 2–8 weeks
Copyright publisher until publication.
1989; bi-annual; 600–800
$9; $5; 40%
80; 6 x 9
ISSN: 1041-9926

POULTRY, A Magazine of Voice

Jack Flavin, Brendan Galvin,
George Garrett
P.O. Box 4413
Springfield, MA 01101
(413) 732-0435

Parodies, satire put-ons, put-
downs of contemporary poetry,
lit & litbiz.

David R. Slavitt, Douglas A.
Powell, Joyce Lamers, Jay Blu-
menthal, Lyn Lifshin, R. S.
Gwynn, J. Argus Huber.

Payment: 10 free copies.
Reporting time: 2–3 months.
Copyright 1st pub rights
1979; 2–3 annually; 1,400
$5; $2
8.

PRAIRIE FIRE

Andris Taskans, Managing Editor
423-100 Arthur Street
Winnipeg, Manitoba, Canada
R3B1H3
(204) 943-9066
Fiction, poetry, essays, book reviews.
A Canadian magazine with a western perspective, featuring new writing and special issues on topics such as ethnic writing, women's writing, genre writing and more.
Sandra Birdsell, Rudy Wiebe.
Reporting time: 3–4 months
Copyright reverts to author upon publication.
1978; 4/yr; 1,000
$22; $6.95; 30%
100; 6 x 9
ISSN: 0821-1124
Canadian Magazine Publishers Assocation

PRAIRIE JOURNAL/of Canadian Literature

Prairie Journal Press
P.O. Box 997, Station G
Calgary, Alberta, Canada T3A3A2
Short fiction, poetry, review, essays, drama.
Literary small press publication.
Fred Cogswell, Lorna Crozier, Mick Burrs, Robin Mathews, Bruce Hunter, John V. Hicks, Shaunt Basmajian, George Amabile, Gary Hyland, Glen Sorestad, Peter Baltensperger, Denniss Cooley.
Payment: Honouraria
Reporting time: 3–6 weeks
Copyright for author
1983; 2 times/ yr; 500
$6; $3; 40%
60; 7½ x 8
Negotiable
ISSN: 0827-2921

PRAIRIE SCHOONER

Hilda Raz
201 Andrews Hall
University of Nebraska
Lincoln, NE 68588-0334
(402) 472-3191
Poetry, fiction, essays, reviews, translation.
PRAIRIE SCHOONER, a literary quarterly, publishes the best writing available from beginning and established writers: short stories, poems, interviews, imaginative essays of general interest, and reviews of current books of poetry and fiction. Scholarly articles requiring footnote references are generally not published by **PRAIRIE SCHOONER**.
Marianne Boruch, Philip Dacey, Brian Swann, Jeanne Murray

Walker, Pat Mora, Dabney Stuart.

Payment: 12 annual writing prizes and grant funds, when available.

Reporting time: 2–3 months.

Copyright held by Prairie Schooner; reverts to author upon request.

1927; 4/yr; 2,000

$15/yr ind; $19/yr inst; $4/ea; 40%

144 pp; 6 x 9

Ad rates: $150/page/4¾ x 7½

ISSN: 0032-6682

Ingram Periodicals, Inc., Total Circulation Services

PRIMAVERA

Editorial Board
1448 East 52nd Street
Chicago, IL 60615
(312) 324-5920

Poetry, fiction, photographs, graphics/artwork.

PRIMAVERA focuses on the experiences of women; publishes both established and unknown writers.

Carol Lee Lorenzo, Doris Lynch, Chitra Divakaruni.

Payment: in copies.

Reporting time: 2 weeks–3 months.

Copyright held by magazine; reverts to author upon publication.

1975; 1/yr; 1,000

$6/yr; $6/ea

5½ x 8½

No ads.

ISSN: 0364-7609

THE PROSPECT REVIEW

Peter A. Koufos, John Cyril Brook, James Betesh
557 10th Street, #3
Brooklyn, NY 11215
(718) 788-5709

Poetry, fiction, drama, everything!

TPR is a literary journal committed to daring; bridging a gap between the unacknowledged poet and writer with those in academia for cultural unity.

E. Ethelbert Miller, Richard Burgin, Jana Harris, Gina Bergaminoe.

Payment: copies.

Reporting time: on or near issue release date.

Copyright reverts to authors upon publication.

1990; bi-annual

$12; $6

86; 6 x 8

Available on request

ISSN: 1049-0426

De Boer

PROVINCETOWN ARTS

Christopher Busa, Raymond Elaran

650 Commercial Street
Provincetown, MA 02657
(508) 487-3167

Poetry, Fiction, Criticism, Essays, Plays, Translation, Interviews, Photographs, Graphics/Artwork.

The documentary voice of the artists and writers who visit Cape Cod, **PROVINCETOWN ARTS** focuses on the phenonmenon of the art colony, not as geographical locus, but as a point of view. A large proportion of this annual book-length magazine emphasizes visual art, exploring the relation of visual art to language.

Alan Dugan, Stanley Kunitz, Carolyn Forche, Anne Bernays, Jason Shinder.

Payment: $25–$125 per poem; $125–300 per story (fiction & nonfiction).

Reporting Time: 2–4 months.

Copyright: Provincetown Arts, Inc.

1985; annually; 5,000

$8; $5; 40%

184; 9 x 12

$650/page; $400/½ page; $250/¼ page

Ingram, DeBoer, Interstate, Cape Cod News

PUCKERBRUSH REVIEW

Constance Hunting
76 Main Street
Orono, ME 04473
(207) 581-3832

Fiction, poetry, reviews, criticism, interviews, essays, graphics/artwork, photographs.

The special focus is on Maine literature and literary figures such as Elizabeth Hardwick, Mary McCarthy. Amy Clampitt, Phillip Booth. The intent is to publish fiction, poetry and reviews by contemporary Maine writers. The purpose is both to reveal and to encourage the literary energy in this isolated state. "Puckerbrush" = new growth.

Angelica Garnett, Ron Welton, Sonya Dorman, Farnham Blair, Sanford Phippen.

Payment: in copies.

Copyright held by magazine; reverts to author upon publication.

1978; 2/yr; 450

$8/yr; $4/ea; 40%

50 pp; 8½ x 11

Ad rates: inquire

PUERTO DEL SOL

Kevin McIlvoy
New Mexico State University
Box 3E
Las Cruces, NM 88003
(505) 646-3931

Poetry, fiction, novel sections,

criticism, essays, reviews, translation, interviews, photographs, graphics/artwork. Though our emphasis is on the Southwest, forty percent of each issue is the poetry, short fiction, artwork, etc. of artists from all over the United States.

Naomi Shihab Nye, Richard Russo, William Stafford, Susan Thornton, Dagoberto Gilb.

Payment: none.

Reporting time: 8–12 weeks.

Copyright held by magazine; reverts to author upon publication.

1960; 1–2/yr; 1200

$6.75/semi-annual ind; $6/semi-annual inst; $5/ea; 40%

150 pp; 6 x 9

Ad rates: $150/page; $90/½ page; $60/¼ page

ISSN: 0738-517X

Q

QUARRY WEST

Kenneth Weisner
c/o Porter College
University of California
Santa Cruz, CA 95064
(408) 429-2155; (408) 429-2951
(messages)

Poetry, fiction, essays, graphics/artwork.

QUARRY WEST combines quality design, graphics, production with about 95 pages of poetry and fiction, plus essays and reviews. We value linguistic and social centeredness, intensity of voice and variety in form, content, intent. "A controversy of poets." We do symposiums, also: #22, Rexroth; #25, Neruda.

Brenda Hillman, Yehuda Amichai, Robert Bly, Lucille Clifton, Bruce Weigl.

Payment: two contributor's copies.

Copyright held by magazine; reverts to author upon request.

1971; 2/yr; 1,000

$12/yr; $5/ea; 40%

110 pp; 6¾ x 8¼

Ad rates: inquire

ISSN: 0736-4628

THE QUARTERLY

Gordon Lish, Ellen F. Torron, Rick Whitaker
201 E. 50th St.
New York, NY 10022
(212) 572-2128; 872-8231

Poetry, fiction, essays, humor. A wide-open venue with particular hospitality for the unaffiliated. Fastest, fairest readings.

Payment: varies.

Copyright held by **THE QUAR-TERLY**; reverts to author upon publication.
1987; 4/yr; 15,000
$40/yr ind & inst; $54/yr Canada ind & inst; $9.95/ea; 40%
256 pp; 5¼ x 8
Ads
ISSN: 0893-3103
Random House

QUARTERLY REVIEW OF LITERATURE

Contemporary Poetry Series
Theodore and Renee Weiss
26 Haslet Avenue
Princeton, NJ 08540
Poetry.

QRL, a new concept in poetry, publishes 4 to 6 prize-winning collections of poetry in each volume, chosen through international competition. Called "the most significant event in years" and "the best bargain in poetry" and applauded as "brilliant." Each issue includes: poetry, long poems, poetic plays, poetry translation, plus introductory essays, photographs, and biographies of each author.

Wislava Szymborska, David Schubert, Nancy Esposito, Larry Kramer, Julia Mishkin.

Payment: $1,000 per accepted manuscript. Reading period: May and November. Please write for more information, with SASE.

Reporting time: 2 months or less.
Copyright held by QRL.
1943; 1/yr; 3–5,000
$20/2 volumes ind; $20/cloth volume inst; $10/ea; 10%
350 pp; 5½ x 8½
Ad rates: $200/page; $125/½ page
ISSN: 0033-5819

QUARTERLY WEST

C.F. Pinkerton, Regina Oost
317 Olpin Union
University of Utah
Salt Lake City, UT 84112
(801) 581-3938

Fiction, poetry, reviews, translation.

We try to publish the best in poetry and fiction, both mainstream and experimental. We conduct a biennial novella competition and also publish reviews and translations. We're not a western genre magazine. Biennial Noyella Competition, send S.A.S.E. for details. We accept multiple submissions (just tell us, please) and read MSS year-round.

Andre Dubus, Ron Carlson, Marvin Bell, Stephen Dobyns, William Stafford.

Payment: fiction $25–$300; poems

and reviews $50 each + 2 cop-
ies and 1 yr. sub.
Reporting time: 2–8 weeks.
Copyright held by magazine; reverts to author upon request.
1976; 2/yr; 1,000
$8.50/yr; $4.50/ea; 25%–40%
140 pp; 6 x 9
Ad rates: $150/page/4⅜ x 7⅞;
$85/½ page/4⅜ x 4
ISSN: 0194-4231

QUILT

Ishmael Reed, Al Young
660 13th Street, #203
Oakland, CA 94612-1241

Poetry, fiction, criticism, essays,
interviews, graphics/artwork.
QUILT is a book-length literary
journal which represents the
quality and diversity of contemporary writing. QUILT is multicultural in focus (featuring
Asian, Afro, Hispanic, European and Native American authors) and gives voice to new as
well as established talent.
Cecil Brown, Frank Chin, Adrienne Kennedy, Harryette
Mullen, Cyn Zarco.
Payment: none.
Copyright reverts to author.
1981; 1/yr; 1,000
$7.95/yr; $7.95/ea; 40%
200 pp; 5½ x 8½
No ads

ISSN: 0277-593X

QUIXOTE

Morris Edelson, Melissa Bondy
1812 Marshall
Houston, TX 77098
(713) 529-7944

Poetry, fiction, criticism, essays,
translation, interviews.
Social criticism/satire/mucking
around.
D. A. Levy, Pablo Neruda, Tuli
Kupferberg, Steve Kowitt, Curt
Johnson.
Payment: in copies.
Reporting time: 6 months.
Copyright held by author.
1965; 12/yr; 300
$15/yr; $2/ea
40–100 pp; 4 x 5–11 x 17

R

RACCOON

David Spicer
P.O. Box 111327
Memphis, TN 38111-1327
(901) 323-8858

Poetry, fiction, criticism, essays,
reviews, translation, interviews,
photographs.

A journal of contemporary literature, with poetry, fiction, essay.
Maurya Simon, Pattiann Rogers, David Romtvedt, Jay Meek, Frank Russell.
Payment: 1 year subscription/poetry; $50/prose, 1 copy.
Reporting time: 6 weeks–3 months.
Copyright reverts to author upon publication.
1977; 3/yr; 500
$12.50/yr; $5/ea; 40%
ISSN: 0148-0162
Small Press Distribution, EBSCO, Faxon

RAG MAG, Black Hat Press

Beverly Voldseth, Editor, Publisher
Box 12
Goodhue, MN 55027
(612) 923-4590
Poetry, fiction, essays, reviews, plays, photographs, graphics/artwork.
Small lit mag. No special focus.
Pat McKinnon, Joan Wolf, Lynne Burgess, Greg Grummer, Karen Wee.
Payment: in copies.
Reporting time: 1 week–2 months, reads Nov. 1–Feb. 1
Copyright held by magazine; reverts to author upon publication.

1982; 2/yr; 150
$10/yr. $5/ea
64 pp; 5½ x 8½
Ad rates: $35/page/4 x 7⅜; $20/½ page/4 x 3½; $10/¼ page/4 x 1¾
ISSN: 0742-2768

RAMBUNCTIOUS REVIEW

M. Dellutri, N. Lennon, R. Goldman, E. Hausler
1221 West Pratt Boulevard
Chicago, IL 60626
Poetry, fiction, photographs, graphics/artwork.
We are an annual literary arts magazine devoted to the publication of new and established writers and artists. We sponsor annual poetry and fiction contests and theme issues. Our next issue is focused on "Heartland Angst."
Elizabeth Eddy, Richard Calisch, Hugh Fox, Richard Kostelanetz.
Payment: 2 issues.
Copyright held by magazine; reverts to author upon publication.
1986; 1/yr; 450
$10/3 issues; $4/sample
48 pp; 7 x 10
No ads
Ingram Periodicals

RARITAN

R. Poirier, Editor; Suzanne K.
  Hyman, Managing Editor
165 College Avenue
New Brunswick, NJ 08903
(908) 932-7887 or 7852
Criticism, essays, reviews, poetry,
  fiction. A comprehensive cri-
  tique of contemporary culture.
Stanley Cavell, Clifford Geertz,
  Vicki Hearne, Edward W. Said.
Payment: $100/article.
Reporting time: 2 months.
Copyright reverts to author in 6
  months.
1981; 4/yr; 3,500
$16/yr, $26/2 yrs ind; $20/yr,
  $30/2 yrs inst; $5/ea; $6/back
  issues; 40%–50%
160 pp; 6 x 9
Ad rates: $275/page/4½ x 7½
ISSN: 0275-1607
DeBoer, Ingram

THE REAPER/STORY LINE
PRESS

Robert McDowell
Three Oaks Farm
Brownsville, OR 97327-9718
(503) 466-5352

RED BASS

Jay Murphy
216 Chartres St.
New Orleans, LA 70130

(504) 522-7758
Poetry, essays, graphics/artwork,
  criticism, reviews, translation,
  interviews, fiction, plays, photographs.
RED BASS seeks to illuminate
  the interface between art and
  politics with a provocative mix
  of visual art/literature/music and
  reviews, with a special emphasis on translations and international work. We have published
  emerging artists and those, such
  as John Cage or Allen Ginsberg, whose reputations are as-
  sured.
Kathy Acker, Etel Adnan, James
  Purdy, Carolee Schneemann,
  Sue Coe.
Payment: in copies, sometimes in
  cash as funds allow.
Reporting time: 3 months.
Copyright held by magazine; reverts to author upon publication.
1981; 2/yr; 2,000
$20/3 issues; $35 inst & overseas;
  $7.50–10 ea; 40%
150 pp; 8½ x 11
Ad rates: $300/page; $175/½
  page; $75/third page page/4 x
  5¼
ISSN: 0883-0126
Ubiquity, Fine Print Distributors,
  Last Gasp, Armadillo

THE RED CEDAR REVIEW

Susan Parker
Department of English

325 Morrill Hall
Michigan State University
East Lansing, MI 48824
(517) 355-7570

Poetry, fiction, graphics/artwork
photography.

Take risks, avoid the mainstream;
love, sex, death as always.
Oddities. Humor. Originality
comes first. SASE required.

Carol Cavallaro, Craig Cotter,
Lyn Lifshin, Hannah Stein.

$10/yr; $5/ea; $2/sample, 40%
Faxon, EBSCO

THE REDNECK REVIEW OF LITERATURE

Penelope Reedy
P.O. Box 730
Twin Falls, Idaho 83303
(208) 734-6653

Fiction, essays, poetry, book reviews.

REDNECK is a magazine of contemporary western American
literature involved in the devel-
opment of the region's literature
through publishing high quality
fiction, poetry, essays, and criticism.

Edward Abbey, Clay Reynolds,
Charlotte Wright, Florence
Blanchard, Leslie Leek, Harald
Wyndham, William Studebaker.

Payment: in copies.

Copyright reverts to author.

1975; 2/yr
$14/yr; $35/3 yrs; $7/ea
100 pp; 8½ x 11. (Fall 89 is tape
and 8½ x 11 booklet.)

REPRESENTATIONS

Stephen Greenblatt, Svetlana Al-
phers, Co-Chairs, Editorial
Board

English Department
University of California
Berkeley, CA 94720
(415) 642-9044

Criticism, essays, translations.

REPRESENTATIONS publishes
critical essays on interdisciplinary topics; disciplines included
are literature, political theory,
art history, and anthropology,
and roughly 50 percent of the
work published is literary criticism. Of the balance, literary
methodology is a substantial
influence in essays in other
fields such as history, political
theory, anthropology, etc.

Natalie Zemon Davis, D. A.
Miller, Louis Montrose, Sabine
MacCormack, Peter Stallybrass,
Audrey Jaffe, Robert Post, Jen-
nifer Nedelsky, Michael Rogin,
Richard Slotkin.

Payment: none.

Reporting time: 6–8 weeks.

Copyright held by University of
California Press.

1983; 4/yr; 2,200
$22/yr ind; $44/yr inst
152 pp; 7 x 9¾
Ad rates: $150/page
ISSN: 0734-6018
B. DeBoer, others

RESONANCE

Evan and Patty Pritchard
P.O. Box 215
Beacon, NY 12508
(914) 838-1217

Essays, graphics/artwork, poetry, review, photographs, fiction, interviews, music and humor.

RESONANCE is a journal of all forms of creative expression inspired by personal spiritual experience. It strives to create a popular forum for communication between artists, scientists and the spiritual community, however it does not promote or denigrate any other organizations, spiritual, educational or otherwise. It is a forum for individual spiritual insight.

Heather Hughes-Calero, Susan Hanniford Crowley. Interviews with Chris Williamson, Madeleine L'Engle, Arun Gandhi, Pete Seeger, David Lanz, Joan Houston, others.

Payment: 1 copy.
Reporting time: 8 weeks.
Copyright held by Evan and Patty Pritchard—compilation only; reverts to author upon publication.

1987; quarterly; 2,000
$12/yr; $3/ea; 40%
52 pp; 8½ x 11
$100/½ page; $50/¼ page; $25/⅛ page
Ubiquity Dist., NY; Homing Pigeon, TX; Armadillo, CA; L-S, San Franciso; Book Tech Dist.; New Leaf Dist. (USA)

RESPONSE: A Contemporary Jewish Review

Bennett Graff
27 W. 20 St. 9th fl.
New York, NY 10011
(212) 675-1168

REVERSE

Jan McLaughlin and Bruce Weber
19 W. 73rd Street #3A
New York, NY 10023
(212) 787-4056

Essays, poetry.

Devoted almost exclusively to essays by poets focusing on issues relevant to poetry. Themes of revent issues: censorship of literature; state of poetry in Florida; forgotten poets. Planning an issue on problems in translation. Includes avante-garde and academic points of view. Often deals with controversial subjects. A poetry journal that thinks.

Carolyn Forche, Barbara Holley, Yvonne Sapia, Jan McLaughlin, Bruce Weber, Lenny Della-Roca.

Payment: $20 upon publication.

Reporting time: 3–4 months.

Copyright held by author.

1988; 2/yr; 300

$6/yr; $3.50/ea; 40%

16 pp; 8½ x 11

$50/¼ page; $25/⅛ page

REVIEW

Alfred J. Mac Adam, Daniel Shapiro, Editors

Americas Society

680 Park Avenue

New York, NY 10021

(212) 249-8950

Fiction, poetry, criticism, essays, reviews, translations, interviews, articles on visual arts and music.

REVIEW presents the best of Latin American literature in English translation. It contains a review section as well as major articles on the Latin American visual and performing arts.

Payment: $100 and up.

Copyright held by the Americas Society (present); Center for Inter-American Relations (back issues).

1967; 2/yr; 5,000

$14/yr ind; $22/yr inst; $7/ea

100 pp; 8½ x 11

Ad rates: $700/page/7¾ x 9¾; $400/½ page/5 x 7

Total Circulation Services (Hackensack, NJ); Ingram Periodicals (Nashville, TN); Inland Book Co. (East Haven, CT)

THE REVIEW OF CONTEMPORARY FICTION

John O'Brien

5700 College Road

Lisle, IL 60532

Criticism, essays, reviews, translation, interviews.

Each issue is devoted to criticism on one or two contemporary novelists.

Upcoming issues are devoted to Angela Carter, Manuel Puig, and William H. Gass.

Gilbert Sorrentino, Robert Creeley, Paul Metcalf, Carlos Fuentes, Toby Olson.

Reporting time: 2 weeks.

Copyright held by magazine; reverts to author upon publication.

1981; 3/yr; 2,800

$15/yr ind; $22/yr inst; $8/ea; 10%–40%

200 pp; 6 x 9

Ad rates: $150/page/5 x 7½
ISSN: 0276-0045
DeBoer, Inland Book Company,
  Small Press Distribution

RFD

Short Mountain Collective
P.O. Box 68
Liberty, TN 37095
(615) 536-5176

Poetry, fiction, essays, reviews,
  interviews, photographs, graph-
  ics/artwork.
RFD focuses on rural gay men in
  related areas of human growth
  and consciousness and is an
  open forum for new ideas, radical views and controversial issues. The scope includes
  articles on alternative lifestyles,
  homesteading skills, collectives,
  gardening, cooking, contact
  letters, poetry, fiction, prisoner
  section, book reviews and
  graphics.
Michael Mason, Harry Hay, Bru
  Dye, Louise Hay, Robin Walden.
Payment: 1 copy of issue published in.
Reporting time: 1–6 months.
Copyright held by author.
1974; 4/yr; 2,700
$22/yr ind 1st class; $15/yr ind
  2nd class; $17/yr inst; $4.25/ea;
  40%

72 pp; 8½ x 11
Ad rates: $350/page/8½ x 11;
  $185/½ page/4¼ x 11 or 8½ x
  5½; $98/¼ page/4¼ x 5½₁₂
ISSN: 0149-709X

RHINO

8403 W. Normal Ave.
Niles, IL 60648
or
Martha Vetreace
1157 E. 56th St.
Chicago, IL 60637
Send 3–5 poems to RHINO or to
  Martha Vertreace. The reading
  period is January to June. Payment is one copy. Sample copies are available at $5.00 plus
  .90 postage. Back issues are
  available for $3 plus postage.
  Please no sentimental verse.
  Strong free verse with fresh
  images!
Copyright held by author.
1976; 1/yr; 500
$5 + .90 postage/ea; 40%
90+ pp; 5½ x 8⅜
No ads

RHODODENDRON

Steven Jacobsen
879 Bell St.
East Palo Alto, CA 94303
(415) 324-0206

Poetry, fiction, reviews, graphics/
artwork.

RHODODENDRON groups
widely differing types of writing
together, in the hopes of effect-
ing a cumulative dynamism and
dialogue. Anything is possible
in **RHODODENDRON**. The
magazine itself is only a vessel
or frame.

Brian Bedard, Laurel Speer, Greg
Boyd, Dan Raphael, Richard
Kostelanetz, Steve Richmond,
Wanda Coleman.

Payment: 3 copies per contributor
upon publication.

Copyright held by Steven Jacobsen; reverts to author upon publication.

1984; 4/yr; 200+
$15/yr ind & inst; $3.50/ea; 40%
40 pp; 8½ x 5½
Ad rates: variable

RIVER CITY (formerly
MEMPHIS STATE REVIEW)

Sharon Bryan
English Department
Memphis State University
Memphis, TN 38152
(901) 678-8888

Poetry, fiction, essays, interviews.
No novel excerpts.

The magazine sponsors the River
City Writing Awards in fiction:
1st prize $2,000; 2nd prize

$500; 3rd prize $300. Send
S.A.S.E. for details.

Fred Busch, Marvin Bell, Mona
Van Duyn, Pattiann Rogers,
Luisa Valenzuela, John Updike.

Payment: varies.
Reporting time: 1 month.
Copyright reverts to author.
1980; 2/yr; 1,000
$6/yr; $4/ea
100 pp; 6 x 9
$40/page

RIVER STYX

Jennifer Atkinson, Quincy Troupe,
Editors; Andrew Haber, Managing Editor
14 South Euclid
St. Louis, MO 63108
(314) 361-0043

Poetry, fiction, interviews, photographs, graphics/artwork.

RIVER STYX is a multicultural
journal of poetry, prose and
graphic arts publishing works
by both established and up and
coming writers and artists, significant for their originality,
quality, and craftsmanship.

Sharon Olds, Grace Paley, Derek
Walcott, Marilyn Hacker,
Howard Nemerov.

Payment: $8/page for literature:
$10/page for photographs or
drawings.

Reporting time: submissions read only in September and October. Copyright held by Big River Association; reverts to author upon publication.
1975; 3/yr; 1,000
$14/yr ind; $24/yr inst; $5/ea; 33%
112 pp; 5½ x 8½
Exchange ads
ISSN: 0149-8851
Ingram

RIVERWIND

C. A. Dubielak, Audrey Naffziger
Hocking College
Nelsonville, OH 45768
(614) 753-3591 ex 2375
Poetry, fiction, non-fiction.
RIVERWIND is more interested in publishing the new poet, the good poet, the challenging, the beautiful, the true as opposed to the well-established and/or predictable. Quality, please.
Simon Percik, James Riley.
Payment: copies.
Reporting time: 4–6 months.
Copyright: Author.
1982; annual; 200
$3.50; $3.50; 60%
80; 6 x 9

ROHWEDDER: International Journal of Literature and Art

H.J. Schact, Nancy Antell, Robert Dassanowsky-Harris
P.O. Box 29490
Los Angeles, CA 90029
(213) 256-5083
Poetry, fiction, reviews, translation, interviews, photographs, graphics/artwork.
A journal of international literature and art, featuring poetry and prose in original language and English translation, black and white photography and graphics, reviews and essays on pictoral and theater arts and events in the Los Angeles area and globally. We are also interested in language oriented work, experimental forms, theoretical writings on postmodernism, open text work and new lyric poetry.
Sarah Kirsch, Pia Tafdrup, Peter Schneider, Juan Felipe Herrera, Susana Thénon, Simon Perchik.
Payment: in copies.
Reporting time: 3 month.
Copyright held by magazine; reverts to author upon publication.
1986; 2/yr; 800–1,000
$12/3 issues ind; $16/3 issues inst; $4/ea
50 pp; 8½ x 11
Ad rates: $300/page/8½ x 11; $170/½ page/5½ x 8½; $90/¼ page/4¼ x 5½; $50/2¾ x 4¼; $30/1¾ x 4¼
ISSN: 0892-6956

S

SAGUARO

Charles Tatum
315 Douglass Bldg
The University of Arizona
Tucson, AZ 85721
(602) 621-7551

Fiction, poetry, essays, auto and biography, no reviews.

Bilingual magazine dedicated to writing by and about Chicano/ Latinos. **SAGUARO** seeks works by both established and unknown writers.

Bernice Zamora, Sandra Cisneros, Joel Huerta, Carmen Tafolla, Maria Herrera-Sobek, Max Aguilera-Hellweg.

Payment: $60 story/essay; $25 poem, plus copies.

Reporting time: variable.

Copyright held by Mexican American Studies & Research Center; reverts to author upon publication.

1984; 1/yr; 500
$8/2 issues; $5/ea.; 20–40%
100; 6 x 9
No ads
ISSN: 0885-5013

ST. ANDREWS/SANDHILLS REVIEW

Steven Smith, Editor
Sandhills Community College
2700 Airport Rd.
Pinehurst, NC 28374

Poetry, fiction, plays, translation, essays, reviews, interviews.

ST. ANDREWS REVIEW publishes fiction, poetry and essays of highest quality from both established writers and promising new authors from all over the U.S. and abroad.

Fred Chappell, Hiroaki Sato, Soichi Furuta, Yukio Mishima, Desmond Egan.

Payment: one copy.

Copyright held by magazine; reverts to author upon publication.

1972; 2/yr; 300
$7/ea; 30%
100 pp; 6 x 9
Ad rates: $200/page/5 x 7; $100/½ page/2½ x 3½; $50/¼ page/1¼ x 1¾
ISSN: 0036-2751

SALMAGUNDI

Robert and Peggy Boyers, Editors; Thomas S.W. Lewis, Associate Editor
Skidmore College
Saratoga Springs, NY 12866
(518) 584-5000, ext 2302

Poetry, fiction, criticism, essays, reviews, translation, interviews.

SALMAGUNDI is an international quarterly of the humanities and social sciences publishing essays and book reviews on literature, contemporary politics, film, dance, and current ideas. General issues also feature original fiction, poetry, photographs and interviews.

George Steiner, Conor Cruise O'Brien, Nadine Gordimer, Christopher Lasch, Susan Sontag, Seamus Heaney.

Payment: none.

Reporting time: 1–5 months.

Copyright held by Skidmore; reverts to author upon publication.

1965; 4/yr; 5,600

$12/yr ind; $20/yr inst; $5/ea; negotiable

160–230 pp; 8½ x 5½

Ad rates: $150/page/4 x 7; $85/½ page/4 x 3½

B.DeBoer, Periodicals In Particular (U.K.)

SALTHOUSE
A Geopoetics Journal

DeWitt Clinton

800 W. Main

Department of English

University of Wisconsin

Whitewater, WI 53190

(414) 472-1036

Poetry, fiction, reviews.

Interest is in poetry, fiction and reviews/criticism which is influenced by a sense of anthropology, geography or history.

Richard Shelton, Jeanne Larsen, Judith Roche, Sybil Woods-Smith, Lynn Shoemaker.

Payment: in copies.

Not reading MSS in 1991. Will announce call for MSS in Poets & Writers in 1992.

Reporting time: 2–3 months.

Copyright held by author.

1975; irregular; 300

$6/ea; back issue is free; 40%

96 pp; 5¼ x 8½

Ad rates: $30/page; $15/½ page

ISSN: 0737-5506

SALT LICK

James Haining

1804 East 38½ Street

Austin, TX 78722

Poetry, fiction, essays, photographs, graphics/artwork.

A thrilling publication since 1969.

Gerald Burns, Robert Trammell, Robert Creeley, Martha King, Susan Firer.

Payment: in copies.

Reporting time: 2–3 weeks.

Copyright reverts to author.

1969; 2/yr; 1,500

$6/yr; $3/ea; 40%
64 pp; 8½ x 11

SAMISDAT

Merritt Clifton
456 Monroe Turnpike
Monroe, CT 06468
(203) 452-0446

Fiction, poetry, essays, reviews, original art.

Environmentally aware, socially and politically conscious litera-ture intended to encourage and inform an audience of activists. (We do not encourage blind submissions–and we are NOT interested in mere rewrites of the daily news.)

Ram Challa, Elliot Richman, Mir-iam Sagan, Robert Harrison.

Payment: 2 complimentary copies.

Reporting time: as soon as possible–two minutes to two weeks.

Copyright reverts to authors.

1973; Quarterly (one regular issue plus four special items usually chapbooks per year); 300

$15/250 pages; $2.50

40–60; 8½ x 5⅕

ISSN: 0226-840X

SAN FERNANDO POETRY JOURNAL

Richard Cloke, Editor; Shirley Rodecker, Managing Editor; Lori C. Smith, Pub. Editor

Kent Publications, Inc.
18301 Halstead Street
Northridge, CA 91325
(818) 349-2080

Poetry.

Seeks to fuse diverse elements of contemporaneity, ranging from evocation of scientific and tech-nical advances–cosmology, sub-atomic inner space–cyber-punk S.F.–with a pronounced interest in poetry of social protest which illuminates the ills of our time, with special emphasis on the perils of nuclear warfare.

Stan Proper, Stratton F. Caldwell, Leigh Hunt, Jack Bernier, Phyl-lis Gershator.

Payment: in copies, discounts on subs.

Reporting time: 2–3 weeks.

Copyright reverts to author.

1978; 4/yr; 500

$10/yr; $3/ea; 20%–30%

100 pp; 5½ x 8½

Ad rates: $50/page/4½ x 7; $25/½ page/4½ x 3½

ISSN: 0196-2884

SAN FRANCISCO REVIEW OF BOOKS

Elgy Gillespie
1109 Geary Street
San Francisco, CA 94109
(415) 771-1252

Criticism, essays, reviews, interviews, graphics/artwork.

A literary review, focusing on one to three themes per issue, with in-depth interviews and articles relating to literature and publishing. Twenty to thirty titles reviewed, with emphasis on new books, including history and non-fiction. Also reviews of nationwide cultural events—dance, art, theatre, film. Open to diverse political opinions.

Ursula K. Le Guin, James D. Houston, M.F.K. Fisher, Jeremy Larner, Larry Bensky, Isadora Alman, Bharati Mukherjee, Isabel Allende, Terry Eagleton.

Payment: variable, in pay and copies; also, trade at local establishments.

Reporting time: 6 weeks–2 months.

Copyright held by magazine; reverts to author upon request.

1975; 4/yr; 5,500

$15/yr ind; $20/yr inst; $4.00/ea; 40%

56 pp; 8¾ x 11

Ad rates: $950/page; $600/ ½ page/7 x 4⅞; $400/¼ page/3⅜ x 4⅞

ISSN: 0194-0724

THE SANTA MONICA REVIEW

Jim Krusoe
1900 Pico Blvd
Santa Monica, CA 90405

Fiction, poetry, essays.

Guy Davenport, Charles Baxter, Robley Wilson, Kathleen Spivack.

Payment: copies.

Reporting time: One to three months.

Copyright first serial rights only.

1988; 2/yr; 1,100

410/yr; $6

128 + ; 8 x 5

Varies

ISSN: 0899-9848

Armadillo, Ubiquity

SATORI

Gary Green, Pat Sims
P.O. Box 318
Tivoli, NY 12583
(914) 757-4443

Fiction, interviews, poetry, essays, photographs, graphics/artwork.

We provide a forum for the work and ideas of artists and writers, both established and previously unpublished, focusing on those from the mid-Hudson Valley region of New York. We are selective in our choices of work, seeking new and unique ideas in fiction, non-fiction, art, and photography. Also featured is a Q & A interview each issue with an artist or writer from the region.

Mikhail Horowitz, Dick Higgins,
Cynde Gregory, Alison
Knowles, Robert Mezey, A.D.
Coleman.
Payment: in copies, upon publication.
Copyright held by magazine; reverts to author upon publication.
1988; 4/yr; 630
$8/yr; $2/ea; 40%; 50% if nonreturnable
20 pp; 8½ x 11
Ad rates: $100/page; $75/½ page;
$50/¼ page
ISSN: 0898-3011

SE LA VIE WRITER'S JOURNAL

Rosalie Avara
P.O. Box 371371
El Paso, TX 79937
(915) 595-2625

Contest winning poems, essays,
short stories, cartoons, book
reviews, articles about poetry,
writing.
A quarterly dedicated to encouraging novice writers, poets and
artists by giving them a chance
to get published and receiving
cash prizes.
Philip Eisenberg, Mary A.
Fowler, Carole C. Koch.
Payment: one copy of issue in
which work appears.

Reporting time: Articles: 2–4
weeks; Contest entries: 90 days.
Copyright: Rosalie Avara, Editor/
Publisher of RIO GRANDE
PRESS.
1987; quarterly; 300+
$14/yr; $4
80+; 8½ x 5
$25/page; $15/½ page; $10/¼
page; $5/⅛ page

THE SEATTLE REVIEW

Donna Gerstenberger
Padelford Hall, GN-30
University of Washington
Seattle, WA 98195
(206) 543-9865, 543-2690

Poetry, fiction, essays, interviews
with writers.
THE SEATTLE REVIEW is a
journal of poetry and prose published twice yearly. We try to
achieve a balance in our pages
between the work of nationally-
known writers and that of
younger writers of promise.
Rita Dove, W.P. Kinsella, Ursula
Le Guin, William Stafford,
Frances McCue, Tina Koyama.
Payment: varies.
Reporting time: 3–4 months; 6
months summer.
Copyright held by magazine; reverts to author upon publication.
$8/yr; $16/2 yrs; $4.50/ea

100 pp; 6 x 9
Ad rates: $90/page/5 x 7; $50/½
  page/5 x 4½
ISSN: 0147-6629

SEEMS
Karl Elder
Lakeland College
Box 359
Sheboygan, WI 53082-0359
(414) 565-3871
Poetry, fiction, essays.
Louis McKee, Scott Owens, Gary
  Pacernick, Katharine Privett,
  Sapphire.
Payment: a copy.
Reporting time: 4–8 weeks.
Copyright held by Karl Elder; re-
  verts to author upon publica-
  tion.
1971; irreg; 350
$12/4 issues; $3/ea
40 pp; 8½ x 7
ISSN: 0095-1730

SEMIOTEXT(E)
Sylvere Lotringer, Jim Fleming
P.O. Box 568
Brooklyn, NY 11211
(718) 387-6471
Fiction, criticism, essays, transla-
  tion, interview, photographs.
Contemporary radical cultural pol-
  itics, "movement" literatures.
  Also sponsors "Foreign

Agents," small book series promoting contemporary radical
  politics and culture, philosophy
  and human sciences.
Michel Foucault, Roland Barthes,
  Felix Guattari, Jean Baudrillard,
  Gilles Deleuze.
Payment: none.
Reporting time: 3 months.
Copyright reverts to author upon
  publication.
1974; irreg; 8,000
$18/3 issues ind; $36/3 issues inst;
  $10/ea; 40%
320 pp; 7 x 9
ISSN: 0093-5779

SENECA REVIEW
Deborah Tall
Hobart and William Smith Col-
  leges
Geneva, NY 14456
(315) 781-3364
Poetry, criticism, translation, in-
  terviews.
Twice a year the **SENECA RE-
  VIEW** publishes poetry and
  prose about poetry, with a spe-
  cial interest in translation.
Seamus Heaney, Rita Dove, Den-
  ise Levertov, Hayden Carruth,
  Cornelius Eady.
Payment: 2 copies.
Reporting time: 4–10 weeks.
Copyright held by Hobart and

William Smith Colleges; reverts to author upon publication.
1970; 2/yr; 600
$8/yr; $15/2 yrs; $5/ea; 40%
90 pp; 5½ x 8½
Ad rates: $75/page/5 x 8
ISSN: 0037-2145
Small Press Traffic

SENSATIONS

David Messineo
2 Radio Avenue A5
Secaucus, NJ 07094

Poetry, fiction, photographs, graphics/artwork.
Payment: none.
Reporting time: 2 months after deadline.
Copyright held by author.
1987; 2/yr; 200
$12/2; $6/ea
50 pp; 8½ x 11
Ad rates: $100/page; $50/½ page; $25/¼ page

SEQUOIA

Annie Finch
Storke Publications Building
Stanford, CA 94305
(415) 362-3420

Poetry, fiction, criticism, interviews, photographs, art.
We are eclectic but like interesting and beautiful language. Feminist, experimental, and new-formalist work is welcome. We are not receptive to typical generic "workshop" writing.
Rita Dove, Seamus Heaney, Susan Howe, Janet Lewis, James Merrill.
Payment: in copies.
Reporting time: 2 months.
Author retains rights.
1892; 2/yr; 500
$10/yr; $5/ea
80–105 pp; 5½ x 8
Ad rates: $100/page; $60/½ page
L & S Distributors

THE SEWANEE REVIEW

George Core
University of the South
Sewanee, TN 37375
(615) 598-1245

Poetry, fiction, criticism, essays, reviews.
America's oldest literary quarterly publishes original fiction, poetry, essays on literary and related subjects, book reviews and book notices for well-educated readers who appreciate good American and English literature.
Hayden Carruth, Louis D. Rubin, Jr., George Garrett, Donald Davie, Malcolm Cowley, L.C. Knights.
Payment: $10–$12/printed page; 60¢/line for poetry.
Reporting time: 4 weeks.

Copyright held by author.
1892; 4/yr; 3,500
$15/yr ind; $20/yr inst; $6/ea
192 pp; 6 x 9
Ad rates: $175/page/4¼ x 7;
$110/½ page/4¼ x 3⅜; $80/¼
page
ISSN: 0037-3052

SHENANDOAH

Dabney Stuart, Editor; Lynn
Williams, Managing Editor
P.O. Box 722
Lexington, VA 24450
(703) 463-8765 (9–12 noon)
Poetry, fiction, essays, transla-
tions, interviews, photographs.
Consider work from both new and
established writers. Annual
prizes in fiction, poetry and the
essay.
Seamus Heaney, Northrop Frye,
Robert Wrigley, Lisa Sandlin,
Shelby Hearon.
Payment: poetry: $2.50/line;
prose: $25/page.
Reporting time: 2–4 weeks.
Copyright held by magazine; re-
verts to author upon publica-
tion.
1950; 4/yr; 2,100
$11/yr; $3.50/ea; 50%
100 pp; 6 x 9
Ad rates: $200/page/4½ x 7;
$100/½ page/4½ x 3½
ISSN: 0037-3583

Armadillo, Fine Print Distributors,
Ubiquity.

SHOOTING STAR REVIEW

Sandra Gould Ford
7123 Race Street
Pittsburgh, PA 15208
(412) 731-7039
Poetry, fiction, essays, reviews,
photographs, graphics/artwork.
SHOOTING STAR REVIEW is
an award-winning illustrated
quarterly that uses the arts to
explore the African-American
experience. **Guidelines available with SASE. Sample copy
($3) is sent with next bulk
mailing unless 9 x 12 envelope
w/$1 postage included.**
Kristan Hunter, Dennis Brutus,
Reginald McKnight, Jerry
Ward, Toi Derricote, Doris Jean
Austin, Marita Golden.
Payment: fiction $30; essays $10
and up; poems $8.
Copyright held by **SHOOTING
STAR REVIEW**; reverts to
author upon publication.
1987; 4/yr; 1,500
$10/yr ind; $15/yr inst; $2.95/ea;
20% consignment, 50% outright
purchase
44 pp; 8½ x 11
Ad rates: $750/page; $425/½
page; $210/¼ page
ISSN: 0892-1407

THE SHORT STORY REVIEW

Dwight Gabbard, Stephen Wood-
hams, Beth Overson, Catherine
Jacob, Melinda Dart, George
Knuepfel

450 Irving St. #4

San Francisco, CA 94122

Fiction.

Founded in 1983, **THE SHORT
STORY REVIEW** publishes
works of fiction.

Molly Giles, Amy Tan, Richard
Cortez Day, William Heinesen,
Sara Vogan.

Payment: none.

Reporting time: 8–12 weeks.

Copyright held by author.

1983; 4/yr; 1,500

$10/yr; $2.50/ea; 40%

20 pp; 10 x 13

Ad rates: $432/page/10 x 13½;
$254/½ page/10 x 6⅝; $149/¼
page/4¹¹/₁₆ x 6⅝

ISSN: 0741-0786

L-S Distributors (San Francisco);
Armadillo (Venice, CA)

SIBYL-CHILD

Nancy Arbuthnot, Saundra Maley

709 Dahlia St. NW

Washington, DC 20012

(202) 723-5468

Established in 1974, **SIBYL-
CHILD** has just gone out of
print. Back issues of

chapbooks—fiction, poetry,
translations—available at $3.50.

Doris Mozer, David Hall, Ann
Slayton, Peter Van Egmond,
William Griffiths, Nan Fry.

5½ x 8

ISSN: 0161-715X

THE SIGNAL

Joan Silva, David Chorlton

P.O. Box 67

Emmett, ID 83617

(208) 365-5812

Poetry, fiction, criticism, essays,
reviews, translation, interviews,
photographs, graphics/artwork.

We would like to create a forum
for inter-disciplinary work,
bridging between literature, art,
music; and ecological, socio/po-
litical concerns. We encourage
submissions in the socio/scien-
tific area; examples would be
archeologic, rare travel experi-
ences/philosophic essays on almost anything, but quality of
thought and expression should
be rigorous and must have literary merit.

Wanda Coleman, B. Z. Niditch,
Jose Bermudez, Alexander
Blok, Robert Peters, Philip K.
Jason, William Studebaker,
Judith Searle, Dick Bakken,
Effie Mihopoulous.

Payment: in copies.

Copyright held by **THE SIGNAL**; reverts to author upon publication.

1987; 2/yr; 425

$10/yr; $6/ea; 40%

50+ pp; 8½ x 11

Ad rates: $100/page/8½ x 11; $65/½ page/8½ x 5½; $35/¼ page/4¼ x 2¾

SILVERFISH REVIEW

Rodger Moody

P.O. Box 3541

Eugene, OR 97403

(503) 344-5060

Poetry, short short stories, reviews, essays, translations, interviews, photographs, annual poetry chapbook contest.

The only criterion for selection of material is quality. In future issues **SILVERFISH REVIEW** wants to showcase essays on creative process as well as translations of poetry from Europe and South America. **SILVERFISH REVIEW** also sponsors an annual poetry chapbook contest.

Ivan Argüelles, Lauren Mesa, Floyd Skloot, Enid Shomer, Robert Ward.

Payment: 5 copies, and $5 per page (when funding permits).

Reporting time: 2–12 weeks.

Copyright held by author.

1979; irreg; 750

$9/3 issues ind; $12/3 issues inst; $3/ea plus $1 postage; 40%

48 pp; 5½ x 8½

Ad rates: $50/page/4¼ x 7½; $25/½ page/4¼ x 4

ISSN: 0164-1085

Spring Church Book Company (chapbooks only), The Faxon Co., Inc; EBSCO; Boley International

SINISTER WISDOM

Elana Dykewomon

P.O. Box 3252

Berkeley, CA 94703

Poetry, fiction, criticism, essays, reviews, interviews, plays, photographs, graphics/artwork by lesbians.

A lesbian/feminist journal of art, literature and politics founded in 1976 by Harriet Desmoines and Catherine Nicholson, passed on in 1981 to Michelle Cliff and Adrienne Rich, in 1983 to Melanie Kaye/Kaye/Kantrowitz and in 1986 to the current editor.

The primary commitment of the magazine is to publish creative work by lesbians from a broad range of racial, ethnic, cultural and class perspectives.

Sapphire, Gloria Anzaldva, Marilyn Frye, Adrienne Rich,

Chrystos, Winn Gilmore, Judith Katz.
Payment: 2 copies.
Reporting time: 6–9 months.
Copyright held by author.
1976; 3–4/yr; 3,000
$17/yr ind; $30/yr inst; $6/ea; 40%
144 pp; 5½ x 8½
Ad rates: $150/page/4½ x 7; $75/½ page/4½ x 3¼; $40/¼ page/2 x 3½
ISSN: 0196-1853
Inland, Bookpeople

SIPAPU

Noel Peattie
23311 County Road 88
Winters, CA 95694
(916) 752-1032

Reviews, interviews, conference news.

Newsletter for librarians, editors, and collectors interested in dissent (feminist, Third World, pacifist, etc.) literature, together with small press poetry. Emphasis on peace and environmental concerns; all must have a print emphasis.

Karl Kempton, Loss P. Glazier, Mary Zeppa, John Daniel, Harry Polkinhorn.
Payment: 5¢/word.
Reporting time: 5 months.

Copyright held by editor; reverts to author upon publication.
1970; 450
$8/yr; $4/ea
36 pp; 8½ x 11
No ads
ISSN: 0037-5837
EBSCO, Faxon, Popular Subscription Service, Turner

SLOW MOTION MAGAZINE

Ona Gritz, Laura Hennessey-Desena, Anne Makeever, Zack Rogow
24 Cornelia St. #3
New York, NY 10014
(212) 228-1359

Poetry, translation (poetry).

SLOW MOTION is a poetry magazine interested in publishing new poets with social interests. We are interested in giving new poets exposure: both local and from other parts of the country.

Ruth Stone, Harry Stessel, Jack Nestor, John Oliver Simon.
Payment: in copies.
Copyright reverts to author upon publication.
1986; 2/yr; 250
$6/yr; $3/ea; 40%
40 pp; 5½ x 8½
No ads

THE SMALL POND MAGAZINE

Napoleon St. Cyr
P.O. Box 664
Stratford, CT 06497
(203) 378-4066

Poetry, fiction, essays, reviews, graphics/artwork.

Features contemporary poetry by new and established writers, but also uses short prose pieces of many genres, plus some art work—black and white only.

Renne McQuilkin, John O'Brien, Heather Tosteson, Barbara S. Parish, H.R. Coursen.

Payment: 2 copies.

Reporting time: 10–30 days, longer in summer.

Copyright held by N. St. Cyr.

1964; 3/yr; 300

$7/yr; $3.00/ea; inquire

40 pp; 5½ x 8½

Ad rates: $40/page/4½ x 7½; $25/½ page/4½ x 3½; $15/¼ page/4½ x 2¼

ISSN: 0031-721X

SNAKE NATION REVIEW

Roberta George, Pat Miller, Janice Daugharty
2920 West Oak
Valdosta, GA 31602
(912) 242-1503

Poetry, fiction, essays, photographs, graphics/artwork.

SNAKE NATION REVIEW is a regional quarterly, founded in the fall of 1989. We encourage writing that addresses all areas of life. We look for good writing that encounters change and character; all subjects are acceptable if it meets our one requirement–well written.

David Kirby, Starkey Flythe, Janet Burroway, Peter Meinke.

Payment: Prize money (editors' choice); 2 copies per contribution.

Reporting time: 6 months.

Copyright: Snake Nation Press.

1989; 2/yr; 500

$12/individual-$20/institution; $6; 40%

100; 6 x 9

$100/page; $50/½ page; $25/¼ page

ISSN: 1046-5006

SONORA REVIEW

Martha Ostheimer, Laurie Schorr, Joan Marcus
Department of English
University of Arizona
Tucson, AZ 85721
(602) 621-8077 or (602) 621-3880

Poetry, fiction, reviews, translation, interviews, criticism, essays.

We're looking for the liveliest new writing we can get our hands

on, including experimental and non-conformist work. Most issues are general in nature, though recent special features have profiled "Crossing Borders: Writing from Alternative Traditions" and "Voices from the Southwestern Landscape."
Jane Miller, David Foster Wallace, Ingrid Smith, Ray A. Young Bear, Tristan Tzara.
Payment: copies, annual prizes.
Reporting time: 2–3 months, longer during summer.
Copyright reverts to author.
1980; 2/yr
$8/yr; $5/ea; $15/2 yrs; 40%
120 pp; 6 x 9

icism of the quality that has earned us several Pushcart nominations, as well as, most recently, election to *The Best American Short Stories 1982* and *Prize Stories 1982: The O. Henry Awards*.
Stephen Dixon, Roseanne Coggeshall, Joyce Carol Oates, Cleanth Brooks, Leslie Fiedler.
Payment: in issues.
Reporting time: 6–9 months.
Copyright held by magazine.
1968; 2/yr; 600
$7/yr ind; $5/ea; 33⅓%
200 pp; 9 x 6
Ad rates: negotiable
ISSN: 0038-3163

SOUTH CAROLINA REVIEW

Richard J. Calhoun
English Department
Clemson University
Clemson, SC 29634-1503
(803) 656-3229

Poetry, fiction, criticism, essays, reviews, translation, interviews.
Listed as one of the twenty most outstanding literary magazines in the United States by the *The New York Quarterly*, **THE SOUTH CAROLINA REVIEW** is now in its third decade of publication. Our primary goal is to continue to publish fiction, poetry, and crit-

SOUTH COAST POETRY JOURNAL

John J. Brugaletta
English Department
California State University Fullerton
Fullerton, CA 92634
(714) 773-2600

Poetry, graphics/artwork.
SOUTH COAST POETRY JOURNAL avoids theorizing so as to remain open to every kind of excellence in poetry, no matter what the style or school. Our standards for excellence, however, are high.
Richard Eberhart, Rita Dove,

Marge Piercy, William Stafford, John Hollander, Denise Levertov, Mark Strand.

Payment: in single copies.

Copyright held by **SOUTH COAST POETRY JOURNAL**; reverts to author upon publication.

1986; 2/yr; 150

$9/yr ind; $10/yr inst; $5/ea; 40%

60 pp; 5½ x 8½

Ads accepted

ISSN: 0887-2074

SOUTH DAKOTA REVIEW

John R. Milton

University of South Dakota

Vermillion, SD 57069

(605) 677-5220, 677-5229

Poetry, fiction, criticism, essays, occasional translation and interviews.

When the material warrants, an emphasis on the American West; writers from the West; Western places or subjects; frequent issues with no geographical emphasis. Periodic special issues on one theme, or one place, or one writer, e.g., Ross MacDonald (Spring 1986).

Edward Loomis, Max Evans, Frederick Manfred, Lloyd Van Brunt.

Payment: in copies.

Reporting time: 2 weeks–2months, slowest in summer.

1963; 4/yr; 600

$15/yr; $25/2 yrs; $5/single copy; 40%

150–190 pp; 6 x 9

ISSN: 0038-3368

THE SOUTH FLORIDA POETRY REVIEW

S.A. Stirnemann

7190 N.W. 21 Street

Fort Lauderdale, FL 33313

(305) 742-5624

Poetry, essays, reviews, interviews.

THE SOUTH FLORIDA POETRY REVIEW, a national poetry triquarterly, publishes the works of well-known poets along with the works of fresh, new talents. We are interested in contemporary poetry of the highest literary quality, work in which there is both a sense of vision and a sense of craft.

Marvin Bell, Christopher Buckley, Mark Jarman, Philip Levine, Gerald Stern.

Payment: in copies; honorarium when available.

Reporting time: 4–12 weeks.

Copyright held by magazine; reverts to author upon publication.

1983; 3/yr; 750

$7.50/yr ind; $9/yr inst; $3/ea;
20%
64 pp; 6 x 9
Ad rates: $100/page/4½ x 7½
ISSN: 0885-0720

THE SOUTHERN CALIFOR-
NIA ANTHOLOGY

Michael Wilds, Melissa Hartman
Master of Professional Writing
Program
University of Southern California
WPH 404
Los Angeles, CA 90089-4034
(213) 743-8255

Poetry, fiction, interviews, graphics/artwork (on cover).

Published through the Master of Professional Writing Program at the University of Southern California, **THE SOUTHERN CALIFORNIA ANTHOLOGY** is a literary journal of fiction, poetry, and interviews. Seventy percent of the pieces are solicited. Volume VII (published April 1989) includes works by: Philip Appleman, Madeline De-Frees, Li Guowen, John Hollander, David Madden, James Merrill, John Frederick Nims, James Ragan, David Ray, Hubert Selby, Jr., Henry Taylor, John Updike, Peter Vierick, Richard Yates.

Payment: 3 copies.

Copyright held by the University of Southern California, Master of Professional Writing Program; reverts to author upon publication.
1983; 1/yr; 1,000
$7.95/yr; 40%
144 pp; 5½ x 8½
ISBN: 0-9615108-5-4
Blackwell North America, Ballen Booksellers, Small Press Disbribution

SOUTHERN EXPOSURE

Eric Bates
P.O. Box 531
Durham, NC 27702
(919) 688-8167

Essays, reviews, interviews, photographs, graphics/artwork.

SOUTHERN EXPOSURE is a winner of the National Magazine Award and is widely respected as the voice of the progressive South. Investigative journalism and oral history are emphasized. Very little fiction or poetry, mostly non-fiction articles on social issues.

Payment: up to $200.
Reporting time: 6–8 weeks.
Copyright held by magazine.
1973; 4/yr; 4,000
$16/yr ind; $20/yr inst; $5/ea;
40%
Ad rates: $400/page; $270/½ page

64 pp; 8½ x 11
ISSN: 0146-809X
Ingram

SOUTHERN HUMANITIES REVIEW

Dan R. Latimer, Thomas L. Wright
R.T. Smith, Poetry Editor
9088 Haley Center
Auburn University
Auburn, AL 36849
(205) 844-9088

Poetry, fiction, essays, reviews.
THE SOUTHERN HUMANITIES REVIEW publishes fiction, poetry and critical essays on the arts, literature, philosophy, religion, and history. Essays, articles, or stories should, in general, range between 3,500 and 5,000 words. Poems should not exceed two pages in length.
Denise Levertov, Louis Simpson, Donald Hall, Peter Green, Yannis Ritsos, Reynolds Price.
Payment: copies and offprints.
Reporting time: 3 months.
Copyright held by Auburn University.
1967; 4/yr; 800
$12/yr; $4/ea
100 pp; 4½ x 7½
Ad rates: $85/page/4½ x 7½;
  $50/½ page/4½ x 3¾
ISSN: 0038-4186

SOUTHERN POETRY REVIEW

Lucinda Grey & Ken McLaurin
Department of English
University of North Carolina
Charlotte, NC 28223
(704) 547-4225

Poetry, review.
Submissions accepted from both established and previously unpublished poets. **SPR** is a natural outlet for poets writing in the South, but has no regional bias. Variety in style and content encouraged.
Susan Ludvigson, Linda Pastan, David Keller, Dave Smith, Marge Piercy.
Payment: in copies.
Reporting time: 6 weeks.
Copyright held by magazine; reverts to author upon request.
1958; 2/yr; 1,100
$6/yr; $3.50/ea; 40%
80 pp; 6 x 9
No ads
ISSN: 0038-447X

THE SOUTHERN QUARTERLY: A Journal of the Arts in the South

Peggy Whitman Prenshaw
University of Southern Mississippi
Southern Station Box 5078
Hattiesburg, MS 39406-5078
(601) 266-4370

Criticism, essays, reviews, interviews, photographs.

A non-profit scholarly journal, **THE SOUTHERN QUARTERLY** includes essays, articles, interviews and reviews on the arts—defined broadly—in the southern U.S. Alternately published general and special issues include research on music, theatre, dance, literature, film, art, architecture, popular and folk arts.

Virginia Spencer Carr, W. Kenneth Holditch, Jessie Poesch, William Ferris.

Payment: none.

Reporting time: 3–6 months.

Copyright held by University of Southern Mississippi; reverts to author upon publication.

1962; 4/yr; 750

$9/yr ind; $16/2 yrs ind; $20/yr inst.; 3/ea; 15%

150 pp; 6 x 9

Ad rates: $100/page/4½ x 6¾; $75/½ page/4½ x 3⅜

ISSN: 0038-4496

THE SOUTHERN REVIEW

James Olney, David J. Smith
43 Allen Hall
Louisiana State University
Baton Rouge, LA 70803
(504) 388-5108

Fiction, poetry, criticism, reviews, interviews.

THE SOUTHERN REVIEW publishes poetry, fiction, criticism, essays, reviews and excerpts from novels in progress, with emphasis on contemporary literature in the United States and abroad, and with special interest in Southern history and culture.

Ernest J. Gaines, Reynolds Price, Lee Smith, W. D. Snodgrass, Jill McCorkle, Albert Gelpi.

Payment: $12/printed page for prose; $20/printed page for poetry; 2 complimentary copies.

Reporting time: 2 months.

Copyright held by LSU; reverts to author upon publication.

1935: original series; 1965: new series; 4/yr; 3,100

$15/yr ind; $30/yr inst; $5/ea ind; $10/ea inst

250 pp; 6¾ x 10

Ad rates: $150/page/4½ x 7½; $90/½ page/4½ x 3⅝; $60/¼ page/4½ x 1⅔

ISSN: 0038-4534

B. DeBoer

THE SOUTHWEST REVIEW

Willard Spiegelman, Editor; Elizabeth Mills, Associate Editor
6410 Airline Road
Southern Methodist University

Dallas, TX 75275

(214) 373-7440

Poetry, fiction, essays, interviews.

THE SOUTHWEST REVIEW is a quarterly that serves the interests of its region but is not bound by them. **SWR** has always striven to present the work of writers and scholars from the surrounding states and to offer analyses of problems and themes that are distinctly southwestern and, at the same time, publishes the works of good writers regardless of their locales.

John Ashbery, Gwendolyn Brooks, Jay Cantor, Millicent Dillon, William Weaver.

Payment: varies.

Reporting time: 1 month.

Copyright held by SMU; reverts to author upon publication.

1915; 4/yr; 1,500

$20/yr ind; $25/yr inst; $5/ea; 40%

144 pp; 6 x 9

Ad rates: $250/page/25 x 42½ picas; $150/½ page/25 x 21 picas

ISSN: 0038-4712

Homing Pigeon, Total Circulation Services

SOU'WESTER

Audrey Parente

411 Main Trail

Ormond Beach, FL 32074

Poetry, especially longer poems, fiction.

Payment: in copies.

Reporting time: 1 month.

Copyright held by Southern Illinois University.

1960; 3/yr; 300

$4/yr; $1.50/ea

88 pp; 6 x 9

ISSN: 0098-499X

THE SOW'S EAR

Errol Hess, Larry Richman (Poetry), Mary Calhoun (Graphics)

245 McDowell Street

Bristol, TN 37620

(615) 764-1625

Poetry, reviews, interviews, graphics, photography.

Contemporary poetry exported from and imported into Southern Appalachia. No nostalgia. We publish both established and new poets, with no restrictions on subject matter or style. We use B & W art to complement poetry.

Marge Piercy, Fred Chapell, Lee Smith, David Huddle, Josephine Jacobsen, Jim Wayne Miller.

Payment: in copies.

Reporting time: 2–3 months.

Copyright reverts to author.

1988; 4/yr; 500

$10/4 issues; $3.50/ea; 40%

32 pp; 8½ x 11

Free classifieds

SPARROW POVERTY PAMPHLETS

Felix and Selma Stefanile
103 Waldron Street
West Lafayette, IN 47906
(317) 743-1991
Poetry.
The one-poet-an-issue magazine, providing a forum for mature poets. We are in the modernist tradition, with its emphasis on craft, shaped language, unity of voice and vision.
Christopher Bursk, Geraldine C. Little, Roger Finch, Gail White, Gray Burr, Ger Killeen.
Payment: $30, plus royalties of 20%.
Sparrow is in reorganization for 1991. For the time, no new manuscripts are being sought. Query, with S.A.S.E. late in 1991.
Copyright reverts to author on request.
1954; 3/yr; 900
$9.00/yr; $2/ea for back copies; 35%
28–32 pp; 5½ x 8½
ISSN: 0038-6588
Small Press Distribution Inc,; Spring Church (for our chapbooks)

THE SPIRIT THAT MOVES US

Morty Sklar
P.O. Box 820
Jackson Heights, NY 11372-0820
(718) 426-8788
Poetry, fiction, photographs, artwork.
We favor work that expresses feeling. Over 95% is unsolicited.
Our *The Casting of Bells* , by Jaroslav Seifert, was followed a year later by the poet's winning the Nobel Prize for literature. In 1985, editor Morty Sklar was awarded a CCLM Editor's Grant. Query first for any theme, and time-frame.
Most recent issue (Dec. 1990) is our special 15th Anniversary collection titled *Free Parking*.
Payment: cash plus copies plus 40% discount on paperbacks.
Reporting time: 1 week–1 month.
Copyright reverts to author upon publication.
1975; 2/yr; 1,500
Vol. 9/$11.20; Vol. 10/$12.60; (special issues are also published clothbound); 40%
64–336 pp; 5½ x 8½
Ads in regular issues only
ISSN: 0364-4014
Inland Book Co.; Bookslinger; Small Press Distribution; Bookpeople; The Distributors

THE SPOON RIVER QUARTERLY

Lucia Getsi, Jerry Pratt, Susan Swartwont

English Department
Illinois State University
Normal-Bloomington, IL 61701
(309) 438-3667

Poetry, translation, interviews, photographs.

With the change in editors, **SRQ** wants poetry that is interesting and compelling. Our standards are high—the acceptance rate is about 2%. Two issues each year contain a chapbook-length feature of new poems by an Illinois poet and an interview and critical introduction to the poet's work.

Bruce Guernsey, Linnea Johnson, John Knoepfle, Richard Jackson, Katherine Soniat, Frankie Paino, William Trowbridge.

Payment: 3 contributor's copies.

Reporting time: 6 weeks.

Copyright reverts to author upon publication.

1976; 4/yr; 500

$12/yr ind; $16/yr inst; $3/ea; 40%

64 pp; 5½ x 8½

Ad rates: $100/page/5 x 8; $50/½ page/5 x 2

ISSN: 0738-8993

Illinois Literary Publishers Association; EBSCO; Ingram

SPWAO (Small Press Writers and Artists Organization) SHOWCASE

Jeannette M. Hopper
P.O. Box 397
Marina, CA 93933

Poetry, fiction, graphics/artwork.

The **SPWAO SHOWCASE** is just what the title says, a showcase for SPWAO members to display their best work, whether it be art, fiction or poetry. Only members of SPWAO may contribute at this time; however, all writers/artists/poets with interests in science fiction, fantasy, or related genres are eligible for SPWAO membership.

Payment: one contributor's copy.

Reporting time: 2 weeks.

Copyright held by magazine; reverts to author upon publication.

1989; 1/yr; $6.95/ea

250 pp; 5 x 7 perfect bound

STILETTO

Michael Annis
P.O. Box 5987–Westport Station
Kansas City, MO 64111

All types except reviews or criticism / "illustrated" / Quality a must. Bold, uncompromising.

All schools, all genres, street poets to academia. Content is our highest priority. Each writer is given a large enough section to clearly demonstrate the author's ability and vision. If you feel like you have a statement to make for posterity, make it here. Apocalyptic vision for an apocalyptic decade.

Antler, Wm. Burroughs, Andrei Codrescu, Diane DiPrima, Diane Wakoski, Anne Waldman.

Payment: 20 contributor copies, First Ed.

Reporting time: to 6 months.

Mss. not selected for **STILETTO** may be considered for inclusion in a companion volume titled *BANNED*.

Copyright reverts to author/artist.

1989; 1–2/yr

$20 1st Ed. collectors hardbound; $12.50 Commercial Ed softcover; 30%

180+ pp; 5 x 11¼

1043-9501

ISSN: By publisher, Howling Dog Press.

STORY

Lois Rosenthal

1507 Dana Avenue

Cincinnati, OH 45208

(513) 871-4933

Short fiction.

STORY is devoted to publishing fine short stories.

Bobbie Ann Mason, Joyce Carol Oates, Robert Ward, Madison Smartt Bell, Alice Adams, Alan Cheuse, Rick De Marinis, William Kotzwinkle.

Payment: $250.

Reporting time: one month.

Copyright: First serial North American Rights.

1989; quarterly; 25,000

$17; $5

128; 6½ x 9¼

ISSN: 1045-0831

Walden, Ingram

STORY QUARTERLY

Anne Brashler, Diane Williams

P.O. Box 1416

Northbrook, IL 60065

(708) 564-8891

Fiction and interviews.

STORY QUARTERLY is looking for great fiction.

Reporting time: 2 months.

Copyright held by magazine; reverts to author upon publication.

1974; 2/yr; 1,500

$12/4 issues; $4/ea; 40%

110 pp; 6 x 9

ISSN: 0361-0144

B. DeBoer, Ingram Periodicals

SULFUR

Clayton Eshleman

210 Washtenaw Avenue

Ypsilanti, MI 48197

(313) 483-9787

Poetry, fiction, criticism, essays, reviews, translation, photographs, graphics/artwork.

Contemporary American poetry, translations, archival materials, book reviews, reproduction of art and photography.

Jerome Rothenberg, John Ashbery, Michael Palmer, William Carlos Williams, Aimé Césaire.

Payment: $30/contribution.

Reporting time: 1–2 weeks.

Copyright held by magazine; reverts to author upon publication.

1981; 2/yr; 2,000

$13/yr ind; $19/yr inst; $8/ea; 40%

250 pp; 6 x 9

Ad rates: $150/page/6 x 9; $85/½ page/6 x 3⅞

ISSN: 0730-305X

Inland; Small Press Distribution; DeBoer, Bookpeople, Armadillo, Small Change.

SUN DOG: The Southeast Review

Jamie Granger

406 Williams Building

Florida State University

Tallahassee, FL 32306

(904) 644-4320

Poetry, fiction, graphic art.

SUN DOG: The Southeast Review reads both fiction and poetry year-round. We are looking for striking images, incidents, and characters rather than particular styles or genres. We also publish the winner and runners-up of the World's Best Short Short Story Contest.

Janet Burroway, David Bottoms, Jesse Lee Kercheval, Leon Stokesbury, Rick Lott, Helen Norris, David Kirby.

Payment: 2 copies.

Copyright held by **SUN DOG**; reverts to author upon publication.

1979; 2/yr; 1,250

$4/ea; 40%

90 pp; 6 x 9

SWAMP ROOT

Al Masarik, Editor; Jill Andrea, Managing Editor

Route 2, Box 1098

Hiwassee One

Jacksboro, TN 37757

(615) 562-7082

Poetry, essays, review, interviews, letters, photographs, graphics, artwork.

Contemporary poetry biased toward clarity, brevity, strong imagery; works that speak strongly of the poet's place; works that show a need to be written.

Naomi Shihab Nye, Ted Kooser, Maurya Simon, Linda M. Hasselstrom, William Klorfkorn, Diane Glancy.

Payment: 3 copies, 1 year subsc.
Reporting time: 1 week–1 month.
Copyright reverts to author.
1987; 3/yr; 1,000
$12, $15 libararies; $5/ea; usual
  discount
86 pp; 6 x 9
ISSN: 1045-7682

SWIFT KICK

Robin Kay Willoughby
1711 Amherst Street
Buffalo, NY 14214
(716) 837-7778

Poetry, fiction, plays, translation,
  photographs, graphics/artwork.
We specialize in unusual formats,
  genres and styles.
Jerry McGuire, Dennis Maloney,
  Simon Perchik, Penny Kemp,
  Maurice Kenny.
Payment: in copies.
Reporting time: varies.
Copyright held by magazine; re-
  verts to author upon publica-
  tion.
1980; 4/yr; 200
$20/4 issues ind; $40/4 issues inst;
  $6 + postage/sample copy
  (checks payable to editor); 40%
ISSN: 0277-447X

T

TALISMAN: A Journal of Contemporary Poetry and Poetics

Edward Foster
Box 1117
Hoboken, NJ 07030
(201) 798-9093

Poetry, essays on poetry and poetics, interviews.
Each issue centers on the poetry
  and poetics of a major contemporary poet and includes a selection of new work by other
  important contemporary writers.
Susan Howe, Charles Bernstein,
  John Yau, Clark Coolidge, Robert Creeley, Rosmarie Waldrop.
Payments: copies.
Reporting time: one month.
Copyright reverts to author upon
  publication.
1988; 2/yr; 650
$9/individuals; $13/institutions;
  $5; 40%
152; 5½ x 8½
$100/page; $50/½ page
ISSN: 0898-8684
Anton J. Mikofsky, Segue, SPD,
  Spectacular Diseases

TAMPA REVIEW

Richard B. Mathews, ed., Don
  Morrill, poetry ed., Andy So-

lomon, fiction ed., Kathryn Van Spanckeren, poetry ed.
Box 19F
The University of Tampa
Tampa, FL 33606-1490
(813) 253-3333
Poetry, fiction, essays, reviews, interviews, photographs, graphics/artwork.
The TAMPA REVIEW is the faculty-edited literary journal of the University of Tampa. It publishes new works of poetry, fiction, non-fiction and art. Each issue includes works from other countries in order to reflect the international flavor of the city of Tampa and its ties to the international cultural community.
Tom Disch, David Ignatow, Elizabeth Jolley, Denise Levertov, William Stafford.
Payment: $10.00 per page.
Reporting time: 12 weeks.
Copyright first serial North American copyrights held by **TAMPA REVIEW** then reverts to author.
Yearly; 500–800
$7.50; $7.95
96; 7½ x 10½
ISSN: 0896-064x

TAPROOT: A Journal of Older Writers

Philip W. Quigg, Enid Graf
Fine Arts Center 4290
University at Stony Brook,
Stony Brook, NY 11794-5425
(516) 632-6635
Poetry, fiction, graphics/artwork, reviews.
Publish the works of older writers; interested in "capturing the stories, poems and recountings of events related to and growing from tradition," as well as the realities of our elders' participation in community life. Publication open to members of Taproot Workshops only.
Payment: 1 copy.
Copyright held by magazine; reverts to author upon publication.
1974; 1/yr; 1,000
$4/ea; 40%
100 pp; 8½ x 11
Ad rates: $500/page; $300/½ page; $175/¼ page
ISSN: 0887-9257

TAR RIVER POETRY

Peter Makuck
English Department
East Carolina University
Greenville, NC 27834
(919) 757-6041
Poetry, reviews.
We are looking for poetry that shows skillful use of figurative language. Narrative poems, short images poems, poems in

closed and open form are welcome. We are not interested in
sentimental, flat statement
verse. Though we often publish
the work of established poets,
we are open to the work of
newcomers as well.

A.R. Ammons, Brenda Galvin,
Sharon Bryan, Jonathan
Holden, Michael Mott, Patricia
Goedicke, Leslie Norris, Mark
Jarman.

Payment: none.

Reporting time: 5–7 weeks.

Copyright reverts to author.

1965; 2/yr; 1,000

$8/yr; $4/ea; 40%

62 pp; 6 x 9

THE TEXAS REVIEW

Paul Ruffin
English Department
Sam Houston State University
Huntsville, TX 77341
(409) 294-1429

Poetry, fiction, criticism, essays,
reviews.

We are interested in the very best
fiction and poetry available; our
non-fiction may be literary, historical, or "familiar." We are
interested principally in reviews
of contemporary poetry and fiction.

Fred Chappell, Richard Eberhart,
George Garrett, Donald Justice,

William Stafford, Richard
Wilbur.

Payment: in contributor's copies
plus one year subscription to
magazine.

Copyright held by magazine; reverts to author upon publication.

1979; 2/yr; 750–1,000

$10/yr ind/inst; $5/ea; 40%

144 pp; 6 x 9

ISSN: 0885-2685

THEATER

Joel Schechter, Editor
222 York Street
New Haven, CT 06520
(203) 432-1568

Criticism, essays, reviews, plays,
translation, interviews, photographs.

Each issue contains the text of a
new play or translation by a
leading contemporary play-
wright. Also interviews with
theatre artists and essays by
theatre artists and critics. Reviews of performance groups
and productions from around
the world.

Athol Fugard, Dario Fo, Eric
Bentley, Jan Kott, Theodora
Skipitares.

Payment: $150 honorarium for
plays; various amounts for articles.

Copyright reverts to author.
1968; 3/yr; 2,000
$20/yr ind; $24/yr inst; $7.00/ea
90–100 pp; 9½ x 9½
Ad rates: $200/page/9½ x 9½
$100/½ page/9½ x 4¾; $60/¼
page/4¾ x 4¾

THEMA

Virginia Howard
Thema Literary Society
Box 74109
Metairie, LA 70033-4109
(504) 887-1263

Fiction, poetry.

Stories and poems must relate to premise specified for each issue. Themes for 1991: The perfect imperfection; Art from the canvas freed; A tattered hat abandoned; It's got to be here . . . Somewhere; Coming in 1992: When the birds stopped singing and more to be announced.

A.L. Sirois, Florrie McMillan, Edith Pearlman, Ann Spiers, Elizabeth Cunningham.

Payment: $25 for short story; $10 for poems, $10 for short-shorts and illustrations.

Reporting time: dependent on deadlines.

Copyright reverts to author.
1988; 4/yr; 200
$16/yr; $5/ea; 40%

200 pp; 5½ x 8½
ISSN: 1041-4851

THIRTEEN

Ken Stone
Box 392
Portlandville, NY 13834
(607) 547-4301

Poetry, fiction, reviews, translations, graphics/artwork.

THIRTEEN is a poetry magazine which specializes in 13-line poetry. We have no special themes or other requirements other than the poem be 13 lines, not including title. All poems should be titled.

Rochelle Holt, Judson Crews, ave jeanne, R. H. Yodice, Sue Saniel Elkind.

Payment: 1 copy.

Reporting time: 2 weeks.

Copyright held by author.
1982; 4/yr; 350
$5/yr; $2.50/ea; 40%
40 pp; 8½ x 11½
No ads
ISSN: 0747-9727
Direct mail by publisher

THIRTEENTH MOON

Judith E. Johnson
English Department
SUNY
Albany, NY 12222

Poetry, fiction, criticism, essays, reviews, translation, interviews, photographs, graphics/artwork.

THIRTEENTH MOON is a feminist literary magazine, placing primary emphasis on the quality of writing. It is specifically interested in work from feminist, lesbian, third-world, and working-class perspectives.

Joanna Russ, Cheryl Clarke, Nelida Pinon, Marie Ponsot.

Payment: in copies.

Reporting time: varies.

Copyright held by 13th Moon, Inc.; reverts to author upon publication.

1973; 1–2/yr; 2,500

$6.50/v ind; $13/v inst; $6.50/ea; 40%

200 pp; 6 x 9⅛

Ad rates: inquire

new poetry, original fiction, and socio-political articles. While based in California, it is aimed at a nation-wide audience.

John Berger, Greil Marcus, Elizabeth Hardwick, Thom Gunn, Christopher Ricks.

Payment: $50–$100.

Reporting time: 3 weeks–2 months.

Copyright held by magazine; reverts to author upon publication.

1980; 4/yr; 8,000

$10/yr; $4/ea; 30%–50%

36 pp; 11 x 17

Ad rates: $600/page/10 x 14; $350/½ page/10 x 7½; $200/¼ page/4½ x 7¼

ISSN: 0275-1410

Ingram Periodicals, Ubiquity

THE THREEPENNY REVIEW

Wendy Lesser

P.O. Box 9131

Berkeley, CA 94709

(415) 849-4545

Poetry, fiction, criticism, essays, reviews, memoirs, graphics/artwork.

THE THREEPENNY REVIEW is a quarterly journal publishing essays on literature, theater, film, television, dance, music, and the visual arts, as well as

THUNDER & HONEY

Akbar Imhotep

P.O. Box 11386

Atlanta, GA 30310

(404) 688-3376

Poetry, fiction, interviews, photographs, graphics/artwork.

THUNDER & HONEY is primarily devoted to poetry and fiction. Future issues will have arts-related articles and some interviews.

Charlie Braxton, Nome Poem,

R.F. Smith, Askia Toure, Jeanne Towns.

Payment: 15 copies.

Copyright held by magazine; reverts to author upon publication.

1984; 4/yr; 1,500

$2.50/yr; 75¢/ea

4 pp; 8½ x 11

Ad rates: $210/page/10 x 16; $120/½ page/10 x 8; $60/¼ page/5 x 4

TIGHTROPE

Ed Rayher
323 Pelham Road
Amherst, MA 01002

Poetry, fiction, translation, graphics/artwork.

We stress excellence and accessibility to unpublished or little published authors. Our format is erratic, but we always emphasize form as well as content.

Steven Ruhl, Linda Burggraf, Gillian Conoley, Lance Liskus.

Payment: inquire.

Copyright held by magazine; reverts to author upon publication.

1977; 2/yr; 350

$10/yr; $6/ea; 40%

40 pp; size varies

TOP STORIES

Anne Turyn
228 Seventh Avenue
New York, NY 10011

Fiction, graphics/artwork.

TOP STORIES is a prose periodical; a chapbook series which (usually) features the work of one author/artist per issue.

Constance DeJong, Lynne Tillman, Susan Daitch, Tama Janowitz, Richard Prince.

Payment: varies.

Reporting time: 1 year.

Copyright held by author.

1979; 3/yr; 1,500

$13.50/yr ind; $14.50/yr inst; $3/ea single issue; $6/ea double issue; 40%

5¼ x 8¼

No ads

TOOK

Edward Mycue
P.O. Box 640543
San Francisco, CA 94164-0543

Poetry, drama, prose, history, criticism, music, food, art.

Laura Kennelly, Owen Hill, Lawrence Fixel, Martha King

Payment: in copies.

Reporting time: one month.

Copyright to the contributors

1988; occasional; 150

$5; $1

8 to 40; 5½ x 4½

$50/¼ page

TOUCHSTONE: Literary Journal

William Laufer
P.O. Box 8308
Spring, TX 77387

Poetry, criticism, essays, reviews, translation, interviews, graphics/artwork.

We are committed to publishing non-fiction, poetry and graphics which commercial magazines no longer publish. We welcome minority viewpoints, and look for imaginative, experimental trends.

Lyn Lifshin, Rebecca Gonzales, Ramona Weeks, Vassar Miller, Arthur Smith, Thomas Kennedy, Walter McDonald, Archie Henderson.

Payment: as finances permit.
Reporting time: 6 weeks.
Copyright reverts to author upon request.
1976; 1/yr; 1,000
$5/ea
48 pp; 5½ x 8, perfect bound
ISSN: 1715-1697
No ads

TRANSFER

Gary Lenhart
248 West 105 Street, Apt. 6D
New York, NY 10025
(212) 691-6590; (212) 866-7595
Poetry, fiction, criticism, essays, translation, interviews, graphics/artwork.

Maureen Owen, Ron Padgett, Christian McEwen, Michael Scholnick, Kimiko Hahn, Pat Nolan.

Payment: none.
Reporting time: varies.
Copyright held by magazine; reverts to author upon publication.
1987; 2/yr; 500
8/yr ind; $10/yr inst; $5/ea; 40%
144 pp; 5½ x 8½
Ad rates: inquire
ISSN: 8095-4054

TRANSLATION

Frank MacShane, Franklin D. Reeve, William Jay Smith
Room 412 Dodge Hall
Columbia University
New York, NY 10027
(212) 854-2305

Poetry, fiction, translation.

TRANSLATION publishes new English translations of significant contemporary works of prose and poetry. Prose excerpts should not exceed 30 pages. Each volume features the literature of a particular language or region.

Payment: in copies.
Reporting time: maximum of 6 months.

Copyright reverts to translator/author upon publication.
1972; 2/yr; 1,500
$17/yr; $8/ea
220 pp; 6 x 9
Ad rates: $500/page
ISSN: 0093-9307

TRIQUARTERLY

Reginald Gibbons
Susan Hahn
Northwestern University
2020 Ridge
Evanston, IL 60208

Fiction, poetry, essays, reviews, translation, interviews, photographs, graphics/artwork.

TRIQUARTERLY is especially dedicated to short fiction, although substantial amounts of poetry are also published regularly in every issue, including long poems. Brief book reviews and occasional essays round out the contents.

Stanislaw Baranczak, Thomas McGrath, Sandra McPherson, Alan Shapiro, Meredith Steinbach, Michael S. Harper.

Payment: $40/printed page, prose; $3/line, poetry.

Reporting time: 2 months.

Copyright reverts to author upon request.

1964; 3/yr; 4,000

$18/yr ind; $26/yr inst; $4/sample; varies
250 pp; 6 x 9¼
Ad rates: $250/page/6 x 9¼; $150/½ page/6 x 4⅝
ISSN: 0041-3097
DeBoer, Ingram Periodicals, Bookpeople, Illinois Literary Publishers Assoc.

TRIVIA: A Journal of Ideas

Lise Weil
P.O. Box 606
North Amherst, MA 01059
(413) 367-2254

TRIVIA publishes writing that puts women at the center and is especially interested in forms that grow out of this intention. Essays, reviews, translations and experimental forms that combine rigorous thinking with uncompromising feminist vision. Articles on language and memory, aging, lesbian ethics, therapy, black lesbian aesthetics, feminism's seduction by New Age philosophy.

Gloria Anzaldua, Nicole Brossard, Michèle Causse, Mary Daly, Jewelle Gomez, Sarah Hoagland, Gail Scott, Christina Thürmer-Rohr.

Reporting time: 4–6 months.

Copyright reverts to author.

1982; 3/yr; 2,000

$14/yr ind; $20/yr inst; $6/ea
120 pp; 5½ x 8½
Ad rates: inquire
ISSN: 0736-928X
Inland, Bookpeople, Ubiquity,
Small Changes

TUCUMCARI LITERARY REVIEW

Troxey Kemper
3108 W. Bellevue Ave.
Los Angeles, CA 90026
(213) 413-0789

Poetry, fiction, essays, nostalgia,
memories, vignettes, humor.
**TUCUMCARI LITERARY
REVIEW** is old fashioned and
the preference is for types of
writing in vogue in the 1930s to
1950s. Most of the poetry is
rhyming, in "standard" forms,
not disjointed phrases and odd-
shaped lines of prose arranged
like poetry. The emphasis is on
writing that "says something."
Alice Mackenzie Swaim, Marian
Ford Park, Bettye K. Wray,
Betty M. Benoit, Patricia M.
Johnson, C. David Hay.
Payment: in copies, upon publication.
Copyright held by author.
1988; bimonthly; 170
$12/yr ind & inst; $2/ea by mail;
40%

40 pp; 5½ x 8½
Ads: free ads for readers

TURNSTILE

Mitchell Nauffts, Sara Gordonson;
poetry
175 Fifth Avenue, Suite 2348
New York, NY 10010

Fiction, poetry, essays, interviews,
photographs, artwork/graphics.
TURNSTILE publishes high-
quality fiction, poetry, essays,
interviews and artistic works. A
passageway for variety and dif-
ference, we encourage new and
emerging writers and artists.
Payment: in copies.
Reporting time: 6–8 weeks.
Copyright reverts to author upon
publication.
1988; 2/yr; 1,200
$22/4 issues; $6.50; 40–50%
128; 6¼ x 9
$150/page; $100/½ page
ISSN: 0896-5951
Deboer, Inland, Bookpeople

TYUONYI

Phillip Foss
Recursos de Santa Fe
826 Camino de Monte Rey
Santa Fe, New Mexico 87501
(505) 852-2734

Poetry, fiction, essays, plays,
translation.

Multi-aesthetic/multi-ethnic literature.

Bernstein, Berssenbrugge, Gunn, Tarn, Olson.

Payment: copies.

Reporting time: 1–3 months.

Copyright held by author.

1985; every 9 months; 800–1,000

$14/2; $7/ea; 40%

150 pp; 8½ x 8½

U

THE UNDERGROUND FOREST—La Selva Subterranea

Joseph Richey, Ann Becker

1701 Bluebell Avenue

Boulder, CO 80302

Non-fiction, poetry, investigative articles, politics.

A bilingual (Spanish-English), hemispheric publication devoted to the dissemination of informed opinions and good writing.

Margaret Randall, Agnes Bushell, Gioconda Belli, Victor Hernandez Cruz.

Payment: 2 copies.

Reporting time: as soon as we can.

Copyright reverts to author.

1986; bi-annual; 2,000

$12; $3; 40%

96; 17 x 5¼

Write for information

ISSN: 1045-3660

Maine Writers and Publishers Association, Ubiquity

UNMUZZLED OX

Michael Andre

105 Hudson Street

New York, NY 10013

(212) 226-7170

Poetry, political.

Library Journal called **OX** "Outrageous and outstanding" because I published Robert Mapplethorpe; given the current climate I'd settle for "lively." We do publish the dead—a forthcoming issue features baroque librettists; plus W. H. Auden, the late Andy Warhol.

John Cage, Robert Creeley, Dan Berrigan, Allen Ginsberg.

Payment: confidential.

Reporting time: varies.

Copyright Michael Andre.

1971; varies; 15,000

$20; $3; varies

150; 5½ x 8½

Call for information

ISSN: 0049-5557

UNIVERSITY OF WINDSOR REVIEW

Joseph A. Quinn

Department of English

University of Windsor
Windsor, Ontario, Canada M9B 3P4
(519) 253-4232 ext. 2303
Poetry, short stories.
Publishes poetry and short fiction.
We subscribe to no particular
school or "ism."
Kenneth Radu, Budge Wilson,
Patrick Roscoe.
Payment: $50/story; $10/poem
Reporting time: 6–8 weeks.
Copyright reverts to author.
1965; b-annual; 450
$12; $6
100; 6 x 9
ISSN: 0042-0352

VERSE

Henry Hart
English Department
William and Mary
Williamsburg, VA 23185
(804) 253-4758

Poetry, criticism, reviews, translation, interviews.
VERSE is a literary journal, begun in Oxford, England (1984),
which publishes poetry in English and in translation. The
focus is on the international
scene, and its main purpose is
to improve the understanding of
the poetries from different countries, especially Britain and the
United States.
Seamus Heaney, James Merrill,
James Dickey, A.R. Ammons,
Galway Kinnell.
Payment: none.
Copyright held by author.
1984; 3/yr; 800
$12/yr; $4/ea; 40%
80 pp; 8¼ x 5¾
Ad rates: $150/page/6 x 4; $75/½
page/3 x 4; $40/¼ page/3 x 2
ISSN: 0268-3830

THE VINCENT BROTHERS
REVIEW

Kimberly A. Willardson
1459 Sanzon Drive
Fairborn, OH 45324
(513) 429-2141

Poetry, fiction, essays, reviews,
photographs, graphics/artwork.
TVBR's purpose is to encourage,
support and promote the work
of poets, artists, and prose writers through the publication of at
least 3 magazines per year. No
focus on one particular theme or
emphasis except that of well-
crafted writing/art. One
"theme" issue per year.
Herbert Woodward Martin, Gwen
Strauss, B.Z. Niditch, Tom
Sheehan, Lyn Lifshin.

Payment: $10 and copy for fiction story; contributors copy for all other pieces.

Reporting time: 3–6 months.

Copyright **THE VINCENT BROTHERS REVIEW**; reverts to author.

3/yr; 250

$12/individual-$15/institutional; $4.40

64; 5½ x 8½

$75/page; $45/½ page; $25/¼ page

ISSN: 1044-615x

THE VIRGINIA QUARTERLY REVIEW

Staige D. Blackford

One West Range

Charlottesville, VA 22903

(804) 924-3124

Poetry, fiction, essays, reviews.

One of the oldest and most distinguished literary journals in the country; contains articles and essays covering economics, art, the sciences, politics, and literature. Publishes high-quality fiction and poetry by established and newer authors. 75–100 brief, tightly-written book reviews per issue.

George Garrett, Jay Parini, Joyce Carol Oates, Mary Lee Settle, Ann Beattie.

Payment: $10/page essays & fiction; $1/line for poetry; $50/essay reviews.

Copyright held by The Virginia Quarterly Review/The University of Virginia; reverts to author upon publication.

1925; 4/yr; 4,200

$15/yr ind; $22/yr inst; $5/ea; 50%

188 pp; 5½ x 8

Ad rates: $150/page/5½ x 8; $75/½ page/5½ x 4 or 2¾ x 8

ISSN: 0042-675X

VISIONS–International, The World Journal of Illustrated Poetry

Bradley R. Strahan, Poetry Editor; Shirley Sullivan, Associate Editor

1110 Seaton Lane

Falls Church, VA 22046

(703) 521-0142

Poetry, reviews, translations, graphics/artwork.

We're international in scope and content. We emphasize the interplay between artwork, poem and appearance of the magazine. We look for strong, well-crafted work that has emotional content (without sentimentality). **VISIONS** publishes issues on special themes (usually once a year). Many of these, including our specials on the "Low Countries" and Francophone poetry, are still in print. We oppose the trend to publish facile word play instead of meaningful poetry. We are always interested in translations, especially from work that has not previously appeared in English and from less translated languages such as: Frisian, Basque, Telegu, Malayan, Gaelic, Macedonian, etc.

Andrei Codrescu, Ted Hughes, Marge Piercy, Marilyn Hacker, James Dickey.

Payment: in copies or $5–$10 when we get a grant.

Read a sample copy ($3.50) before submitting work

Reporting time: 1–3 weeks.

Copyright held by VIAS; reverts to author upon publication.

1979; 3/yr; 750

$14/yr; $4.50/ea; 30%–40%

56 pp; 5½ x 8½

ISSN: 0194-1690

VOICES INTERNATIONAL

Clovita Rice

1115 Gillette Drive

Little Rock, AR 72207

(501) 225-0166

Poetry, essays, photographs, graphics/artwork.

VOICES INTERNATIONAL focuses on high literary quality poetry, accepting for publication poetry with strong visual imagery and haunting impact. We encourage the beginner and have no preference in subject matter (as long as in good taste) if it presents a fresh approach and special awareness.

Bob Evans, Nome Mann, Jeanne Norris, Barbara Weekes.

Payment: in copies.

Reporting time: averages 6 weeks.

Copyright held by magazine.

1966; 4/yr; 325

$10/yr; $2.50/ea

32 pp; 6 x 9

VOLITION

Bonnie Lateiner

Lateiner/Vortex/Volition

Box 314

Tenants Harbor, ME 04860

(207) 372-6458

Poetry, short stories, excerpts from longer prose pieces, elemental/primal concerns.

VOLITION dramatically presents strongly contrasted current fiction, poetry and prose works. The magazine exhibits variations of American writing.

Fielding Dawson, Duncan McNaughton, Al Young, Simone O, Tama Janowitz.

Payment: in copies.

Copyright reverts to author.

1982; 1/yr; 500
$4/ea; 20%–40%
50 pp; 7 x 8
Inland, Segue, Small Press Distribution

VORTEX: A Critical Review
Bryce Milligan
627 E. Guenther
San Antonio, TX 78210
(817) 477-1777

Poetry, fiction, criticism, essays, reviews, translation, interviews, photographs, graphics/artwork.

We see the "Vortex" of our review as being in Texas, a funneling down from the U.S. and Canada and a funneling up from Latin America. The idea is to promote literary discourse in this hemisphere. This also means a particular emphasis upon writing in Texas. The emphasis is on real criticism of literary matters and essays on cultural topics. AFFINITIES, a literary supplement is included in each issue and features mostly poetry and a lot of that in translation.

Carlos Fuentes, Donald Hall, Octavio Paz, John Howard Griffin, Rainer Schulte.

Payment: no, but may begin soon: $50 for longer work, $25 for reviews and poetry (upon publication).

Reporting time: 30 days or less.
Copyright held by Robert Bonazzi, Latitudes Press; reverts to author upon publication.
1986; 4/yr; 1,000
$10/4 issues ind & inst; $3/ea; 40%
40 pp; 8½ x 11
Ad rates: contact magazine or CLMP for ad rates
Small Press Distribution, Inc.; Texas Circuit

VREMYA I MY (TIME AND WE)
Victor Perelman
409 Highwood Avenue
Leonia, NJ 07605
(201) 592-6155

Russian language literature and commentary. Fiction, essays, poetry, criticism, translation, graphics/artwork, interviews, photographs.
$59/yr ind; $86/yr inst; $19/ea; 40%

W

WASHINGTON REVIEW
Clarissa Wittenberg, Editor; Mary Swift, Managing Editor; Pat

Kolmer, Jeff Richards, Beth Joselow, Anne Pierce, Editorial Board
P.O. Box 50132
Washington, DC 20091
(202) 638-0515
Poetry, fiction, essays, reviews, plays, interviews, photographs, graphics/artwork.
Bi-monthly tabloid-size journal of arts and literature including poetry, fiction, book and art reviews, essays on the arts, original art work. Emphasis on arts of Washington, D.C. One special issue on single topic each year.
Terence Winch, Doug Lang, Lee Fleming.
Payment: $15–20/review, $50–100/article if we have it.
Reporting time: 2 months.
Copyright held by magazine; reverts to author upon publication.
1975; 6/yr; 1,500
$12/yr; $8.50/yr inst; $20/2 yrs; $2/ea; 40%
Ad rates: $250/page/16 x 11¼; $175/½ page/8 x 11¼; $135/⅓ page/7⅜ x 8
ISSN: 0163-903X

WATERWAYS

Barbara Fisher, Richard Alan Spiegel
393 Saint Pauls Avenue
Staten Island, NY 10304
(718) 442-7429
Poetry, graphics.
We publish poets of all ages and types provided we like their work and it pertains to our monthly themes. Our page size is small to encourage portability and accessibility.
Joanne Seltzer, Robert Lima, Arthur Winfield Knight, Albert Huffstickler, Ida Fasel.
Payment: 1 copy.
Reporting time: 1 month.
Copyright held by Ten Penny Players; reverts to author upon publication.
1977; 11/yr; 100–200
$20/11 issues; $2/ea; 40%–60%
48 pp; 7 x 4¼
ISSN: 0197-4777

WEBSTER REVIEW

Nancy Schapiro
Webster University
470 East Lockwood
St. Louis, MO 63119
(314) 432-2657
Poetry, fiction, essays, translation, interviews.
WEBSTER REVIEW emphasizes translations of contemporary fiction, poetry and essays. We look for quality original work in those categories. We are partic-

ularly open at this time to non-
fiction of a general literary
nature.

William Stafford, Jared Carter,
Barbara Lefcowitz, Charles Edward Easton, Etelvina Astrada.

Payment: in copies.

Copyright held by magazine; reverts to author upon publication.

1974; 2/yr; 1,100
$5/yr; $2.50/ea; 40%
104 pp; 5½ x 8½
ISSN: 0363-1230

WEST BRANCH

Karl Patten, Robert Taylor
Bucknell Hall
Bucknell University
Lewisburg, PA 17837
(717) 524-1853

Poetry, fiction, reviews.

A twice-yearly magazine of poetry, fiction, and reviews.

David Citino, Barbara Crooker,
Harry Humes, William Kloefkorn, Helena Minton.

Payment: 2 copies and 1 year subscription.

Reporting time: 6–8 weeks.

Copyright held by magazine; reverts to author upon publication.

1977; 2/yr; 500
$7/yr; $11/2 yrs; $4/ea
88–106 pp; 5½ x 8½

No ads
ISSN: 0149-6441

WEST HILLS REVIEW

William Fahey
246 Old Walt Whitman Road
Huntington Station, NY 11746
(516) 427-5240

Poetry, essays, photographs,
graphics/artwork.

Good lyric poetry. Prose related to
Walt Whitman.

John Ciardi, Dave Smith, Gay
Wilson Allen, David Ignatow,
Edmund Pennant.

Payment: none.

Reporting time: 3 months.

Copyright held by magazine; reverts to author upon publication.

1979; 1/yr; 500
$5/yr; $5/ea; 50%
125 pp; 5 x 8

WESTERN HUMANITIES
REVIEW

Larry Levis, Richard Howard,
Barry Weller
341 OSH/ University of Utah
Salt Lake City, UT 84112
(801) 581-6070

Poetry, fiction, criticism, essays,
reviews, non-fiction.

We print fiction, poetry, film and
book reviews, articles on the

humanities (we prefer 2–3M words). Our standard is excellence; we publish work by established writers as well as new writers.

Mary Oliver, Charles Simic, Francine Prose, Sandra McPherson, Philip Levine, Joseph Brodsky.

Payment: $50/poem; $150/story-criticism-review.

Copyright held by **WESTERN HUMANITIES REVIEW**.

1947; 4/yr; 1,100

$18/yr ind; $24/yr inst; $5/ea; 40%; 50% to distributors

96 pp; 6 x 9

No ads

ISSN: 0043-3845

WHETSTONE

Sandra Berris, Marsh Portnoy, Jean Tolle

P.O. Box 1266

Barrington, IL 60011

(708) 382-5626

Poetry, short stories, novel excerpts, essays, photography, art.

Prefer to see 3–5 poems or up to 25–30 pages of fiction or nonfiction. Feature one guest artist. Include SASE. Especially interested in showcasing Illinois artists, but receptive to others.

Ellyn Bache, Robert Klein Engler, John Jacob, William Kloefkorn, Paulette Roeske, Jeanne M. Walker, Lucia Getsi.

Payment: 2 copies.

Reporting time: 3 months.

Copyright reverts to author.

1983; 1/yr; 500

$5 + $1 post; $5/ea; no disc.

96 pp; 5⅞ x 9

Will consider ads for 1991 issue.

Barrington Area Arts Council, bookstores, some Hallmark stores

WHISPERS

Stuart David Schiff

70 Highland Ave.

Binghamton, NY 13905

(607) 729-6020

Fiction, criticism, reviews, graphics/artwork.

WHISPERS is a literary magazine of fantasy and horror. The journal publishes original fiction and art as well as news and reviews.

Stephen King, William Nolan, Ray Bradbury, Harlan Ellison, Ray Russell.

Payment: varies.

Reporting time: 1–3 months.

Copyright held by Stuart David Schiff; reverts to author upon publication.

1973; 2/yr; 3,000

$10/yr ind; $12/yr inst; $6/ea; 40%

176 pp; 5½ x 8½
Ad rates: $90/page/4⅜ x 8; $50/½
   page/4¾ x 4½; $30/¼
   page/4¾ x 2¼

WHITE CLOUDS REVUE
Scott Preston
P.O. Box 462
Ketchum, ID 83340

Poetry, one prose piece in 4 issues
so far.

WCR is a serially-issued journal
   specifically interested in delin-
   eating and suggesting trends in
   inter-mountain American West
   Poetics, divergent from those
   foisted on hapless readers &
   writers by the homogenized tyr-
   anny of regional MFA syn-
   dromes and syndicates.
Charles Potts, Ed Dorn, Rosalie
   Sorrels, Bruce Embree, Peter
   Boweb, Brooke Medicine Ea-
   gle.
Payment: several copies.
Reporting time: 2 weeks–2
   months.
Copyright reverts to author.
1987; 1½/yr; 200+
$12/4 issues; $3.50/ea; 30%
28–44 pp; 7 x 8½

WHOLE NOTES
Nancy Peters Hastings
P.O. Box 1374

Las Cruces, NM 88004
(505) 382-7446

Poetry.

WHOLE NOTES features work
   by unknown or beginning writers as well as established poets.
   It is intentionally kept small so
   that it is affordable—and highly
   readable. Writers whose work
   has appeared in it are Keith
   Wilson, Carol Oles, Greg
   Kuzma, Ted Kooser, Bill Kloefkorn.
Payment: in copies.
Copyright: Nancy Peters Hastings.
1984; 2/yr; 400
$6/yr ind, inst; $3/ea; 40%
20 pp; 5½ x 8½
Ad rates available. Contact CLMP
   for information.

THE WILLIAM AND MARY REVIEW
William Clark
Campus Center
College of William and Mary
Williamsburg, VA 23185
(804) 253-4895

Poetry, fiction, criticism, interviews, photographs, graphics/
   artwork.

THE WILLIAM AND MARY
   REVIEW is an internationally-
   distributed literary magazine
   published by graduate and undergraduate students of The

College of William and Mary, without faculty supervision or censorship. It is the express purpose of **THE WILLIAM AND MARY REVIEW** to publish the work of established writers as well as that of—and with an emphasis on—new, vital voices.

Amy Clampitt, Julie Agoos, Carole Glickfeld, David Ignatow, Dana Gioia.

Payment: in copies.

Copyright held by College of William and Mary, and Editor; reverts to author upon publication.

1962; 1/yr; 5,000

$4.50/yr ind; $8/yr inst; $5/ea; 40%

120 pp; 6 x 9

ISSN: 0043-5600

WILLOW SPRINGS

Nance Van Winckel, Editor

MS-1

Eastern Washington University

Cheney, WA 99004

(509) 458-6429

Poetry, fiction, essays, reviews, translation, graphics/artwork, interviews.

WILLOW SPRINGS is committed to the imagination and the power of language fully engaged in the act of telling. We publish high quality poetry, fiction, translation, essays, and art.

Russell Edson, Thomas Lux, Alberto Rios, Madeline DeFrees, Olga Broumas, Jane Miller, Donald Revell.

Payment: 2 copies on publication.

Reporting time: 6 weeks.

Copyright reverts to author.

1977; 2/yr; 1,000

$8/yr; $4/ea; 40%

104 pp; 6 x 9

Ad rates: $125/page/4¼ x 7; $75/½ page/4¼ x 3½; $50/¼ page/2⅛ x 3½

ISSN: 0739-1277

Pacific Pipeline, Small Changes

WIND

Quentin R. Howard

R.F.D. #1, Box 809K

Pikeville, KY 41501

(606) 631-1129

Poetry, fiction, criticism, reviews from small presses only.

Focus and emphasis are on the writers who have something special to say: nothing cold and lifeless. **WIND** is highly eclectic; any form, subject matter or approach.

Hale Chatfield, John Svehla, Philip Miller, Carolyn Osborn, Frances Sherwood.

Payment: in copies.

Reporting time: 2–4 weeks.
Copyright held by author.
1971; 2/yr; 450
$7/yr ind; $8/yr inst; $2.50/ea
82 pp; 5½ x 8¼
ISSN: 0361-2481
Hawley Cooke Booksellers

WINDFALL

Ron Ellis
Friends of Poetry
c/o Department of English
University of Wisconsin
Whitewater, WI 53190
(414) 472-1036
Poetry.
We are interested in short, intense, highly-crafted poems in any form. Longer poems occasionally considered. No xerox or dot matrix.
William Stafford, Ralph Mills, Francine Sterle, Sheila Murphy, Joanne Hart.
Payment: contributor's copies.
Reporting time: 8 weeks.
Copyright held by Friends of Poetry; reverts to author upon publication.
1979; 2/yr; 400
$5/yr; $3/ea
40 pp; 5½ x 8½
ISSN: 0893-3375

THE WINDLESS ORCHARD

Robert Novak
English Department

Indiana University
2101 East Coliseum
Fort Wayne, IN 46805
(219) 483-6845
Poetry, criticism, review, photographs, graphics/artwork.
Our muse is interested only in the beautiful, the sacred, and the erotic. Excited, organic forms, with thinking and feeling done in imagery and epigram.
Ruth Moon Kempher, Elliot Richman, Mike Martone, Michael Emery.
Payment: 2 copies.
Reporting time: 1 week on.
Copyright reverts to author.
1970; irregular; 320
$8/4 issues; $3/ea
52 pp; 5½ x 8
No ads

WITHOUT HALOS

Frank Finale, Lora Dunetz, Barbara Finale, Denise Hughes, H.G. Stacy, W. Swayhoover, W. Toensmann, Rich Youmans
P.O. Box 1342
Pt. Pleasant Beach, NJ 08742
Poetry, graphics/artwork.
We consider all types of poetry—mainstream, avant-garde, haiku, light verse, etc. We judge each poem not on a poet's name but on the passion it displays, the honesty of its roots.

Geraldine C. Little, Harold Witt,
Emilie Glen, Stephen Dunn,
Gail White, Sallie Bingham.
Payment: 1 copy.
Reporting time: 3–4 months.
Copyright held by author.
1983; 1/yr; 1,000
$5.00/ea
88 pp; 8½ x 5½
No ads
ISSN: 1052-3162

WITNESS

Peter Stine
31000 Northwestern Highway
Suite 200
Farmington Hills, MI 48018
(313) 626-1110

Fiction, essays, poetry, interviews,
photographs, graphics/artwork.

WITNESS presents nationally
known writers, as well as new
talent, and highlights the role of
the modern writer as witness.
The magazine features a diverse
selection of writings—fiction,
poetry, essays, journalism,
interviews—and regularly de-
votes every other issue to illu-
minating a single subject of
wide concern.

Gordon Lish, Joyce Carol Oates,
Robert Coover, Lynn Sharon
Schwartz, Madison Smartt Bell.

Payment: $6/page for prose,
$10/page for poetry.

Reporting time: 2–3 months.
Copyright held by Witness; reverts
to author upon publication.
1987; 3/yr
In spring 1990 **WITNESS** will be
published tri-annually. Subscription rates: $15/3 copies per
year; $6/single copies
160 pp; 6 x 9
Ad rates: $100/page/5 x 7; $60/½
page/5 x 3½
ISSN: 0891-1371
Bernhard DeBoer, Inland Book
Company

WOMAN POET

Elaine Dallman
P.O. Box 60550
Reno, NV 89506
(702) 972-1671

Poetry, criticism, photos, interviews.

The West, the East, the Midwest,
the South.

Marilyn Hacker, Lisel Mueller,
Judith Minty, Rosalie Moore,
Mona Van Duyn, Josephine
Jacobsen

$12.95/ea paperback; $19.95/ea
hardcover. Resale discount varies.

Inland

WOMEN & PERFORMANCE:
A JOURNAL OF FEMINIST
THEORY

Editorial Board; Jill McDougall,
Managing Editor

721 Broadway/Sixth Floor
New York, NY 10003
(212) 998-1625

Essays, criticism, plays, reviews, interviews, translation.

Hélène Cixous, Marianne Goldberg, Ann Gavere Kilkelly, Karen Laughlin, Phyllis Zatlin.

$12/yr ind; $25/yr inst; $7/ea; $9/ea back issues; 40%

THE WOMEN'S REVIEW OF BOOKS

Linda Gardiner
Wellesley College Center for Research on Women
Wellesley, MA 02181
(617) 431-1453

Reviews, poetry.

In-depth reviews of books by and about women, in all areas, both academic and general-interest; feminist in orientation but not committed to any one brand of feminism or any specific political position.

June Jordan, Diane Wakoski, Gerda Lerner, Michelle Cliff, Jane Marcus.

Payment: varies, $50 minimum.
Reporting time: 1 month–6 weeks.
Copyright held by Women's Review; reverts to author upon publication.
1983; 11/yr; 12,500

$16/yr ind; $30/yr inst: $2/ea; 40%

28 pp; 10 x 15

Ad rates: $1,210/page/10 x 15; $650/½ page/10 x 7½; $335/¼ page/4¾ x 7½

ISSN: 0738-1433

THE WORCESTER REVIEW

Rodger Martin
6 Chatham Street
Worcester, MA 01609
(508) 797-4770; (603) 924-7342

Poetry, fiction, criticism, essays, graphics/artwork, photographs.

We look for quality poetry and fiction, and also articles and essays about poetry that have a New England connection.

Richard Eberhart, Judith Steinbergh, Walter McDonald, William Stafford, Kathleen Spivack.

Payment: 2 copies plus honorarium dependant upon grants.
Reporting time: 12–16 weeks.
Copyright held by Worcester Review of the Worcester County Poetry Assoc.; reverts to author upon publication.
1973; 2/yr; 1,000

$10/yr; $5/ea; 40%

80 pp; 6 x 9

$195/Full page display; $100/½ page; $55/¼ page

ISSN: 8756-5277

THE WORMWOOD REVIEW

Marvin Malone
P.O. Box 4698
Stockton, CA 95204-0698
(209) 466-8231

Poetry, reviews, translation, graphics/artwork.

Poetry and prose-poems reflecting the temper and depth of the present time. All types and schools from traditional-economic through concrete, dada and extreme avant-garde. Special fondness for prose poems and fables. Each issue has a yellow paper section devoted to one poet or topic. One chapbook per year.

Charles Bukowski, Lyn Lifshin, Ronald Koertge, Gerald Locklin, Judson Crews.

Payment: 3–6 copies of magazine or cash equivalent.

Copyright held by Wormwood Review Press; reverts to author upon request.

1959; 4/yr; 700
$8/yr ind; $10/yr inst; $4/ea; 40%
48 pp; 5½ x 8½
ISSN: 0043-9401

THE WRITERS' BAR-B-Q

Editorial Board: Timothy Osburn, Becky Bradway, Gary Smith, Marcia Womack, and Myra Epping

924 Bryn Mawr Boulevard
Springfield, IL 62703
(217) 525-6987

Fiction, photographs, graphics/artwork.

THE WRITERS' BAR-B-Q publishes stories and novel excerpts. Our preference is for realistic work that has strong characterization and story. We are looking for excellent, spirited, daring writing from all genres. We encourage work by gays and lesbians, people of color, and other writers who may have trouble fitting into the usual venues. Our idea is to publish good stories, and to have fun doing it. **THE WRITERS' BAR-B-Q** is a potluck of styles, subjects and characters. Almost all stories are fully illustrated.

Lowry Pei, Sharon Sloan Fiffer, Michael C. White, Martha M. Vertreace, Shannon Keith Kelley, Nolan Porterfield, Deborah Insel, Paul Lisicky.

Payment: 3 copies, upon publication.

Copyright held by Sangamon Writers, Inc.; reverts to author upon publication.

1987; 1–2/yr; 1,000.
$10/yr; $5/ea.
100 pgs; 8½ x 11
Ad rates: $75/½ page/4½ x 7½; $50; inquire.
Bernhard DeBoer

WRITERS FORUM

Alex Blackburn, Editor; Craig Lesley, Bret Lott, Fiction Editors; Victoria McLabe, Poetry Editor

University of Colorado at Colorado Springs

Colorado Springs, CO 80933-7150

(719) 599-4023

Poetry, fiction.

We want the finest in contemporary short story and poetry, with some focus and emphasis on the trans-Mississippi West with its varieties of place and experience.

Gladys Swan, Ron Carlson, Frank Waters, Kenneth Fields, David Ray.

Payment: none.

Reporting time: 3–6 weeks.

Copyright held by UCCS; reverts to author upon publication.

1974; 1/yr; 1,000

$8.95/yr ind; $7.20/yr inst; $8.95/ea

200 pp; 8½ x 5½

WRITER'S JOURNAL (formerly The Inkling)

Valerie Hockert

P.O. Box 9148

N. St. Paul, MN 55109

(612) 433-3626

Essays, poetry, reviews, criticism, interviews, commentaries, writing techniques.

Provides writers and poets with practical advice and guidance, motivation and authorative instruction in the craft of writing. Includes book reviews, essays, poetry, legal advice and references.

Dennis E. Hensley, Marilyn Bailey, Betty Ulrich, Ester M. Leiper, Herman Holtz, Ken Strandberg.

Payment: variable.

Reporting time: 2–6 weeks.

Copyright held by Minnesota Ink, Inc., reverts to author upon publication.

1980; 6/yr; 35,000

$18.00/yr; $3/ea; 50%

48 pp; 8 x 10½

Ad rates: $675/page/6¾ x 9; $355/½ page/6¾ x 4½ or 3⅛ x 9

ISSN: 0891-9759

Ingram, Armadillo, Homing Pigeon, ARA, Bernhard DeBoer, MPG

WYOMING, THE HUB OF THE WHEEL . . . A Journey for Universal Spokesmen

Dawn Senior, Managing Editor; Lenore A. Senior, Founding & Consulting Editor.

Box 9

Saratoga, WY 82331

(307) 326-5214

Poetry, fiction, graphics/artwork, essays, translation, photographs.

WYOMING, THE HUB OF THE WHEEL . . . A Journal for Universal Spokesmen attempts to reach a general audience interested in peace, humanism, the environment, society, and universal messages. Each issue is devoted to the themes of Peace, The Human Race, Positive Relationships, and the Human Spirit and all its Possibilities.

Graciany Miranda-Archilla, B.J. Buckley, Eugenio de Andrade, Virginia Love Long, Rodney E.J. Chang.

Payment: 1 copy, contributor discounts.

Reporting time: 6 weeks.

Copyright held by magazine; reverts to author upon publication.

1985; 1–2/yr; 300

$10/yr; $6/ea; 40%

100-148 pp; 6 x 9

No ads

ISSN: 0884-2930

X

XANADU: A Literary Journal

Mildred M. Jeffrey, Barbara Lucas, Pat Nesbitt, Editors; Barry Fruchter, Jeanne K. Welcher, Virginia R. Terris, Consulting Editors; Lois V. Walker, Business Manager

Box 773

Huntington, NY 11743

(516) 741-7188

Poetry, essays.

XANADU publishes contemporary poetry and literary criticism.

Karen Swenson, David Ignatow, Edmund Pennant, William Stafford.

Payment: 1 copy per contributor.

Reporting time: 3 months.

Copyright reverts to author upon publication.

1975; 1/yr; 300

$4/ea plus $1 postage/handling; 20%–40%

64–76 pp; 5½ x 8½

ISSN: 0146-0463

Y

YARROW

Harry Humes, Editor; Arnold Newman, Associated Editor

English Department

Kutztown University

Kutztown, PA 19530

(215) 683-4353

Poetry, interviews.

A journal of poetry.
William Pitt Root, Gerald Stern,
  John Engels, Gibbons Ruark,
  Lola Haskins, Fleda Brown
  Jackson, Sally Jo Sorenson.
Payment: in copies.
Reporting time: 1 month.
1981; 2/yr; 350
$5/2 yrs; $1.50/ea
36 pp; 6 x 9

YELLOW SILK: A Journal of Erotic Arts

Lily Pond
P.O. Box 6374
Albany, CA 94706
(415) 644-4188
Fiction, poetry, essays, reviews,
  translations, photography,
  graphics/artwork, cartoons, fine
  arts, science fiction, humor.
YELLOW SILK publishes erotic
  literature and arts. "All persua-
  sions; no brutality." Literary
  and artistic excellence combines
  with healthy eroticism in this
  beautiful alternative to pornography.
Kotzwinkle, Shange, Paz, Hacker,
  Soto.
Payment: 3 copies, 1 year subscription, and varying cash payments.
Reporting time: 3 months.
Copyright reverts to author after
  one year following publication;

YS keeps non-exclusive reprint
  and anthology rights.
1981; 4/yr; 16,000
$28/yr ind; $35/yr inst; $7/ea;
  40%
52 pp; 8½ x 11
ISSN: 0736-9212
Bookpeople, Inland, Ingram,
  Ubiquity

YET ANOTHER SMALL MAGAZINE

Candace Catlin Hall
Box 14353
Hartford, CT 06114
(203) 549-6723
Poetry.
YASM publishes short, imagistic
  poems—special interest in lesser
  known poets— started broadside
  inclusion highlighting a single
  poem.
Lyn Lifshin, Charles Darling, Pat
  Bridges, Sister Mary Ann
  Henn, Neil Grill.
Payment: in copies.
Reporting time: November; read-
  ing period is Aug. 1 to Oct. 31.
Copyright reverts to author.
1981; annual; 300
$1.98/ea
8–12 pp; 11 x 17
ISSN: 0278-9442

Z

ZUKUNFT

Dr. Joseph Landis, Joseph
  Mlotek, Matis Olitzki
25 East 21st Street
New York, NY 10010

Poetry, fiction, criticism, essays,
  reviews.

The **ZUKUNFT** is an independent
literary publication. It serves as
a vehicle for writers from many
countries and is concerned with
problems of Jewish life throught
the world. In 1982 the **ZUK-
UNFT**, the oldest continously
published Yiddish journal in the
world, celebrated its 90th anniversary. It has served to stimulate literary creativity for
several generations throughout
Yiddish speaking communities.

Copyright held by Congress for
  Jewish Culture; reverts to author
  upon publication.

1892; 10/yr; 2,500
$20/yr ind; $1.50/ea, 20% for
  agencies
44 pp; 7½ x 10½
Ad rates: $100/page; $50/½ page;
  $25/¼ page

ZYMERGY

Sonja A. Skarstedt
P.O. Box 1746, Place Du Parc

Montreal, Quebec, Canada H2W2R7

Poetry, fiction, essays, book reviews.

High-quality, innovative, imaginative, writing; all facets. International, all races and creeds,
feminist, political (though not
political-for-political-sake writing e.g. "sloganism"). Not accepting submissions until after
September 1, 1991.

Ralph Gustafson, Louis Dedek,
  Phyllis Webb.

Payment: copies.
Reporting time: Two weeks.
Copyright in care of **ZYMERGY**
  for the author.
1987; bi-annual; 500+
$10; $6
160; 6 x 9
$80/page; $40/½ page; $25/¼
  page
ISSN: 0835-0264
Canadian Magazine Publishers
  Association

ZYZZYVA

Howard Junker
41 Sutter Street, Suite 1400
San Francisco, CA 94104
(415) 255-1282

Poetry, fiction, essays, plays,
  translations, photographs,
  prints, drawings.
West Coast writers, artists, and
  publishers.

Francisco X. Alarcón, Isabel Allende, Dorianne Laux, Tess Gallagher, August Kleinzahler, Barry Lopez.
Payment: $50–$250.
Reporting time: prompt.
Copyright held by magazine; reverts to author upon publication.
1985; 4/yr; 3,500

$20/yr ind; $28/yr inst; $7/ea
144 pp; 6 x 9
Ad rates: $450/page/5 x 7¾; $275/½ page/5 x 3¹³/₁₆; $150/¼ page/2⁷/₁₆ x 3¹³/₁₆
ISSN: 8756-5633
Bookpeople, Ingram Periodical, Inland Book, Small Press Distribution

INDEX BY STATE

NORTH CAROLINA

NORTH DAKOTA